Preventing Child Abuse and Neglect
Through Parent Education

Preventing Child Abuse and Neglect Through Parent Education

by

N. Dickon Reppucci, Ph.D.
University of Virginia
Charlottesville

Preston A. Britner, Ph.D.
University of Connecticut
Storrs

Jennifer L. Woolard, M.A.
University of Virginia
Charlottesville

·P A U L·H·
BROOKES
PUBLISHING C°

Baltimore • London • Toronto • Sydney

Paul H. Brookes Publishing Co.
Post Office Box 10624
Baltimore, Maryland 21285-0624

Typeset by Maryland Composition Company, Inc., Glen Burnie, Maryland.
Manufactured in the United States of America by
Thomson-Shore, Inc., Dexter, Michigan.

Library of Congress Cataloging-in-Publication Data

Reppucci, N. Dickon.
    Preventing child abuse and neglect through parent education / by N. Dickon
Reppucci, Preston A. Britner, Jennifer L. Woolard.
       p.   cm.
    Includes bibliographical references and index.
    ISBN 1-55766-289-4
    1. Child abuse—Virginia—Prevention.   2. Child abuse—Prevention.
3. Parenting—Study and teaching—Virginia.   4. Parenting—Study and
teaching.   I. Britner, Preston A.   II. Woolard, Jennifer L.   III. Title
HV6626.53.V8R47   1997
362.76′7′09755—dc21
                                                97-9036
                                                CIP

British Library Cataloguing in Publication data are available from the British Library.

Contents

About the Authors

N. Dickon Reppucci, Ph.D., Department of Psychology, University of Virginia, Gilmer Hall, Charlottesville, VA 22903-2477. Dr. Reppucci received his doctoral degree in clinical psychology from Harvard University in 1968, was a psychology faculty member at Yale University from 1968 to 1976, and became Professor of Psychology at the University of Virginia in 1976. Since then, he has served the Psychology Department as Director of the Program in Research and Clinical Community Psychology (1976–1980), coordinator of the Community Psychology program (1980–present), and Director of Graduate Studies (1984–1995). As President of APA's Division 27 (The Society for Community Research and Action) in 1986, Dr. Reppucci initiated the Biennial Conferences on Community Research and Action. He is a Fellow of the American Psychological Association, the American Psychological Society, and the American Association of Applied and Preventive Psychology. He has served on several editorial boards, including the *American Journal of Community Psychology*, *Journal of Consulting and Clinical Psychology*, and *Professional Psychology,* and was Associate Editor of *Law and Human Behavior* (1986–1996). Dr. Reppucci has served on National Institute of Mental Health Internal Review Committees concerned with violence and antisocial behavior and with life-span development and preventive intervention, the Virginia Advisory Council on Prevention and Promotion (1985–1992), and the Executive Committee of the National Consortium on Law and Children and The Child Maltreatment section of APA's Division 37. His books include *The Sexual Abuse of Children* (Jossey-Bass, 1988) and *Prevention in Community Mental Health Practice* (Brookline Books, 1991), both coauthored with Jeffrey Haugaard. Author of more than 100 professional works, Dr. Reppucci's most recent articles have been concerned with juvenile delinquency, preventing child abuse, and adolescent decision making in legal contexts. In 1991, he was honored as the Outstanding Scholar in Psychology by the Virginia Association of Social Scientists.

Preston A. Britner, Ph.D., School of Family Studies, University of Connecticut, 348 Mansfield Road, U-58, Storrs, CT 06269-2058. Dr. Britner is Assistant Professor in the School of Family Studies at the University of

Connecticut. He received his doctoral degree in Developmental Psychology from the University of Virginia in 1996. Dr. Britner has published on a number of topics related to the social development and adaptation of children and their families. Specific research areas include child care and the continuity of child environments; the integration of attachment and family systems theories involving preschool children with and without special needs; child maltreatment prevention and correlates; professionals' decision making with respect to foster care placements, especially following maltreatment; and developmental, legal, and social policy issues related to children and families.

Jennifer L. Woolard, M.A., Ph.D. candidate, Department of Psychology, University of Virginia, Charlottesville, VA 22903-2477. Ms. Woolard has published articles on adolescent development in legal contexts, mental health needs of juvenile delinquents, and antisocial behavior. Her research interests focus on adolescent development in context and violence prevention. Recent and ongoing research projects address community interventions for family violence prevention, adolescent development and decision making, juvenile delinquency, child maltreatment prevention and intervention, and policy regarding children and families.

Foreword

What do we know about the rationale for, substance of, and outcomes of programs that deal with and/or prevent child abuse? That question, of course, implies that we have a responsibility to distinguish between what we know and what we need to know. That distinction is too frequently glossed over as we understandably feel and respond to pressures to act (i.e., to do *something* that we hope will be effective). The hallmark of the helping professions is that their practitioners do the best they can on the basis of what they think they know to render an effective service. As any such practitioner will attest, problems always are more complicated than they initially seem, desired outcomes are too frequently elusive or nonexistent, available knowledge is of questionable validity, and one is left to one's own devices to figure out how things might be done differently. And there is one other thing that bedevils the practitioner in the field of child abuse: He or she is in a relatively new field in which independent assessments of service programs are very few and far between.

This book is unusual in several respects. First, the Virginia Department of Social Services had the wisdom—and, I would say, the courage—to ask a group of researchers independently to assess the department's parenting programs aimed at preventing child abuse. *That* is unusual. Second, the researchers took seriously the responsibility to describe in detail how 5 of 25 parenting programs were locally created, who were the creators, how they defined and utilized community resources, what problems they encountered and how well they coped with those problems, and what judgments could be made about how and why these programs varied in effectiveness. Third, the researchers approached each of the 25 sites sensitively and sympathetically but dispassionately (i.e., they were well aware that the program developers were operating in uncharted territory; they had nothing resembling an empirical basis to serve as concrete guidelines). Fourth, the researchers went beyond description and assessment to provide guidelines for the collection of data of potential usefulness not only to the Virginia programs but also to similar programs elsewhere. Of particular practical importance is an appendix in this book that addresses "the most frequently asked questions about implementation and outcome evaluation" (e.g., how to recruit and retain clients, how to organize an advisory board, how to obtain funds).

This book will be of great interest and help to those who have responsibility for child abuse programs. It should also be of practical import for anyone interested in prevention and parent education and, not the least, to those who consult to these programs.

How public policies arise and are implemented is a fascinating, complex process in which opinion plays as much of a role as fact, and I would say that personal opinion plays far more potent a role than fact. When the problem for which a public policy is being formulated is relatively new (in terms of public recognition) and concerns behavior that offends the morality of any sane person, it is understandable that opinion will goad us to action that, however well-intentioned, glosses over what we do not know about the factual basis of our actions. This book achieves the purpose of beginning to provide a more solid, empirical basis for what we should do in the future. The authors know full well that they have not provided "final" answers; that the more you know, the more you need to know. They have done their job carefully, honestly, and very well.

Seymour B. Sarason, Ph.D.
Professor of Psychology Emeritus
Yale University
New Haven, Connecticut

Acknowledgments

We extend our thanks to the Virginia Family Violence Prevention Program, for funding our evaluation; Ann Childress, Virginia Department of Social Services, for her assistance with the entire evaluation process; the parent educators and parents at each of the 25 sites that we visited, for their helpful cooperation; and Sarah L. Cook, Peter A. Dillon, Heather O'Beirne Kelly, Deborah J. Land, Sharon G. Portwood, and Deborah Schutte, members of the evaluation team who contributed much to the project design, data collection, literature reviews, and drafts of earlier versions of some of the chapters in this book. Finally, we acknowledge the Psychology Department at the University of Virginia, which housed and facilitated us throughout the entire research process, and the Center for Advanced Studies at the University of Virginia, which provided a Sesquicentennial Fellowship to the first author during the spring of 1996.

To

my mother, Bertha Elizabeth Reppucci [NDR]

Suzanne [PAB]

Will [JLW]

Preventing Child Abuse and Neglect
Through Parent Education

Introduction

In 1994, child protective services in 48 states received more than 2.9 million reports of alleged child maltreatment (U.S. Department of Health and Human Services, National Center on Child Abuse and Neglect [NCCAN], 1996). Of these, 1,011,628 children were determined to be victims of abuse and neglect. From 1990 to 1994, the number of substantiated victims increased by almost 27%. Across these years, neglect was the predominant type of maltreatment, with the number of neglect victims being consistently more than twice the number of physical abuse victims, the next most common type of maltreatment. Almost half of the children were 8 years of age or younger, and almost 5,400 children died as a result of the maltreatment. Based on data from 41 states, nearly 80% of perpetrators of child maltreatment were parents (NCCAN, 1996). These statistics indicate that child maltreatment is a social problem of staggering proportions. In addition, numerous empirical studies have documented a relation between abuse and maladaptive behaviors in children (see comprehensive review by Becker et al., 1995). Becker et al. (1995) pointed out that the effects of child maltreatment are widespread and often manifest themselves differently depending on the age of the child (e.g., physically abused infants and preschoolers may show problems with attachment, whereas school-age children may display decreased self-esteem, social withdrawal, and depression); likewise, neglected children frequently demonstrate significant deficits in cognitive, social-emotional, and language development. The statistics regarding incidence and prevalence in conjunction with the findings regarding the psychological and social consequences of child maltreatment clearly suggest that preventing child maltreatment should be a national goal.

Three types of prevention—primary, secondary, and tertiary—typically are identified. Primary prevention consists of interventions to prevent a specified problem, such as child maltreatment, from ever happening; secondary prevention usually suggests early identification and early intervention to keep the problem from continuing; and tertiary prevention aims to reduce the severity and effects of the problem after it has occurred by some means of rehabilitation and treatment. Family support programs, in general, and parent education programs, in specific, are unique in that they can be used for all three types of preventive interventions. Beginning in the 1960s with the identification of the "battered child syndrome" (Kempe, Silverman, Steele, Droegemueller, & Silver, 1962) and the passage of child abuse reporting laws in all 50 states between 1962 and 1967 (Reppucci & Aber, 1992), public policy has encouraged state intervention "in the best interests of the child" when the parents are unable or unwilling to perform their child-rearing roles adequately. One result has been the development of parent education programs of various types and prevention orientations throughout the United States. Although many parent education programs have been designed to enhance family functioning generally, especially in "high risk" groups (e.g., unmarried adolescents) with the continued documentation of the incidence and prevalence of child abuse and neglect, more and more of these programs are designed explicitly to prevent child maltreatment and family violence. Their underlying assumptions are that if parents' stress can be reduced, if their knowledge of child development can be improved, and if their social coping skills and supportive networks can be enhanced, then parenting strategies will be improved, and many forms of child maltreatment may be prevented (Willis, Holden, & Rosenberg, 1992). These programs have become the most popular and prevalent form of intervention for preventing abuse and neglect.

Parent education and family support programs to enhance parental competencies, resources, and coping skills have been implemented as promising strategies to prevent child abuse and may be viable alternatives to a coercive child protection system centered on investigation and treatment after the abuse has occurred. Although such programs, both state supported and private, have expanded and diversified since the mid-1970s, little actually is known about either their implementation or their effectiveness (Wolfe, Reppucci, & Hart, 1995). In 1985, Rosenberg and Reppucci summarized the prevention literature as being at a primitive level with little solid evidence of effectiveness. Nevertheless, because of the tremendous need, programs have proliferated without a basis of research findings. As cutbacks in social services have become normative in the 1990s, however, it is critical for such research to occur. If development and implementation of parent education and family support programs are to continue, then program staff must engage in the systematic evaluation of long-term effectiveness of parent education on parental behavior, efficacy of family support programs to increase social support, and identification of characteristics and training of home visitors and parental educators critical to successful programs. Such research could play a role in defining public policy regarding the delivery of preventive and supportive services to families in need.

In 1993, the Community Research Group (CRG) at the University of Virginia was provided with the opportunity to gather systematic information on parent education and family support programs for the prevention of abuse and neglect throughout Virginia. As with the United States as a whole, Virginia had experienced an ever-increasing number of complaints of alleged child abuse and neglect. In fiscal year (FY) 1993, there were 36,460 complaints of alleged child abuse and neglect received by local departments of social services. Of these, 6,563 were classified as "founded" complaints (i.e., showed clear and convincing evidence) of child abuse and neglect, involving 10,108 children; and 3,137 were classified as "reason to suspect" complaints (i.e., maltreatment suspected, but the evidence did not meet the clear-and-convincing standard), involving 4,555 children. In-depth information was collected by child protective services workers in local departments of social services on a statistically valid random sample of complaints in FY 1992. Of the founded and reason-to-suspect cases that indicated a need for services, the second most frequently identified service needed was parenting education (43%) (Virginia Department of Social Services, 1993).

The Virginia Department of Social Services asked our group to conduct a process evaluation of the 25 parenting programs statewide that it was funding through its Family Violence Prevention Program. When sufficient data were available, the goal was to assess outcome also. The programs varied in focus and the range of clients served. Several drew from the general population and consequently reflected the low to mid–socioeconomic status (SES) of the surrounding communities. Client groups ranged from urban African American parents to rural Caucasian mothers, and many of the client groups were racially mixed. Several programs specifically targeted teenage mothers. The courts, Department of Social Services, Child Protection Services, and other community groups routinely referred clients to several of the programs. A majority of the programs offered parent education classes structured around the popular Systematic Training for Effective Parenting (STEP) (Dinkmeyer & McKay, 1976, 1982) or the Nurturing Program curricula (Bavolek & Comstock, 1985); several others had developed curricula of their own. Classes usually were arranged in a series of weekly sessions; however, some programs offered monthly topical seminars instead. Many programs provided a separate parent support group, such as Parents Anonymous, and some programs incorporated a parent support group in their parenting classes. Some programs also included a home-visiting component that varied in its purpose and frequency. Many programs provided child care, and several offered programs specifically for children.

The CRG was asked to evaluate the various approaches used by these child abuse and neglect prevention programs in order to develop guidelines for replicating successful approaches, to help existing programs with self-evaluation, and to aid the Department of Social Services in choosing model approaches and programs for funding based on actual and potential effectiveness. After initial site visits to all 25 programs, five model programs were identified for intensive evaluation. This subset was selected to be representative of the larger group on a number of criteria, including standard parent education classes, home-visiting programs, child care/parent education programs, mentor programs, and parent support groups. Target groups and urban/rural issues also were varied. A final report was prepared that included recommendations for the programs, the Department of Social Services, and the Virginia state legislature.

As a result of this experience, we have learned a great deal that may be valuable to parent educators, social services personnel and administrators, and researchers and practitioners of many backgrounds (e.g., psychology, social work, education, public health) who are involved with the prevention of child abuse and neglect. Thus, this book is directed at a large and diverse audience. It has three major goals: 1) to present in a concise and thorough manner the existing knowledge base; 2) to describe the Virginia research project and the lessons learned from it, including the provision of some concrete materials that may be useful to agencies or groups in the process of creating and evaluating such programs; and 3) to provide recommendations for practitioners, researchers, and administrators and to urge the adoption of a public policy focused on prevention.

The book is divided into three parts. The first part follows this introductory chapter and focuses on parent education. Chapter 2 is a concise review of what we know and what we don't know about parent education and family support programs as vehicles for preventing maltreatment. Chapter 3 reviews the literature regarding the various approaches of parent education, areas of focus (e.g., parenting knowledge versus stress and support), and the published curricula that are available and widely used. Special attention is devoted to the evaluation of these curricula and the assumptions underlying parent education. In Chapter 4, we differentiate needs, process, and outcome evaluations and how and why the prevention educator should engage in all three. Details of process and outcome evaluations are provided as are guidelines for collecting data that are of potential usefulness for the programs themselves. We also discuss several critical issues that we prepared as topical briefs to help program personnel in Virginia with implementation. These briefs, which we include in full in Appendix A for easy use as handouts by program personnel, address the most frequently asked questions about implementation and outcome evaluation (e.g., how to recruit and retain clients, how to organize an advisory board, how to obtain funds). Finally, Chapter 5 focuses on measurement tools for self-evaluation. The most frequently used, best validated, and simplest evaluation tools (from knowledge of child development to parenting attitudes to markers of parenting stress) are reviewed for their utility in evaluating various program types (see also Appendices B and C). We prepared these chapters because, much to our surprise, when we started our own research project we could find no single volume that contained adequate discussions of these basic issues. In fact, it was difficult to find critical reviews in either journals or books regarding the parent education and family support literature or the curricula.

The next three chapters focus on describing what we learned from our own research project in Virginia. Chapter 6 provides an overview of diverse parent education efforts in Virginia, which we believe can be considered representative of many of the programs that exist throughout the United States. It also provides information that should prove useful for effective consultation. Chapter 7 presents four case studies of the creation of successful parent education programs. Sarason (1972), in his book *The Creation of Settings and the Future Societies,* described the need for detailed descriptions regarding the creation of human services programs. His point was that just as case studies of individuals have proved extremely useful to clinical practitioners and theorists, such program creation descriptions, although rare, could be tremendously useful to program developers. We hope that these case studies, each of which emphasizes a particular issue, provide insight and guidelines for program staff and administrators about problems and issues that appear regularly and must be confronted and dealt with whenever a program is created. Chapter 8 provides a description of the outcome evaluation of a program for adolescent, low-income, urban, unmarried mothers and their infants that documents reduced child maltreatment by program participants versus a matched control group over a 3-year period. Because of its outcome success, we share both the steps used in the evaluation and an outline of the curriculum (see Appendix D) of this program (which could be adapted by parent educators). This description demonstrates how evaluation, which often is resisted by practitioners as too time consuming, provided direct benefits to the program itself (e.g., grant re-funding and additional contracts for program implementation).

The final two chapters summarize our recommendations and conclusions. Chapter 9 provides a synthesis of what we have learned from the research literature and the Virginia project about the key components of successful programs. Lessons learned from these sources are translated into concrete goals for practitioners and administrators and into practical guidelines for consultants and evaluators. Chapter 10 focuses on general goals for public policy relevant to the prevention of child maltreatment and how to influence public policy. We conclude by encouraging the adoption of a central focus on prevention as the priority for state and national policy aimed at eliminating child maltreatment.

Parent Education and Family Support for the Prevention of Child Maltreatment

What We Know and What We Don't Know

with Sarah L. Cook

As researchers and service providers uncover evidence of the alarmingly high incidence and prevalence of child abuse and the negative consequences that follow, an urgent need for prevention emerges. Although estimates vary because of study methodology (e.g., official statistics, clinical samples, survey data), one survey (Wolfner & Gelles, 1993) found that at least 62% of children experience some form of minor violence (i.e., pushed, grabbed, or shoved; slapped or spanked), and 11% experience some form of severe violence (i.e., kicked, bitten, or hit with a fist; hit or almost hit with an object; beat, burned, or scalded; threatened or assaulted with a gun or a knife).

The consequences of child maltreatment are diverse. Abused children are believed to be at higher risk for developmental and behavior problems because these outcomes often are associated with disturbances in the parent–child relationship (Wolfe, 1987). The concomitants of parental mistreatment, such as low self-esteem and mistrust of others, can result in negative physical, behavioral, and psychological consequences in childhood (Becker et al., 1995). Problems associated with abusive childhood experiences include heightened aggression toward peers, poor self-control, and lower self-competence. These effects may continue throughout development, leading to long-term problems that continue into adulthood (Wolfe, 1987).

Sarah L. Cook is a Ph.D. candidate in community psychology at the University of Virginia, Charlottesville.

Many policy makers, service providers, and university researchers have recognized the need for primary prevention, using programs that put in place structures and contexts that provide stability and coping skills for individuals before problems arise (Seidman, 1987). Therefore, child abuse prevention programs are defined as those that target families who have not experienced child maltreatment. The goal of these programs is to reduce the incidence of neglect and physical and sexual assault, thereby averting the devastating consequences that so often follow.

Many programs have been developed in the name of child abuse prevention, but there is little evidence to indicate actual prevention. Many programs, such as classes for adolescent mothers and their babies, should be considered interventions because they target groups already identified as at risk. Other programs that many professionals refer to as preventive actually are treatment oriented, including programs that focus on families known to the child protection system. As a result, existing research does not adequately address whether many child abuse prevention programs are effective (Wolfe, Reppucci, & Hart, 1995). One reason for this lack of empirical evidence is that the value of prevention research often is understated. Without solid empirical evaluation, it cannot be known whether child abuse prevention programs truly reduce the incidence of child maltreatment. Assessing the efficacy of prevention programs is imperative in communities that depend on these efforts as one of their primary responses to child abuse (Reppucci & Haugaard, 1988). Furthermore, prevention research may aid in enhancing existing or developing new models of sexual and physical aggression. As Seidman (1987) stated,

> Prevention and intervention research provides fertile ground for discovery, hypothesis-generation, and theory comparison. . . . [I]n the course of observing our interventions unfold, we can begin to discover the patterns of causality and linkages between variables and their contextual embeddedness. (p. 3)

Fortunately, efforts at child abuse prevention can be informed by an existing body of theory and empirical research on the causes and nature of child maltreatment (Becker et al., 1995). It is widely accepted that no single factor causes a parent to mistreat a child. Instead, multiple factors, including social and economic variables (e.g., unemployment, underemployment), stress or transition periods (Olds & Henderson, 1989; Wolfe, 1987; Zigler, Hopper, & Hall, 1993), history of family violence, social support and social isolation (e.g., parental stress; formal, informal, and family supports), and sociocultural values and mores (e.g., acceptance of family violence), are implicated in most etiological models of maltreatment (Egeland, Jacobvitz, & Sroufe, 1988; Olds & Henderson, 1989; Vondra, 1990). In order to aid families, we must intervene at the individual, family, community, and societal/cultural levels (Wolfe, 1987). Given such complex patterns, parent education programs face the difficult task of selecting points of intervention.

Historically, specialized child protection programs have emanated from social services departments and have been coercive in nature (Melton et al., 1995). *Coercive* characterizes the nature of agencies that mandate services to families after a report of abuse or neglect, with the threat of further intervention if the maltreatment issues are not resolved. Some localities have developed community-based child protection teams composed of professionals in the medical, legal, and human services fields who identify children in need of protective services and treatment as well as advise child protection agencies about casework and policy. They work in coordination with the larger child protection system, which includes courts, police, schools, and mental health agencies. Many programs have been funded by departments of social services but implemented by other community agencies in a noncoercive fashion.

This chapter describes the nature and efficacy of available parent education and family support programs, including home visiting, as examples of noncoercive, neighborhood-based, child-centered, and family-focused child protection programs. We discuss issues of development, implementation, and evaluation in an attempt to place these programs within the framework of the policy proposed by the U.S. Advisory Board on Child Abuse and Neglect (U.S. ABCAN) (1991, 1993). These programs provide voluntary access to help for families in urban, suburban, and rural communities. We highlight promising strategies, identify barriers to effective prevention, and suggest future directions for prevention research. Our goal is twofold: 1) to provide a representative, although not exhaustive, review of available programs and evaluation studies and 2) to demonstrate that such programs may have the potential to achieve the same goals as those of coercive agencies.

This broader definition of child protection programs includes voluntary, neighborhood-based, child-centered, and family-focused programs, as proposed by U.S. ABCAN (1991, 1993). Existing family support and parent education programs that promote child and family welfare fit this description. (See Appendix A for the topical brief "Parent Education as a Preventive Intervention.") These programs provide voluntary education and support services and most often operate apart from the formal child protection system. Although many family support and education programs may not consider themselves child abuse and neglect treatment and prevention programs per se, most of them incorporate similar strategies.

Thus, child protection programs can be placed on a continuum from prevention to treatment. Community-based parent education programs exemplify primary prevention (geared toward all parents in a community), family support programs (often for groups at high risk, such as single, teen parents) embody early intervention techniques, and multidisciplinary teams typically focus on rehabilitation and treatment goals (after maltreatment has occurred). Although the programs intervene at different points on the continuum, they all share the common goal of promoting healthy children and families. Programs on the prevention and early intervention end of the continuum, however, make a valuable contribution to a federal child protection policy that concentrates on re-ducing child maltreatment by strengthening neighborhoods and families. The emphasis on strengthening families at the neighborhood level is crucial, as maltreatment takes place in both a social and a psychological context (Garbarino & Kostelny, 1992). Research echoes this assertion (Wolfner & Gelles, 1993).

Although these programs are innovative in their methods, family support centers strongly resemble, in philosophy and structure, settlement houses of the 19th century as organizations for the development of strong families and communities. The home-visiting concept also began in the 19th century and continued into the early 20th century (Garbarino & Kostelny, 1992). In the 1950s and 1960s, community action agencies' neighborhood service centers, such as the Gray Areas program of the Ford Foundation (Garbarino & Kostelny, 1992), developed in this tradition.

PARENT EDUCATION

Basic parent education is perhaps the simplest of the several prevention strate-gies we review; we devote Chapter 3 to a more extensive review of the as-sumptions underlying parent education and evaluation of the specific curricula available. Parent education programs are based on the assumption that beliefs about child development, care, and rearing are linked to parent practices, an as-sumption that has received empirical support (Luster & Youatt, 1989; Wandersman, 1987; Wiehe, 1992). Thus, parent education programs typically include instruction in child development and rearing and aim to explore indi-viduals' perceptions and attitudes about parenting (Wolfe et al., 1995). Parents who have against them founded (i.e., proven or documented) reports of mal-treating their children often are presumed to have less knowledge about child developmental milestones and norms and to make more negative attributions to their child's behavior. These presumptions are borne out in some studies (e.g., Daro, 1988; Zigler et al., 1993) but contradicted in others (Rosenberg & Reppucci, 1983). Thus, the utility of parent education in preventing abuse re-mains an important topic of discussion. Interest in *universal* parent education for adults has increased since the mid-1970s, perhaps because traditional par-ent education programs are directed toward small and select groups, such as parents at high risk for maltreating their children, instead of toward a broad spectrum of new and potential parents.

Another type of preventive educational class should be mentioned, al-though it is not discussed in this book (because of our focus on adult clientele and prevention models): parent education classes geared toward youth. The ideology behind parent education classes geared toward youth (sometimes re-ferred to as family life education) is that educating school-age children and adolescents about child-rearing roles and responsibilities prior to parenthood decreases the risk of child maltreatment by these children as adults (Wekerle & Wolfe, 1993). In other words, it is a model for primary prevention (Bartz, 1980). The National Children's Bureau describes parent education as "a continuous process, starting with birth and early childhood and going through school days, adolescence and committed relationships, pregnancy and parenthood itself" (O'Connor, 1990, p. 85) with education tailored appropriately to developmental tasks. Often, the programs are reality based, offering experiential learning with infants and small children in on- or off-site child care centers (Luster & Youatt, 1989). They sometimes are incorporated into existing classes, such as personal and social education, moral education, home economics, and a variety of primary school classes (O'Connor, 1990).

Although broad-based programs are available, family life education has remained a neglected area of the school curriculum. This low status is ironic considering that many educators strongly believe that the family is an important part of the educational process and a stabilizing influence on society (O'Connor, 1990). The political context makes it less ironic in that many parents want less intrusion into "family life" by the schools. A parents' rights amendment, being advocated by conservative legislators, states that the rights of parents to "direct the upbringing and education of their children shall not be infringed" (Frankel & Reibstein, 1996, p. 58).

The Efficacy of Parent Education

Parent education programs rarely have been evaluated. Studies are beginning to suggest, however, that participation in parent education programs is associated with a variety of outcomes including parents' knowledge of children's emotional, social, cognitive, and physical development; their awareness of resources available to them and the level of commitment needed to function as effective parents; their knowledge of health care practices, such as the importance of immunizations and prenatal and postnatal care; and observers' ratings of parenting-related behavior (Luster & Youatt, 1989; Morgan, Nu'Man-Sheppard, & Allin, 1990; Wekerle & Wolfe, 1993). Some programs also examine outcomes related to social competence, such as self-concept, conflict resolution, and social support, which most likely enhance parental competence (Wekerle & Wolfe, 1993). One program explored the effects of parent education on the marital dyad (Winans & Cooker, 1984).

Most results indicate that parent education (directed toward parents or parents-to-be) is effective in enhancing parenting knowledge and attitudes when taught in groups (Luster & Youatt, 1989; Wekerle & Wolfe, 1993). Some programs report a decrease in authoritarian attitudes (Richett & Towns, 1980) and an increase in responsible decision making (Gritzmacher, Schultz, Shannon, & Watts, 1981), confidence in parenting ability (Gritzmacher et al., 1981; Kline, Grayson, & Mathie, 1990), and belief in children as people

(Lewko, Carriere, Whissel, & Radford, 1986). Most programs that incorporated experiential learning demonstrated behavior changes, such as an increase in active listening skills (Wekerle & Wolfe, 1993). Although these initial results are promising, the significance of these programs in preventing abuse and neglect is not yet clear (Clarke-Stewart, 1983; Powell, 1984; Wolfe, Reppucci, & Hart, 1995). (See Chapter 3 for a review of parent education curricula and their specific evaluations.)

Studies of family life education programs (directed toward adolescents) have reported that students receiving parent education evidenced gains in self-concept (Doino & Haskins, 1985), conflict resolution, and social support (Lewko et al., 1986). Longitudinal studies that incorporate direct measures of parental behavior are needed to determine whether parent education received as an adolescent influences future parental behavior and thereby promotes positive parent and child outcomes (Cooke, 1990).

FAMILY SUPPORT PROGRAMS

Community-based family support programs offer families a comprehensive variety of services and activities designed to strengthen families and neighborhoods through social networking. These programs, which may or may not have physical locations in neighborhoods, are similar to settlement houses and multipurpose neighborhood service centers in several ways. First, they work closely with families whom they serve and seek to provide tangible and readily available help. Second, families who frequent support programs take part in the delivery of services by helping others become a part of a network. Third, family support programs take into account the ethnic and cultural background of those whom they serve. These characteristics reflect the voluntary "neighbor helping neighbor" aspect of U.S. ABCAN's (1991, 1993) federal policy proposal.

The rationale for community-based family support programs is based on four factors. First, communities are responsible for protecting children because individual treatment for parents as a solution to child maltreatment is not effective (Gentry & Brisbane, 1982). Second, the structure of today's families is drastically different from that of past decades because of social, economic, and cultural changes. These changes include the entry of more women into the workforce; the feminization of poverty; diminishing earnings of men; more liberal welfare benefits; and altered attitudes about sex, marriage, and families (Elwood, 1988). Third, community and family networks that sustained previous generations are less available because of massive family relocations that have resulted in a loss of social ties, community connections, and extended family support (Cochran & Woolever, 1983; Weissbourd & Grimm, 1981; Zigler & Black, 1989). Fourth, services to families have emphasized treatment to the detriment of prevention (Gentry & Brisbane, 1982; Weissbourd &

Grimm, 1981). In many states, families qualify for supportive services only if they are actively involved with the child protection system by a report of maltreatment (Kamerman & Kahn, 1990). In conjunction with these factors, the established linkage between maltreatment and stresses and supports in neighborhoods (Garbarino & Crouter, 1978; Garbarino & Kostelny, 1992) has underscored the need for community-based support programs to assist families who lack traditional links to extended kin in developing new networks in their community (Weissbourd & Grimm, 1981). In many localities, family support programs developed because formal social services were unable to meet these needs (Zigler & Black, 1989).

Conceptually, family support programs are based on an ecological model that leads to programs that intervene at multiple levels—for example, the individual, family, community, and society—and thus reject the notion that child maltreatment has a singular etiology (Thompson, 1995). Moreover, their goal is to empower families by promoting constructive child-rearing forces and reducing destructive ones, thereby enhancing the capacities of families (Cochran & Woolever,1983; Weissbourd & Kagan, 1989). Family support programs espouse that parents are most capable of appropriate parenting when they have proper education and support. Therefore, family support meets children's needs through meeting the needs of their parents.

Family support programs usually are either community or university based. Both types recognize the importance of working with families in the context of their community (Zigler & Black, 1989). Although there is no typical family support program, the programs usually provide one or more of the following: education about child development, nutrition, health, and parenting skills; support groups; drop-in centers; home visits; child health screening; and child care relief (Weissbourd & Kagan, 1989; Wekerle & Wolfe, 1993). They usually are staffed by some combination of professionals, paraprofessionals, and volunteers. Many strive to match the cultural backgrounds of the families whom they serve (Weissbourd & Kagan, 1989).

A number of states have started to view the development of family support centers as an important part of their prevention efforts. For example, Maryland's Friends of the Family (FOF) is a network of family support centers, which was designed to reduce the state's high teen pregnancy and child maltreatment rates. Programs vary, but all provide parenting education and child development information, social support services, and help to parents interested in completing their GED (cited in Allen, Brown, & Finlay, 1992). Similarly, the Minnesota Early Childhood Family Education Program (ECFE) offers center-based parent discussion groups and parent–child activities, in addition to home visits, for parents of children under the age of 5 in most school districts (Seppanen & Heifetz, 1988). Connecticut focuses most of the attention of its Parent Education Support Centers on teenage, low-income, and African American and Hispanic parents (cited in Allen et al., 1992).

The Efficacy of Family Support Programs

The empirical rationale for community-based family support programs, although not widely established, is growing (see Wekerle & Wolfe, 1993, for a detailed summary). Maternal and child outcome studies focus on increasing birth weight, increasing school success, increasing community resource use, reducing criminality (Zigler & Black, 1989), enhancing overall parental capacities (Rosenberg & Reppucci, 1985), improving maternal/child mental and physical health (Hardy & Streett, 1989; Olds & Kitzman, 1990), improving positive parent–child interaction (Andrews et al., 1982; Epstein & Weikart, 1979), and reducing incidents of abuse and neglect (Armstrong & Fraley, 1985; Teleen, Herzog, & Kilbane, 1989). Evidence from outcome studies suggests that individualized, multilevel family support programs are effective in promoting healthy families compared with less intensive services (Dubowitz, 1989; Garbarino & Kostelny, 1992; Hardy & Streett, 1989; Lutzker, Wesch, & Rice, 1984; Olds, Henderson, Chamberlain, & Tatelbaum, 1986; Olds & Kitzman, 1990; Rosenberg & Reppucci, 1985; Thompson, 1995; Wekerle & Wolfe, 1993). This suggestion is supported across programs directed toward different types of parents—for example, "procedurally defined at-risk" parents, new and expectant parents, and adolescent parents—with the effects on parental outcome most pronounced in programs that include home visiting with parents with the highest risk of maltreatment (e.g., single parents, adolescent parents, parents with premature infants, parents at a socioeconomic disadvantage) (Wekerle & Wolfe, 1993).

The majority of positive gains in maternal behavior outcomes are found through indirect measures such as probing parenting attitudes and knowledge, but some positive gains also are found through direct measures, such as observing mother–child interactions (Wekerle & Wolfe, 1993). Some programs report a lower incidence of child abuse and neglect reports (Lutzker et al., 1984; Olds et al., 1986), whereas others report fewer emergency room visits due to injury, often an indicator of neglectful child supervision (Hardy & Streett, 1989; Olds & Kitzman, 1990). Unfortunately, there is little information on short-term maternal adjustment as an outcome variable (Wekerle & Wolfe, 1993), a factor that many programs claim is critical to promoting healthy children and families.

Evidence for child outcomes is mixed. Most programs report only modest, short-term, cognitive gains when detailed curricula about child development are included; furthermore, few studies have demonstrated long-term impact of family support programs on child development (Wekerle & Wolfe, 1993). Nevertheless, studies that examine health outcomes are promising. Some programs are effective in improving women's health-related behaviors during pregnancy, with a resulting increase in children's birth weight and gestational age (Hardy & Streett, 1989; Olds & Kitzman, 1990). Moreover, these positive health behavior effects appear to last beyond the perinatal period. Some studies report an increase in the utilization rate of sick-child clinics (Dawson, Van Doorninck, & Robinson, 1989; Olds & Kitzman, 1990), whereas others report a decrease with a corresponding increase in well-child clinic visits (Hardy & Streett, 1989). These findings may reflect an increased understanding of children's health care needs.

More research, however, is needed to demonstrate the long-term effectiveness of family support on maternal and child outcomes (Barth, 1991; Thompson, 1995). Longitudinal studies need to be conducted to determine whether improving parenting attitudes and knowledge induces behavior change. Garbarino and Kostelny (1992) cited a variety of programs whose outcome data are not yet available but should soon add to the research base.

Zigler and Black (1989) called for research to focus not only on children's cognitive development but also on social competence. Moreover, research on fathers' participation is almost nonexistent (Wekerle & Wolfe, 1993). Furthermore, little research focuses on whether family support programs increase positive social support networks and consequently improve family functioning; this is somewhat surprising considering the ideology behind family support—that increased support will improve outcomes.

Beyond systematic outcome research, there is a great need for policy-relevant research (Roberts, Wasik, Casto, & Ramey, 1991), including cost–benefit analysis (Kagan, Powell, Weissbourd, & Zigler, 1987), of which there is almost none, and studies on program implementation, process evaluation, and how family support programs can fit into existing social services structures (Zigler & Black, 1989). Some of this research is under way. For example, Project LINK is a community-based program addressing the multiple needs of substance-using pregnant and parenting women and their families in Virginia (Geller, 1991). In place is a strong external evaluation designed by university researchers including process, implementation, and outcome variables.

The Harvard Family Project (Seppanen & Heifetz, 1988) provides an in-depth look at how family support can fit into existing community services and suggests community education as an appropriate base for family support programs. Also, Miller and Whittaker (1988) provided direction regarding how family support could be integrated into child welfare and protective services.

Finally, programs report information about how families initiate involvement with family support. One program in England reported that self-referrals to a family walk-in center significantly exceeded other types of referrals (Pillai, Collins, & Morgan, 1982). The Healthy Start Program in Hawaii reported that 95% of new mothers who were offered home-visiting services accepted them (Breakey & Pratt, 1991; Thompson, 1995). Likewise, it would be helpful to know utilization rates of family support centers. Although these examples are encouraging, more information is needed.

HOME-VISITING PROGRAMS

Home-visiting programs provide services in the form of social support; parent education; and crisis intervention for promoting healthy pregnancies, infants, and mothers and preventing child abuse and neglect. Because services are brought to and offered in the home, home visitors may be able to reach families who are not able to gain access to family support programs (Garbarino & Kostelny, 1992). Home-visiting programs have existed since the 1950s, and although several states now support them through Medicaid (Olds & Kitzman, 1990), few have received sufficient funding (Hardy & Streett, 1989).

Home-visiting programs are guided by several assumptions that are shared with family support programs: 1) parents usually are the most consistent caregivers for their children; 2) parents can respond positively and effectively to their children when parents are given the knowledge, skills, and support necessary; and 3) parents' emotional and physical needs must be met in order for them to be effective parents (Wasik, Bryant, & Lyons, 1990). Most of these programs have developed in coordination with hospitals or public health prenatal clinics and serve mothers and infants in the prenatal, perinatal, and/or postnatal period through home visits by health professionals (usually public health nurses) (Dawson et al., 1991; Dubowitz, 1989; Olds et al., 1986; Olds & Kitzman, 1990; Siegel, Bauman, Schaefer, Saunders, & Ingram, 1980; Wald & Cohen, 1988), paraprofessionals such as trained perinatal coaches and parent aides (Darmstadt, 1990; Dubowitz, 1989; Siegel et al., 1980), or trained volunteers (Atkins, 1986; Hardy & Streett, 1989; Harrison, 1981). In addition, one treatment-oriented program, developed in a university setting, utilized graduate students trained in behavioral methods of change (Lutzker et al., 1984), whereas another program (Harrison, 1981) was a collaborative effort among a Junior League organization, a prevention council, and a citizen advocate group for family support programs.

Services offered through home-visiting programs depend on the skill level of the visitor and the program's underlying assumptions about preventing negative outcomes. For example, if a program assumes that isolation and psychosocial stress are causes of child maltreatment, then the visitor may fulfill primarily a supportive, social role (Olds & Kitzman, 1990). In contrast, if the assumption is that parents lack adequate knowledge of child development, then the visitor may serve as an educator and model appropriate interaction with the infant. Of course, the visitor may serve dual roles. As the visitor's role complexity increases, the education and training level of the visitor also must increase (Wasik et al., 1990).

Before examining the effectiveness of these programs, three factors—appropriateness of target groups, unintended consequences, and problems in the identification of families at risk for maltreating their children—warrant attention because of their potential impact on the interventions. Harrison (1981) suggested that some interventions are inappropriate for several types of groups, for example, parents with mental illness; parents intent on surrendering an infant for out-of-home care; parents with degenerative illnesses, such as multiple sclerosis; parents who appear to be heavily influenced by a cohabitant who abuses their children; and parents termed "recidivists," who continually abuse their children despite treatment. Although Harrison's suggestions may be accurate, she provided no empirical data to support them. Intuitively, it makes sense that parents firmly committed to surrendering a child would not be receptive to a home visitor, and in cases in which a cohabitant is abusing another's children, child protective services need to intervene immediately. In contrast, parents with mental or physical illness and their children might benefit from home-visiting services, if the parents are not actively psychotic, suicidal, or abusing substances. Little is known, however, about the effectiveness of home-visiting programs with special risk groups such as substance-abusing mothers or mothers with mental illness (Olds & Kitzman, 1990). The evaluation of Project LINK (mentioned previously; Geller, 1991) may provide initial insight into the effectiveness of home visiting with a substance-abusing group.

Some authors (e.g., Newberger, 1983) have suggested that unintended consequences may result from intervention, although sparse data exist to support these claims. For example, Olds et al. (1986) reported negative effects for a treatment group of middle-class, married mothers (specifically, extended family members were disturbed by the intervention), a group that generally is considered at low risk and that seldom is the target of home-visiting programs. Moreover, as Garbarino (1986) pointed out, the psychological and social costs associated with prevention programs may appear in the form of "conflict and heightened need for community development and social network change as components of positive interventions aimed at the parent-child relationship" (p. 145). To deal with these concerns, researchers should evaluate for unintended consequences (Olds et al., 1986).

Accurately identifying families at risk for maltreating is of critical importance. Referrals to existing home-visiting programs result from parents being labeled as "at risk" by virtue of age, marital status, socioeconomic status, or previous referral to a child protection agency. Although many of these characteristics correlate with child abuse and neglect, the risk of false positives is quite high (Leventhal, Garber, & Brady, 1989). Incorrectly labeling a family as being in need of services may lead to unintended negative consequences, such as stigmatizing them or creating feelings of inadequacy. Olds and Kitzman (1990) pointed out that available resources do not allow precise targeting of families who would be most likely to benefit from intervention; however, a universal approach to home visiting, whereby services are offered to all families in communities, such as the Hawaii Healthy Start program (Breakey & Pratt, 1991), would circumvent this problem by removing the "stigma of eligibility" present in many social services programs (Vondra, 1990). (See

Bryant, Lyons, and Wasik, 1990, for a thoughtful discussion of ethical issues in home visiting.)

The Efficacy of Home-Visiting Programs

Olds and Kitzman's (1990) comprehensive review of home-visiting programs focused on studies of randomized home-visitation trials with families at environmental risk for maternal and child health problems, which, broadly defined, included child abuse and neglect as well as developmental delays. They concluded that home-visiting programs have the greatest chance of success if they include the following three characteristics. First, they should be based on an ecological model incorporating material, social, behavioral, and psychological services and should focus on improving both maternal and child outcomes. Programs based solely on a social support model that assumes poor maternal and child outcomes as a result of high levels of psychosocial stress generally are not as effective as programs based on a more comprehensive ecological model (Dubowitz, 1989; Hardy & Streett, 1989; Olds & Kitzman, 1990; Rosenberg & Reppucci, 1985; Siegel et al., 1980).

Wolfe et al.'s (1995) review of eight studies that focused their education and training efforts largely on new and expectant first-time parents during the perinatal and postnatal periods found greater gains in parental rather than child outcomes (unless child stimulation was specifically targeted) and increased efficacy of intensive home visitation (1–3 years). Moreover, they found support for matching treatment length to subject need or risk (i.e., parents at high risk benefit more from intensive, long-term interventions). Several studies of programs that focused on providing teen parents with basic knowledge of child care and child development (e.g., Field, Widmayer, Greenberg, & Stoller, 1982; Field, Widmayer, Stringer, & Ignatoff, 1980) found that children of home-visited mothers were more interactive and positive than children of control mothers and that home-visited mothers reported greater educational attainment and fewer subsequent pregnancies. Wolfe et al. (1995) concluded that although suggestive, the (maltreatment) preventive potential of these interventions is uncertain because neither child abuse reports nor child health variables were measured.

Second, home-visiting programs need to be designed with a focus on the ecology of the family during pregnancy and early childhood. In other words, home visiting must occur frequently and extend over a period of time long enough to be able to address the factors that influence child and maternal outcomes (Olds & Kitzman, 1990). Several studies support timing and duration of home visits as a crucial factor (Larson, 1980; Siegel et al., 1980), with early and extended contact between mother and visitor contributing to successful intervention. As Hardy and Streett (1989) noted, only after daily crises in the lives of poor families were resolved (e.g., threat of eviction; lack of heat;

money for diapers, food, and formula) could the mothers' attention become focused on parenting and health issues. In turn, home visitors often became valued and trusted resources, advocates, and friends.

Third, to increase positive outcomes and to prevent stigmatizing individual families, home-visiting programs must target entire communities of families at greatest risk for negative outcomes. This is consistent with the results of previously mentioned programs. Olds and Kitzman (1990) believed that because individual families cannot be accurately targeted, intervention efforts should focus on communities with high rates of poverty and/or single and adolescent parents because of their lack of personal and social resources. Universal programs designed with different numbers of sessions and levels of intensity for families depending on risk may be a nonstigmatizing and feasible solution. If resources are limited, then it also may be essential to delimit target groups further. For example, although there is no direct evidence that home-visiting programs affect first-time mothers differently than they affect mothers of later-born children, it may make sense to focus efforts on first-time mothers because the intervention effects may carry over to subsequent births (Olds & Kitzman, 1990). Olds et al. (1986) reported a study in which first-time mothers with the intervention actually had fewer subsequent births. Of course, it also could be true that additional children increase stress on mothers enough that the impact of the intervention may be diluted.

In addition to careful investigation of home-visiting programs that incorporate the characteristics noted by Olds and Kitzman (1990), other intervention components deserve study. For example, identifying the characteristics of effective home visitors and type of training that they need may be critical (Dawson et al., 1991; Roberts et al., 1991). The most effective trials appear to be those utilizing employed nurses (Olds & Kitzman, 1990), college-educated women who were once members of the community served by the program (Hardy & Streett, 1989), and psychology graduate students trained in behavioral methods (Lutzker et al., 1984), but very little is actually known about this issue.

Studies of cost-effectiveness also are needed to assess whether home-visiting programs pay for themselves through averted expenditures for future medical and psychosocial services. Comparing the cost of home visiting with an emergency room visit as a result of child maltreatment, Hardy and Streett (1989) concluded that the cost of averted medical expenses was greater than the total cost of the home-visiting program. Cost-effectiveness obviously is determined by the outcome measures chosen. For example, although emergency room costs were included in this analysis, costs associated with child maltreatment in terms of child protective services and law enforcement were not. If these costs were included with costs for maltreatment cases that become court involved, projected savings would undoubtedly skyrocket.

Finally, the home-visiting evaluation literature has focused on short-term change despite the goal that ecological interventions address proximal *and* distal causes of child maltreatment. Evaluations of home-visiting interventions would be more conclusive if they incorporated short- and long-term evaluation (Rosenberg & Reppucci, 1985). The strongest statement that an intervention program could make is that its preventive effects lasted throughout the greatest period of risk for child maltreatment, namely the first few years of the child's life (Zigler et al., 1993). Therefore, future research should incorporate longitudinal designs.

CONCLUSION

The concept of child-centered, neighborhood-based child protection programs warrants serious attention by policy makers, researchers, and service providers. Voluntary programs such as parent education and family support programs, including home visiting, appear promising as strategies for preventing child abuse and neglect and may be viable alternatives to a coercive child protection system centered on investigation and treatment. As Wolfe et al. (1995) pointed out, "Overall, those programs that span from 1 to 3 years and provide a personalized approach (e.g., home visits) stand out as being most successful in achieving the desired outcomes and most successful with higher-risk individuals" (p. 12).

The implementation of ABCAN's federal policy proposal may allow overburdened and taxed child welfare service providers to concentrate their efforts on families that are the most seriously isolated and in need—those for whom family support programs with an endless amount of home visitation would not be effective.

Child-centered, neighborhood-based programs are the cornerstone of ABCAN's recommendations. Without further systemic restructuring of supporting agencies' goals in relation to child maltreatment, however, family support and home-visitation programs could become overwhelmed. These programs cannot function alone and are not designed to do so. It must be recognized that family support and home visitation work best when they empower families to develop the skills and knowledge necessary to recognize their strengths and weaknesses and then to seek and effectively utilize services.

Critical to the continuing development and implementation of parent education, family support, and home-visiting programs are systematic research and evaluation. We have identified several crucial areas to study: long-term effectiveness of parenthood education on parental behavior, efficacy of family support programs to increase social support, and identifying the characteristics and training of home visitors that are critical to successful programs. All studies should include outcomes measures of the incidence and prevalence of child maltreatment as one indicator of program efficacy. In addition, Zigler and Black's (1989) call for policy-relevant, cost–benefit, process, and implementation research should be met. This research could play a role in redefining the delivery of prevention and supportive services to families from mandated intervention to voluntary services.

Curricula and
Their Evaluation

Assumptions Underlying
Parent Education

chapter • 3

In the 1960s, a governmental shift in policy encouraged state intervention "in the best interests of the child" when the parents were unable to perform their child-rearing role adequately (Dokecki & Moroney, 1983). Since then, parent education programs of various types and orientations have been initiated throughout the United States. Many of the programs are designed to prevent or end child maltreatment or family violence by improving family functioning. Programs, both state supported and private, have expanded and diversified. Copyrighted curricula have been used extensively throughout the United States and have been endorsed by child abuse councils and task forces. After adequate time to implement evaluations and because of trends toward greater fiscal accountability, parenting programs now must face the difficult task of justifying their funding with evidence of their efficacy in preventing family violence.

This chapter explores some of the aspects of parent education programs, which have been theorized to be useful in preventing child abuse and neglect. The chapter is divided into four sections: 1) a brief summary of the rationale behind approaches to parent education, 2) a critical review of the existing body of empirical literature related to parent education in general, 3) an examination of the major specific parent education curricula in use in Virginia and the evaluation data available for those curricula, and 4) some broad-based recommendations and calls for further research efforts from experts in the field of child maltreatment prevention.

The authors thank Peter A. Dillon for his contributions to an earlier draft of this chapter.

WHY PARENT EDUCATION?

Given the state of knowledge about the etiology of family violence, does it make sense to expect parent education programs to prevent abuse? It can be argued that these programs benefit families in two separate but related ways: 1) by increasing parenting knowledge of child development and effective discipline and 2) by decreasing parental distress through expanding social support networks.

Parenting Knowledge

Justifications for parent education as an intervention for improving family functioning (generally) and preventing abuse and neglect (specifically) have been based on developmental research on socioeconomic status (SES), deprivation, critical periods, interactions between child and mother (at the expense of other caregivers), and laboratory manipulations. Clarke-Stewart (1983) noted the limitations of each line of inquiry in relation to parent education, but she observed that these lines of research converge on the conclusion that parental behavior does affect development throughout childhood. Frank and Rowe (1981), for example, concluded that teaching mothers about the emotional development of young children will minimize the occurrence of child abuse in groups at high risk (e.g., parents from low-income or isolated settings, teen mothers), on the basis of findings that abusive parents have more inappropriate expectations and demands for their children.

Although these empirical studies of abusive parents' knowledge of typical child development are few in number (Rosenberg & Reppucci, 1983), mental health professionals working with these parents commonly noted that many cases of child abuse resulted from inappropriate expectations of children's abilities (Altepeter & Walker, 1992). Parents who interpret developmental limitations as deliberate noncompliance are likely to experience frustration and anger in dealing with their children (Belsky & Vondra, 1989). For example, the difficult phases of colic, awakening at night, separation anxiety, exploratory behavior, negativism, poor appetite, and toilet-training resistance have been described as the "seven deadly sins" of childhood (Schmitt, 1987). These are frustrating for any parent, but in the context of families at high risk for maltreating their children and who are not prepared to cope with them, these behaviors are likely to precipitate harsh punishment or episodes of abuse. It is one goal of parent education programs to prevent abuse by teaching parents to expect and deal with such difficulties.

Education about nonviolent disciplinary alternatives is another advantage of parenting classes. Parent education programs provide a means for parents to learn effective parenting practices from sources other than their own upbringing. Bavolek and Comstock (1985), for example, wrote in their Nurturing curriculum that "to offset the generational perpetuation of dysfunctional parenting practices, education in appropriate parenting and child rearing is viewed as the single most important treatment and intervention strategy" (p. 3).

If physical abuse itself is conceptualized as an inappropriate and extreme form of discipline, then it follows that abusive parents typically lack an awareness of appropriate discipline; some studies have supported this notion (Barrick, 1988; Zigler, Hopper, & Hall, 1993). Other studies, however, have found these parents to be surprisingly knowledgeable about discipline alternatives and describe typical responses to misbehavior that very often are appropriate techniques (Kadushin & Martin, 1981; Rosenberg & Reppucci, 1983). In stating that parent education is a worthwhile means of preventing family violence, one must be careful not to assume that abusive parents as a group have poor parenting skills (Rosenberg & Hunt, 1984). Given the resilience demonstrated by children when rearing environments are improved, however, knowledge of child development and basic child-rearing practices may lessen the stress of parenting for the parent and improve the child's chance for healthy development, in spite of the presence of other "risk" factors (Bartz, 1980; Showers, 1991). Feshbach and Feshbach (1978) went so far as to call for mandatory parent education for *all* teenagers.

Stress Support

If the dissemination of parenting information alone could be expected to be effective prevention, then the many books in print related to child rearing could be hypothesized to prevent abuse. Parent education programs provide this information in a social context, either through parenting group formats or through individual home visitors. Above and beyond the delivery of information on parenting skills, the social support functions of parent education programs are essential components of comprehensive prevention services (Olds & Henderson, 1989). The transition to parenthood has been associated with the negative stress factors of increased physical demands, strains on the marital relationship, emotional stresses, and the realization of opportunity costs and restrictions, especially for young, single parents (Belsky, Ward, & Rovine, 1985). An ecological ("real world") paradigm of looking at abuse prevention emphasizes the situational nature of abuse and suggests that the most salient risk factors may be the situational demands that place the highest levels of stress on those who are predisposed to abuse, in the absence of sufficient support systems (Altepeter & Walker, 1992). Approaches that seek to reduce situational stressors vary from support systems with ambiguous or broad-based goals to specific behavior modification programs designed to change a particular type of behavior—for example, parent workshops to encourage children's altruistic behavior (Patrick & Minish, 1985). Parent education classes for adolescent and adult parents are viewed as important means of removing "nonfacilitating environments" from family members' lives (Anastasiow, 1988, p. 64).

Other parent groups focus more on humanistic support of parents at risk by means of informal discussion and linkage to appropriate community services in an ecological attempt to pay attention to the parents' relevant social contexts (Powell, 1984). Whereas traditional parent education classes assume that the dissemination of knowledge will translate into changes in behaviors and attitudes (although there is no systematic evidence that this is the case), the support approach assumes that the provision of social support will have a positive effect on family functioning (Powell, 1989). Social support may need to be matched to specific stressors in order to be effective, however (Coyne & DeLongis, 1986; Tetzloff & Barrera, 1987). Felton and Berry (1992) suggested that groups may serve different supportive functions than individuals. Powell (1989) discussed the value of "kitchen talk," or informal conversations, during which group members grow closer by sharing experiences. Unfortunately, it is unclear whether parent support programs are effective in reducing stress and, if they are, which characteristics of the program are effective and which specific stressors are being reduced. Whether increasing parenting knowledge leads to decreased parental stress or whether parenting groups directly alleviate stress, teasing out the differential effects of parent education and support orientations requires careful research.

EVALUATING EFFECTIVENESS

Evaluating child abuse prevention programs is an extremely difficult process (Rosenberg & Reppucci, 1985). An initial step is deciding on outcome variables to be measured. A direct measure of outcome might be the number of founded cases of abuse among program participants. Indirect measures of effectiveness, such as changes in parental stress, knowledge of child development, or changes in children's behavior (just to name a few), are more easily obtained. Simple pre- and postprogram measures of these variables can point out changes within the sample of participants; however, factors other than the program itself, such as familiarity with the repeated measures, participants' exposure to information from the media rather than from the class, or a natural tendency for extreme levels of distress to decrease over time (many other possible "third variables" exist), could account for these changes. In addition, short-term changes in knowledge or behavior may or may not translate into long-term change or prevention. Therefore, in order to attribute the cause of change to the program in an empirically valid manner, participants must be randomly assigned to a parent education group or to a control group (which does not take part in the program) and followed longitudinally. Documented changes in the parent education group that exceed changes in the control group represent empirical support for the effectiveness of the program. Many practical difficulties (e.g., high service loads, already-overworked staff) make this type of data collection challenging but not impossible for already-busy service agencies. Such studies of multiple programs using a variety of curricula, formats, and orientations would constitute a strong body of literature in support of parent education in preventing family violence.

Do Programs Work?

Most parenting programs remain untested with adequate control groups, if they have been studied at all (Olds & Henderson, 1989). Moreover, the majority of evaluations have been simplistic (Clarke-Stewart, 1983). The database is limited, and the variety of programs makes generalizability difficult; overall, answers are lacking to questions of program effectiveness (Powell, 1984). Clarke-Stewart (1983), nevertheless, concluded that evaluations of parent programs generally have yielded positive outcomes as a variety of parent intervention programs have been associated with elevated IQ levels (sometimes long term) in children. In contrast, a review of 48 studies involving humanistic (focusing on support), behavioral (focusing on discipline), and Adlerian (focusing on child development knowledge and parenting skills) programs found resultant parental attitude changes to be inconsistent and related to the measurement instruments; methodological problems abounded in the studies, and behavior changes were not shown to result from program participation in most cases (Dembo, Sweitzer, & Lauritzen, 1985). This suggests that further research is vital to establishing empirical links between parent education and behavior changes, especially for child abuse and neglect.

Studies by Wolfe and colleagues (Wolfe, Edwards, Manion, & Koverola, 1988; Wolfe, Sandler, & Kaufman, 1981) represent rare attempts at studying the efficacy of behavioral parent training as a secondary prevention strategy. In this research, parents (identified as at risk for child maltreatment) who completed a 9-week behavioral training program were more likely to show improvement on several parenting risk factors at posttest and be rated better by case workers at a 12-month follow-up than were parents who received only a 9-week informational intervention. Unfortunately, the results of this work, like so many other lines of inquiry, are plagued by questions of sampling and have yet to be replicated.

Most of the evaluation studies just discussed consisted of simple pretest and posttest designs without a control group and represent important initial steps in establishing the efficacy of the programs; however, clinical psychologists for decades have been training parents in behavior management techniques as a treatment for conduct disorder in children. Because of the similarity of the curricula and outcome variables commonly targeted by prevention programs and by clinicians, a brief summary of this body of literature seems relevant. Parent training interventions in a variety of formats and theoretical orientations have been evaluated in hundreds of outcome studies (Kazdin, 1987) and generally are considered to be among the most effective treatments for conduct disorder (Gurman, Kniskern, & Pinsof, 1986). Whereas only about half of the studies used a control group (Rogers Weise, 1992), most that have used adequate experimental control have demonstrated significant improvement in the behavior of the identified child or in the parenting skills of the participants (Baum & Forehand, 1981; Kazdin, 1987; Parsons & Alexander, 1973; Patterson, Chamberlain, & Reid, 1982; Webster-Stratton, 1984).

Although the effectiveness of parent training as an intervention does not translate into direct support for the efficacy of parent education as prevention, it does offer encouragement. For example, the impact of parent training has been found to be broad, affecting siblings of targeted children and parental psychopathology. This suggests that educating parents can have preventive effects that generalize beyond targeted children with conduct disorder (Kazdin, 1987). The question of how well this clinical literature generalizes to parent education prevention programs is open to debate. For example, it could be argued that because families under clinically significant distress may feel a strong motivation to alter their parenting practices, the intervention has greater potential for positive impact. It also could be argued that parent education as a means of prevention may show even greater success in that parents who are not in crisis will be less emotionally overwhelmed and more receptive to information. Given the relative weakness of the body of literature demonstrating the efficacy of these prevention programs, the clinical literature on parent training provides some additional credibility to the argument that parent education can prevent family violence.

How Do Programs Work?

Simple pretest and posttest comparisons cannot explain the processes by which family functioning changes. It is unclear to what extent programs are being implemented according to the curricula, getting through to parents, resulting in desired changes in parental and child behavior, and having a lasting impact (Clarke-Stewart, 1983). Intervention in the form of parenting classes typically has been viewed as present or absent, without any consideration of the variety of parents' experiences in evaluating the effectiveness of the program (Powell, 1989). Variables such as the parents' demographic characteristics, social network ties, input or involvement, facilitators' training, the nature of the parent–facilitator role, program length, and program setting must be considered in order to understand better the mechanisms of any changes resulting from parent education. The degree to which curricula are modified (versus strictly adhered to) is an important area of study in evaluating curriculum effects, given the wide variety of implementation practices in the field. Other possibilities for studying the process of change include investigating the influences of parents' own childhood experiences on their child rearing (Powell, 1984). In attempting to "break the cycle of abuse," several attachment theorists (e.g., Crittenden & Ainsworth, 1989; Egeland, Jacobvitz,

& Sroufe, 1988) have emphasized the importance of working through the parents' memories of their own abuse as children before dealing with the demands of parenting. According to these theorists, parent education needs to focus on integrating the parents' own attachment experiences, how they view their child, and how those relationships influence their view of child rearing (Egeland et al., 1988).

Do Certain Types Work Best?

Studies of curricula, length of program, program intensity, and instructional techniques often have been confounded and have yielded inconclusive results (Clarke-Stewart, 1983). There is wide variability in "parent education," including support groups, community resource networking, home-based programs, and the more traditional lecture/discussion courses. Though diverse approaches may be effective (depending on one's criteria), identifying a "best" type of program has been unsuccessful; it may be more important to identify under which conditions program models are effective (Powell, 1984). With respect to the clients who actually are served, Powell (1989) suggested that parents' participation in various types of support and education groups is related to levels of environmental stress, social networks, and parents' dispositional or demographic characteristics.

No conclusive evidence exists to suggest that parent-focused programs are more effective than child-focused programs (Clarke-Stewart, 1983), nor are there any cost–benefit studies that directly relate to parent education. The Perry Preschool project used a long-term follow-up of experimental and control groups to evaluate the costs and benefits of parent training and quality early childhood education for children who are at risk for abuse or neglect in terms of a variety of outcomes at 15 and 19 years of age (Barnett, 1985; Schweinhart & Weikart, 1988). The designers of the program were able to conclude that the program, on the basis of its strong methodological foundation, was both important for long-term social functioning and cost-efficient because of its effects on education, income, criminal behavior, welfare benefits, and so forth; however, it is not possible to separate the parent and child components of this model prevention program.

Haskins and Adams (1983), using the existing literature, found no evidence that would allow them to conclude that parent education was any more effective than other social programs or that the classes should be rated highly on criteria of preference satisfaction, efficiency, or freedom from social stigma. Other researchers (e.g., Clarke-Stewart, 1983; Olds & Henderson, 1989; Powell, 1989; Rosenberg & Reppucci, 1985) were less pessimistic about the potential of parent education in preventing abuse and other negative outcomes, but they maintained the need for more comprehensive ecological approaches and more stringent evaluation techniques.

PARENT EDUCATION CURRICULA

The parent education field is maturing and expanding, with many orientations falling under the rubric of parent education. Kramer (1990) suggested that the three perspectives of humanistic, behavioral, and Adlerian programs have had the most impact on the parenting education literature. Like the programs reviewed next, most of the parenting approaches (e.g., Parenting Skills [Abidin, 1982]; Parent Effectiveness Training [Gordon, 1970]; Parents of Young Children [Wetzel, 1990]) involve 9–15 sessions of lecture and discussion, with a focus on teaching democratic parenting methods, improving the parent's self-concept, and (ultimately) improving the behavioral functioning of all family members. Other "educational" programs are more rooted in support and, in fact, more closely resemble support groups such as Parents Anonymous (see Fritz, 1989).

Evaluations comparing the various parent education orientations have yielded tentative support for the use of parent education. For example, Cole (1986) noted that simple evaluative research generally has supported the effectiveness of the humanistic and Adlerian parenting groups. Adlerian approaches generally involve the teaching of democratic parenting methods in which the purposes or goals of a behavior are analyzed; the interconnected nature of thoughts, feelings, and behaviors are used to describe the mutual influences of parents and children on one another (Cole, 1986). Nystul (1982) summarized several studies in which parents in more behavior-oriented programs displayed more physical contact with their children than did controls or parents in Adlerian parent classes. Showers (1991) found that the use of child behavior management flash cards (featuring developmental and behavioral expectations) in a parenting class with pregnant and parenting teens resulted in changes in the teens' knowledge base that were sustained over 3 months. Other studies (e.g., Barrick, 1988) have found parent education classes, as they are currently delivered, to be poorly targeted, sparsely attended, and generally ineffective in changing the knowledge of abuse indicators or appropriate expectations for those parents who did regularly attend.

On the whole, parent education shows some promise as an indirect means of preventing child maltreatment, with improved knowledge potentially leading to attitude and behavior changes. Most published materials for abuse and neglect prevention programs, however, have undergone little or no experimental testing. The different curricula also vary in terms of reading level and difficulty, target groups, and approaches that may be more or less effective with various participant groups (Kramer, 1990). Before discussing recommendations related to the implementation of programs, four of the most popular parent education programs (Active Parenting, the Nurturing Program, Parents as Teachers, and Systematic Training for Effective Parenting) in the United States and in Virginia are reviewed in greater detail.

Active Parenting

Active Parenting (Popkin, 1989) is a 6-session video-based delivery system for teaching basic parenting skills. There are few content differences from other Adlerian programs (i.e., those that focus on the role of the family and context in the child's environment) such as STEP (Dinkmeyer & McKay, 1976, 1982), but the videotaped role plays are used liberally with in-class practice activities and discussions. The potential for modeling needed skills or behaviors from the videotapes is appealing to some behavior-oriented researchers (Kramer, 1990).

Popkin (1989) reported that 97% of 274 parents experienced desired changes in their own parenting after completing the 6-week course in a 1984 field test of the program. Participants were predominantly white (92%), well-educated (67% had a college degree), older (mean age of 40.7 years), and female (74%). Generalizability is limited because of the restricted sample. Buroker (1993) documented short-term parenting behavior changes in participants but used no control group. In a review of the Active Parenting program, Cole (1986) noted that the program was designed for relatively well-adjusted families and not intended to remedy situations involving abuse or neglect. The program also makes no provisions for children or families with special needs. Cole concluded that the program is well-designed for teaching basic parenting skills but that sound research on the effectiveness of the program is needed.

The Nurturing Program

The Nurturing Program is a 15-session Adlerian parent education program with versions suitable for use with parents and their children under the age of 5 (Bavolek & Dellinger-Bavolek, 1989) and ages 4–12 (Bavolek & Comstock, 1985). The program advocates that all members of the family must be involved in the treatment condition to precipitate change, yet growth in the parent must be achieved before growth in the parent–child interaction can occur (Bavolek & Comstock, 1985).

The Nurturing Program is the most widely used curriculum among Virginia Family Violence Prevention Program (VFVPP) grantees, partly because training for the curriculum is available through the advocacy group Prevent Child Abuse–Virginia (PCA–V) and because the curriculum materials, purchased by the Commonwealth with federal challenge grant money, are available. Parents Anonymous in Virginia originally selected the curriculum and set up a number of Nurturing Programs on the basis of its attractive format and apparent efficacy, as demonstrated through research by the program's originators and cited in the curriculum's manuals.

Some instrumentation for evaluating process change and satisfaction with the program are included with the curriculum. The Family Social History Questionnaire is a self-report questionnaire designed to tap demographics and past and current abuse for the participant, his or her spouse or partner, and the children. Parents may be asked weekly to complete the Nurturing Program Family Log, a form on which they note how they, their children, and their family are changing as a result of their participation in the program, and the Program Evaluation Form, which taps their feelings about the session. The authors of the curriculum note that attention also should be paid to attendance, participation, and completion of home practice exercises in evaluating program process. There also is a modified version for use with teen parents.

The standard outcome assessment tool of program effectiveness included with the Nurturing curriculum is the Nurturing Quiz, a 25-item pre- and posttest of knowledge of appropriate child development—each item has "only one right answer" (Bavolek & Dellinger-Bavolek, 1989, p. 24). The Adult-Adolescent Parenting Inventory (AAPI) (Bavolek, 1984) is an instrument, independent of the Nurturing curriculum, recommended for pre–post comparisons of 32 statements about parenting and raising children on the constructs of inappropriate expectations, empathy, corporal punishment, and parent-child role reversal.

Incorporating role playing, rehearsal, and attempts to support parents as they implement skills and tactics during the Nurturing Program may assist parents in learning the desired skills for behavior changes (Kramer, 1990). The research cited in the curriculum's manuals, however, is limited to simple pretest and posttest assessments of short-term knowledge and attitude change. There are no data from controlled studies to support the effectiveness of either program implementation or behavior change outcomes for the Nurturing curriculum.

Parents as Teachers

The Missouri-based Parents as Teachers (PAT) curriculum has grown from a four-site pilot program to a statewide program operating through the public school system, in addition to most other states and a few other countries. More extensive and broad based than some of the strict parent education curricula, PAT consists of home visits; parent meetings; systematic monitoring of children's medical and developmental status; and referrals to government agencies, such as social services, as needed. Although each program is implemented differently (from target group to recruitment strategy to curriculum), a statewide evaluation (without control groups) suggested that the program was successful in identifying early child risks and improving child school performance and parent knowledge of child development, except in the case of non–English-speaking mothers with less than a high school education (cited in Allen, Brown, & Finlay, 1992; Zigler et al., 1993).

Systematic Training for Effective Parenting

Systematic Training for Effective Parenting (STEP) (Dinkmeyer & McKay, 1976; 1982) is a 9-week, 2-hours-per-session, Adlerian-based parent program consisting of lectures and discussion skills training, with an emphasis on communication skills. STEP also provides parents with some basic counseling skills that they can use with their children.

The program is very popular across the United States, but evaluative research is limited (Cole, 1986). In one attempt to evaluate the STEP program, a sample of 28 middle- to upper-class Australian mothers from intact families were randomly assigned to a control (no class) or experimental (9-week STEP class) condition. Following participation in the class, STEP mothers (by self-report) were more democratic, encouraged more verbalization, and were less likely to be strict with their children than were control group mothers (Nystul, 1982). The small and homogeneous sample limits the extent to which the conclusions may be applied to other groups. In another Australian sample (Allan, 1994), STEP participants reported that they were better able to control angry reactions and to understand their children's behavior. Given the limitations of existing evaluations, the lack of research validating this widely used program has led some critics to conclude that STEP has "no empirical support" (Kramer, 1990, p. 525). There is a body of research, however, that consistently finds short-term knowledge and attitude change among parents who have completed the STEP program (Brooks et al., 1988; Dinkmeyer, McKay, & Dinkmeyer, 1990; Hammett, Omizo, & Loffredo, 1981; Jackson & Brown, 1986; Nystul, 1982; Summerlin & Ward, 1981; Williams, Omizo, & Abrams, 1984).

Summary

Although there may be some evidence of changes in attitudes, knowledge, or behaviors resulting from parent education classes, none of the programs reviewed have been compared with control groups to evaluate their effectiveness in preventing abuse and neglect. Such studies would be time consuming and costly but extremely valuable. We can only assume that parent education serves as a means of primary prevention for child maltreatment.

RECOMMENDATIONS FOR PARENT EDUCATION

Based on extensive study of Minnesota's Early Childhood Family Education programs (many of which have been in operation since the early 1970s), Seppanen and Heifetz (1988) found that the programs that served families at risk most successfully had several characteristics in common: 1) formal and informal communication occurred across community organizations, such that parent education and support services did not compete with other services; 2) staff were successful in locating multiple funding sources; 3) programs served the needs of parents and children (see also Bavolek & Comstock, 1985; Kramer, 1990; Powell, 1989); and 4) staff relied on group process techniques more than on a fixed syllabus of topics. Powell (1989) also noted a shift from standardized, curriculum-based classes to individualized programs that are culturally responsive and contextually relevant to the family. In addition, Powell argued for the implementation of programs with sustained contacts (i.e., at least 3 months) in order to achieve the most pervasive and sustained effects on family functioning. This recommendation calls into question the effectiveness of short parent education classes that are not accompanied by long-term follow-ups or other contacts.

Furstenberg, Brooks-Gunn, and Chase-Lansdale (1989), in their review of maltreatment prevention efforts geared toward teen mothers, concluded that parenting education programs in home-visiting and center-based programs can be successful in improving teens' (as well as adults') parenting skills and their children's development. They, too, emphasized the need for coordinated services for children of teens and children in poverty, the importance of good child care as a potential source of enhancement of the quality of life for both mothers and children, and the need to abandon the notion of teen mothers as a homogeneous population.

Olds and Henderson (1989) called for a multifaceted approach to preventing maltreatment. They concluded that education about children's competencies and demands is an important part of abuse prevention but that it must be accompanied by efforts to give support and reduce the situational problems that are interfering with the parents' child rearing. This suggests that parent education should be considered one component of a larger, more comprehensive abuse and neglect prevention strategy.

Substance Abuse Component

Most parent education curricula fail to address the issue of substance abuse. Because substance abuse is known to affect some of the clients served and can interfere severely with good parenting (Wolfe, 1991), some human services projects amend their curricula to cover this topic or augment their parenting classes with occasional seminars focusing on substance abuse; other programs make referrals to appropriate agencies. The absence of a strong substance abuse component may limit a program's ability to reach its intended clientele or effect long-term change in those clients with substance abuse problems.

Relationship with State Service Agencies

Many maltreatment prevention programs operate from within their local Department of Social Services (DSS) or Community Services Board/Community Mental Health Center (CSB/CMHC), benefiting from that agency's resources; some, however, avoid mentioning such associations publicly because of the stigma attached to DSS in some communities. Often, local DSS and CSB agencies and courts provide referrals, and, in return, many projects provide information about clients to these entities. Most of the published curricula fail to give guidelines on how to modify the parenting classes given different types of clientele (or mixed groups of "known" abusers and "nonabusers") or deal with the issues of confidentiality and which information will be shared with other organizations. In terms of evaluations, it also is important to consider past history of abuse when evaluating the effectiveness of a given program because abusers are more likely than nonabusers to commit a violent act (Wolfe, 1991).

CONCLUSION

Parent education appears to be a promising strategy for influencing parental attitudes and short-term behavior change; less is known with respect to long-term change or its effectiveness in preventing child maltreatment. Given the diversity of programs and participants, all tentative conclusions about the effectiveness of parent education must be taken with a healthy dose of skepticism. Clearly, further methodologically sound evaluative research is necessary for us to understand more about the processes and outcomes of various parent education and support programs and the parents whom they serve.

Evaluation for the Prevention Educator

Although many service providers and policy makers agree that evaluation is an important component of any service program, in reality few effective evaluations are required, funded, and implemented for child abuse treatment and prevention programs (Starr, 1990). A number of practical barriers may serve to prevent systematic evaluation of prevention programs. Barriers include lack of funding, lack of time, and lack of knowledge. Given the realities of limited funding and staffing for most prevention programming, including child abuse and neglect prevention, the desire to focus scarce resources on direct services is understandable. The lack of evaluation, however, truly does a disservice in the long run to service providers, policy makers, and, especially, program recipients. Policy makers want to fund programs that work, service providers want to meet their clients' needs effectively, and clients want to have their problems addressed. None of this can happen effectively and efficiently without the knowledge gained from some form of evaluation.

This chapter introduces the concept of evaluation for child abuse prevention programs. First, we talk openly about the misconceptions of implementing evaluation techniques and show that the long-term benefits outweigh the short-term costs. Second, goals and objectives are highlighted as key components of any evaluation process. Third, three types of evaluation are introduced—needs, process, and outcome. For each type, we review its purpose, the type of information it provides, and implementation considerations.

COMMON MISCONCEPTIONS ABOUT EVALUATION

It is important to acknowledge up front that there are costs and benefits associated with implementing evaluation techniques. Sometimes common misconceptions can cause the negative impact of evaluation to be exaggerated and the benefits that accrue to be ignored.

1. *"Evaluation just criticizes my program and points out the problems. We are doing the best that we can with what we have."* Evaluation is not designed just to expose problems. A good evaluation examines a program in its entirety. The general intent of an evaluation is documentation—systematically describing how a program works within its current situation. Certainly, an evaluation is designed to uncover program difficulties. The reality is that programs that undertake evaluation must be willing to uncover areas that may need improvement. A program has to take that risk in order to improve! Moreover, evaluation also can uncover unanticipated and undocumented benefits of programs. For example, if a parent education program increases parental knowledge (the stated goal) but serves the indirect purpose of empowering parents to become more involved in their child's schooling, then that program benefit also needs to be documented.

2. *"What my program does can't be measured or reduced to a bunch of numbers. We know it works. We don't need an evaluation to tell us that."* Evaluation is not just about reducing a program to a bunch of numbers. Sometimes it *is* hard to capture the experience of client successes without telling their stories. That is why evaluation techniques can incorporate quantitative (numerical) and qualitative (non-numerical) information. Both are critical for understanding a program. For almost every program, however, some aspects can be measured in a systematic, numerical way. For example, parent education workshops can be measured in terms of the types of information conveyed, the number of new ideas, the knowledge of the participants, and the changes in parenting behavior that occur after participation. Similar measurements can occur for home-visiting programs and other types of education techniques. Moreover, numbers can be important for helping people *outside* of the program to understand it. Numbers can improve presentations to oversight agencies, advisory boards, national organizations, community groups, and funding agencies.

3. *"Evaluation doesn't have any relevance. It creates lots of paperwork and reports that end up sitting on a shelf somewhere."* If evaluation is not used to its fullest potential, then there is a chance that it may end up gathering dust on a shelf. The key is making evaluation work *for* a program. Evaluation information can work on two levels. On a day-to-day level, information obtained from sound, evaluative techniques can help ensure that a program is meeting its intended purpose. It also can help a program remain flexible and adapt to the changing needs of clients. For example, evaluating what clients learn each week in an educational program can help shape the next week's activities—reviewing material that was not understood, addressing important concerns, or covering new topics. In the

larger scope, evaluation data also can serve to justify program efforts to policy makers and other funding sources. Solid information about clients, program activities, and outcome measures provides a comprehensive picture of program achievements and may help providers acquire additional or continued funding. Scarce financial resources require that program efficacy justify significant expenditures. If a parenting education program can document its clientele, service delivery, and changes in outcome measures, then it might be more competitive in a grant funding decision or a round of governmental budget cuts than would other existing programs based solely on good ideas without good data.

Evaluation is an ongoing process that can be integrated into the continued existence of a prevention program. The products of an evaluation can help program administrators serve clients better by delineating which aspects of the program are successful and which aspects need adjusting or reformulating. Evaluation also can provide the information necessary to justify to external decision makers a program's continued existence. The next section discusses how to facilitate effective evaluation and the types of information that different evaluations can provide.

FACILITATING EVALUATION:
PROGRAM GOALS AND OBJECTIVES

Before an evaluation can be put into place and information collected about a program, several things must happen. The most important activity often can be the most difficult—identifying concrete program goals and objectives. Goals are general statements that specify the end condition that should occur as a function of the program (Price & Smith, 1985). The goals must be clearly specified so that they can be translated into operational terms and therefore measured through specific objectives (Kaufman & Zigler, 1992; Price & Smith, 1985; Weiss, 1972). Concrete goals and objectives should be created for a number of reasons:

- *Goals and objectives make the purpose and intended impact explicit.* Without delineating and agreeing on what the activities of a prevention program are, staff may not all be working toward the same activities and outcomes. Clear goals and objectives can help ensure that all people involved with the project are on the same page. They also provide the measures of impact and outcome—program success can be defined and measured in terms of meeting goals and objectives.
- *Returning to the goals and objectives during the course of service delivery can remind staff of the intended activities and outcomes.* If the program is no longer focusing on the original goals and objectives, then this indicates

that either 1) the program has unnecessarily strayed from its intended purpose and needs to get back on track; or 2) the program is intentionally changing in response to something (e.g., changes in target group, potential duplication of services), and, perhaps, goals and objectives need to be reformulated.

• *Goals and objectives enable staff to communicate more effectively about accountability.* Accountability is both internal, in terms of management and staff responsibility, and external, in terms of the criteria by which project success is judged. Determinations of whether goals and objectives have been met can provide feedback to program administrators regarding strengths and weaknesses of implementation. This feedback also can be used to provide to potential and current funding agencies concrete measures of success, as well as to determine areas that deserve more attention.

Goals and objectives should be flexible statements about intended results that connect the program to the larger purpose. For example, the goals of a parent education program may be to increase parents' capability to raise their children effectively or to increase parents' capacity to cope effectively with parent–child conflict. Goals and objectives are related and should be useful, practical, and compatible with each other (Weiss, 1972):

Agency purpose:

- General statement with room for flexibility
- Sets the general mission for the agency
- Seldom changed

Program goal:

- General statement of results intended with room for flexibility
- States intent to carry out programs as means to achieve agency purpose
- Seldom changed but more often than purpose

Program objective(s):

- Specific statement with criteria for evaluation built in
- Changed every program budget period (year)

Service goal:

- General statement of the desired end
- Stated for each service unit (e.g., case, group)

Service objectives:

- Specify conditions or behaviors that are intended as outcomes and time for appearance of outcome
- Stated for each service incident (Price & Smith, 1985, p. 49)

Objectives are more specific statements of outcomes that reflect progress toward or achievement of a goal within a specific time frame (Price & Smith, 1985). Objectives should be measurable, specify the desired end condition, and specify the criteria that determine whether the desired result has been achieved. It is important that the means to achieve objectives are delineated (Kaufman & Zigler, 1992).

Price and Smith (1985) suggested that two types of objectives should be formulated: program objectives, which make the desired outcome explicit, and service objectives, which specify how resources will be provided to clients. For example, one outcome objective for parent education may be that 80% of parents completing the Nurturing Program in 1996 will have an accurate understanding of parenting practices as measured by the posttest. The corresponding service objective may be that 80% of the parents participating in the August–November Parent Nurturing class will demonstrate an accurate understanding of parenting practices as measured by a minimum score of 80% correct on the posttest. These objectives are useful because they state very concrete criteria by which success can be demonstrated. When specifying objectives, a number of issues should be considered, including the nature and content of objectives, the target group, the time frame of the expected effect (long versus short term), the interrelatedness of objectives, and the potential for unintended consequences, among others (Rossi, Freeman, & Wright, 1979).

Making goals and objectives concrete requires an understanding and consensus among appropriate administrators and staff with regard to acceptable outcome criteria. Although this type of consensus and level of concreteness may be difficult to reach, setting goals and developing objectives are important because they help identify the project mission, and they provide a check as to whether program activities mesh with program goals and objectives. And, of course, they provide the concrete outcomes by which programs can evaluate their effectiveness. Goals and objectives should be created at the design phase, after a needs evaluation has been conducted (see next section); however, it is never too late to clarify a program's intent. Existing programs can benefit from new goals and objectives, although they must be created within the context of ongoing programming.

TYPES OF EVALUATION

Evaluation is an ongoing process that can be integrated into a prevention program. Depending on the intended use of information obtained from an evaluation, one or more types of evaluation may be appropriate. Needs, process, and outcome evaluations each serve a different purpose for a prevention program, although they may overlap in time frame.

Needs Evaluation

Prevention programs are founded on the premise that the community is in need of some form of prevention services. The idea for a new program can be generated from a variety of sources—perceptions of community members or service providers, changes in agency priorities, media reports of social problems, or government initiatives, among others. Although the pressure to start a program can be great once an idea has been generated, thoroughly evaluating the community's needs is an important first step. A more complete understanding of a community's needs and resources will provide a stable framework upon which a successful prevention program can be built.

The needs evaluation process involves gathering information from a variety of sources about a variety of topics (see Table 1). Before a needs assessment is conducted, the people or agency involved in developing the prevention project usually has some idea of the target group, the broad categories of intervention that might be useful, and the negative aspects of the condition to be prevented. For example, an agency might have an idea to target teen mothers with some sort of educational/support intervention to alleviate some of the stress and lack of parenting knowledge of young mothers. With that very broad background of ideas, the next step in program planning is the needs evaluation itself. Important steps in the needs evaluation process include the following:

1. *Describe the target group* (age, sex, socioeconomic characteristics, geographic distribution).
2. *Identify major stresses* affecting the target group.
3. *What problems* (as a result of stress) within the target group should be reduced or eliminated with a prevention intervention?
4. *What skills* does the target group need to develop to cope with stress/crisis?
5. *Identify the agencies or groups* in the community that must be involved in planning for this target group. Which person(s) need to be involved?
6. *What steps will be taken to secure the interest and cooperation* of the community groups or agencies?
7. *Establish several tentative objectives* for the intervention project.
8. *Identify intervention strategies* to achieve these objectives.
9. *How will the program be evaluated* to identify needed *administrative* changes while the project is under way?
10. *How will the project be evaluated* to determine the extent to which *intervention objectives* have been met for the target group?
11. *What level of resources* (information, money, support, space, expertise) will be needed? What sources for these resources should be approached? (Price & Smith, 1985, p. 30)

These questions are then applied to the relevant services. Perhaps the most time-consuming part of a needs evaluation is assessing local services to determine where gaps exist. Programs already involved with the service community may be somewhat familiar with available services. If not, then staff

Table 1. Needs evaluations

Purpose: To identify unmet service needs for various groups in the community
Question answered: *What* do we need to do?
Information provided:

- Current service delivery and target groups
- Gaps in service delivery and underserved groups
- Obstacles and facilitators related to new service provision

Implementation considerations:

- Requires familiarity with the community and service delivery systems
- Requires gathering information from a variety of sources
- Becomes an important precursor to program development and implementation

members may want to make initial contacts with easily identifiable groups or agencies, such as a Community Services Board or Community Mental Health Agency, Department of Social Services, or local advocacy groups. Regardless of the starting point, it is important to speak with service providers and other interested parties about their own agencies as well as their familiarity with other community services and needs. This assessment can be done formally, with standardized interview or survey protocols, or informally, through discussions with relevant people.

Koss and Harvey (1991) identified five dimensions by which existing local services can be assessed:

- *Availability:* What is being offered?
- *Accessibility:* Which people can actually receive the services?
- *Quantity:* How many programs are offered, and how many people can be served?
- *Quality:* How good is the available programming?
- *Legitimacy:* Does the community believe in the providers and services?

For example, a needs assessment of parent education services could be applied to available parent education classes, support groups, outreach activities, workshops, and home-visiting programs, as well as other educational activities in a given community. Although it may appear to delay the implementation of a good program, needs assessments are crucial to an accurate understanding of the community's needs. Without such an understanding, even the best-intentioned program may fail because it was implemented improperly or failed to meet existing needs. Information from a thorough needs evaluation can strengthen funding applications and provide a solid foundation for effective programming.

Process Evaluation

Once a needs evaluation has been completed, the goals and objectives have been defined, and the program has begun, a process evaluation can provide information about the way in which the program is being implemented (see Table 2). Monitoring the implementation process can serve as a method of quality control for the intervention in deciding whether the service is delivered in the intended manner. If parent support groups are intended to serve as the primary service for parents, but attendance suggests that most parents are involved with the program's child care service, then any successes or failures of an outcome evaluation may not necessarily be attributed to the support groups. Modifications of original proposals are not intrinsically negative. Indeed, adapting a program to a particular community's needs can be vital to the success of a program. If changes are made in the course of service delivery, however, then process evaluation data gathered to assist in program replication must reflect those changes, and goals and objectives must be modified accordingly.

A number of questions regarding program implementation can guide a process evaluation. They should focus on comparing the intended or planned service delivery with the program as it is actually being implemented.

- Are participants successfully retained for the duration of the program?
- Are program goals and objectives clear, concrete, and measurable? Is programming consistent with the goals and objectives?
- Are program orientations appropriately matched to participants?
- Are programs implemented according to the original intent and design? If not, then are the modifications appropriate?
- Are appropriately trained staff and/or volunteers utilized to implement programs?
- What kinds of data are maintained by the programs regarding program implementation? Are data used to modify programming when appropriate?

Use of terms such as *appropriate, effective,* and *successful* indicate that some criteria must be developed—either by the evaluator, program staff, or both—by which implementation can be evaluated.

Examining the process can determine whether the appropriate target group is being served and how effectively the program is reaching it. Target groups may go unserved for a number of reasons, including potential clients' lack of awareness of services; practical barriers, such as access to transportation or program costs; or lack of appropriate referrals from other agencies. Even if target groups are reached, information from a process evaluation may suggest that particular program strategies are inappropriate or ineffective. A standard parent education program may reach the targeted group of low-education mothers, but the curriculum format may rely too heavily on verbal

Table 2. Process evaluation

Purpose: To determine how a program is being implemented compared with intended implementation

Question answered: "Are we doing what we *intended* to do?"

Information provided:

- Whether and how target group is being served
- Consistency between current method of service delivery and intended service delivery
- Data on program implementation

Implementation considerations:

- Requires concrete, measurable program goals and objectives as well as information-gathering procedures
- Requires willingness to uncover areas of program design and implementation that need improvement
- Requires ability to gather information from a variety of sources, including staff, clients, and other community agencies

---

and reading skills and thus exceed the literacy levels of participants. This type of mismatch, if uncorrected, may lead to retention problems.

At this point, unintended consequences of a program, both positive and negative, may be discovered. An educational workshop series designed for parents at risk of maltreating their children may have unintended labeling effects, preventing some parents from identifying themselves as needing services or leading parents who do attend to view themselves as inadequate. Conversely, a program that relies on volunteer "program graduates" to facilitate discussion may serve the unintended purpose of empowering and educating those volunteers as well as the program participants.

Outcome Evaluation

An outcome evaluation is designed to assess the effectiveness or impact of a project in terms of its goals and objectives (see Table 3). More common, the outcome evaluation ultimately should help answer the question, "Does this program make a difference?" Of any type of intervention, effective outcome evaluation research for prevention programs is perhaps the most difficult to conduct. This is true for several reasons: the complexities of working with agency staff and clients, obtaining information from many different people, and trying to contact clients after a program is completed.

Moreover, it is difficult to measure true prevention because if something is prevented successfully, then "nothing happens." Behavior changes associated with positive outcomes (e.g., preventing child abuse), however, can be measured. Improvements in parenting skills may demonstrate effects for years, and improved child outcomes may not surface until adolescence or

Table 3.   Outcome evaluation

Purpose: To assess effectiveness or impact of program in terms of goals and objectives

Question answered: *"How* is our program making a difference in the community?"

Information provided:

- Specific changes in appropriate client indicators (e.g., knowledge, attitudes, and behavior related to risk for child abuse)
- Whether objectives have been achieved and whether changes are related to the program or intervention
- Which aspects of the program work for particular types of clients

Implementation considerations:

- Facilitated by continuous data collection and information tracking regarding goals and objectives
- Requires client follow-up to examine long-term change
- May require additional expertise to put into place and analyze data

---

adulthood. In the shorter term, true knowledge and behavior change must be demonstrated to last beyond the intervention itself—tracking participants for extensive follow-up can be difficult. These difficulties do not make outcome evaluation impossible; instead, they underscore the need for systematic planning and assessment to ensure that outcome evaluations are valid and useful.

Parent education programs designed to prevent child abuse can utilize a number of outcome indices:

- *Stress:* individual- and family-level stress; parenting stress and general life stress, including poverty and unemployment; the control of anger and use of coping strategies
- *Developmental expectations:* lack of knowledge of child development, skill limitations, inappropriate expectations
- *Child management:* poor parent–child interactions, skill limitations, problem-solving limitations, ineffective child control, poor disciplinary techniques
- *Social support:* family and government/social services support, lack of knowledge of available resources, inability to gain access to resources, insularity

Individual programs can measure success by adopting a "small wins strategy" (Weick, 1984). Weick's small wins approach divides a program's activities into smaller achievable goals that establish the foundation for an ultimate long-term or comprehensive goal. This strategy involves identifying particular factors associated with child abuse that an intervention tries to affect and measuring change.

It is easy (especially for funding sources and legislators) to get caught in the trap of using the ultimate outcome measure—the reduced incidence of child abuse—as the only true outcome measure. Child abuse prevention is the ultimate goal of most programs, but it is important to recognize that child abuse is a complex phenomenon occurring within the interaction of individual, family, and social forces. True reduction in the incidence of child abuse will depend on comprehensive, multifaceted, long-term strategies. Certainly, it is hoped that participants in parent education programs are less likely to abuse their children than other groups at similar risk. Indeed, the number of abuse incidents among program participants may be an appropriate outcome measure (with caveats of confidentiality, permission, etc.). Outcome evaluations of parent education programs, however, should take a broader view of appropriate outcome measures, both short-term and long-term.

Ultimately, an effective outcome evaluation should provide information on whether objectives have been achieved, what specific changes have occurred, and why those changes occurred. The need for specific, concrete, measurable objectives is underscored here. Useful objectives will lead to outcome measures that can document change in the level of the criterion variable *before* and *after* the intervention, preferably compared with a control group. Participants in a special home-visiting program may demonstrate higher scores on parenting behavior assessments and knowledge tests than a group of parents who were provided only the normal services, such as access to parenting resource materials.

Data can be used to identify the program elements that are most effective. If educational programming creates behavior change only when in the context of larger comprehensive family services, then short-term parenting programs may not be an effective sole strategy for child abuse prevention. Outcome data can show which parts of a program are working and where resources should be targeted. Moreover, the data can document program worth to external funding agencies, a crucial component of competitive grant applications.

CONCLUSION

The three types of evaluation—needs, process, and outcome—all require a commitment to constructive feedback. This commitment can entail some financial, administrative, and time costs; nevertheless, a proper evaluation can provide both short-term and long-term benefits. The short-term benefits include useful feedback, which can help administrators modify their interventions to serve clients better. Long-term benefits include information about the overall effectiveness of educational interventions, which can be used to improve programming and justify current or expanded funding needs. The short- and long-term benefits of evaluation can be realized only if considerable thought and effort are directed toward developing concrete, measurable goals and objectives. A key component of any type of evaluation is measurement. The next chapter provides some hints to effective measurement and data collection in parent education programs.

Measurement Tools
for Self-Evaluation

chapter • 5

Effective evaluations depend on the ability of staff and evaluators to gain access to existing sources of data and, in many situations, create new sources by documenting program activities and outcomes. Although it may take time and effort to identify appropriate data sources and put data collection procedures into place, the information gained can be tremendously helpful. From reviews of scientific literature on child maltreatment and parent education, interviews with program staff, and a statewide process evaluation, we have identified a variety of sources, instruments, and issues that may facilitate effective measurement and data collection. First, we review the general sources of data to which prevention program staff members may have access. Second, we make specific suggestions for measurement tools and strategies that are useful for each of the evaluation types reviewed in Chapter 4. Third, we raise some specific concerns for maltreatment prevention programs that collect and use data from their clients and communities.

DATA SOURCES

Data for needs, process, and outcome evaluations can come from a variety of sources. Each source has its benefits and drawbacks, reinforcing the need for multiple sources of information. Rossi, Freeman, and Wright (1979) identified four main sources of data: 1) observation, 2) service records, 3) service provider information, and 4) program participants.

Observation

Direct observation can be utilized to obtain information about services and their delivery. A narrative method documents activities, providing a descriptive record of the intervention. For example, an observer would generate a narrative of activities during a parent–child play session. A more structured method utilizes a rating scheme or a standard set of questions that are answered during the course of observation. Observational methods provide direct information about the intervention, but the training required to obtain reliable observers may be too time consuming. Qualitative data can be difficult to analyze. Moreover, the very act of observation may lead participants to act differently. Parents may not speak as freely in a support group with an observer present.

Service Records

Often, a wealth of data already exists in a program's client records and service documentation. Relevant information sometimes can be obtained from the records of other service agencies such as the health department, criminal justice services, and social services with client permission and confidentiality considered. Community-level statistics, such as the incidence of teen pregnancy or child abuse, also can be helpful in defining the extent of a problem (needs evaluation) or, although more difficult, documenting change following intervention (outcome evaluation).

If service records are not kept by a program, then they usually are relatively easy to introduce into the current system. Of course, documentation needs must be balanced with a realistic appraisal of time and organizational constraints of the program. Data from these records often are inexpensive and efficient, permitting the use of a prestructured data form. If records vary in structure or are incomplete, however, then systematic data collection can be difficult. Data storage also can become an issue—service records stored on computer may be much easier to access than paper forms.

Service Provider Information

Staff can serve as an important resource for data, especially in process evaluations. They may easily identify differences between what the program should be doing and what it actually accomplishes. Information can be obtained through interviews, narrative reports, or rating forms. Service providers also have a unique perspective about their clientele, which may not be captured from any other source.

Program Participants

The easiest and most common form of information obtained from program participants is satisfaction ratings. Although satisfaction ratings can provide some feedback regarding the utility of the service and suggestions for modification, they are only one type of information that clients may be able to provide. Self-administered questionnaires and interviews can probe in further detail about the services provided as well as which services the clients actually use. Outcome measures such as pre- and post-questionnaires, follow-up studies, tests of knowledge, and behavior can demonstrate whether any changes occurred and, if proper control groups are used, how likely it is that change occurred as a result of the intervention.

Other Community Members

One source not mentioned by Rossi et al. (1979) but crucial to understanding the context in which a program operates are other community members. This category can include advisory boards, other service providers and professionals, key community leaders, and the general public. Just as these people can provide information regarding existing services during a needs evaluation, they also can explain community perceptions of the program being evaluated. Service providers can discuss interagency collaboration and turf issues. Members of the general public can talk about awareness of the program, its visibility in the community, and its reputation. Survey, self-report, and interview formats are useful here, with the inherent cautions mentioned for each in the previous sections.

CHOICE OF MEASURES AND INTEGRATION INTO SERVICE DELIVERY

Once evaluation is accepted as a component of prevention programming, the evaluation process must be integrated into the service delivery process. Written measures must be appropriately matched to the program and serve several purposes. The measures not only should be scientifically valid and useful for data analysis, but they also must be useful and appropriate for the clients and program staff. As such, they should be of reasonable length, validity, and reading level, and they should not have complicated scoring systems. Information obtained from the measures should provide feedback to the staff, which can be used, if appropriate, during the course of service delivery. For example, a knowledge test given after a class on child development could highlight areas that need to be reviewed during the following week's class to clarify points that were missed. Likewise, measures of stress during a parent support group could suggest topics for further discussion. The purpose of each evaluation suggests potential data sources.

Needs Evaluation Data

A needs evaluation is designed to identify unmet service needs for various groups in the community. In essence, data from a needs evaluation provide a "statistical portrait" or snapshot of the existing community. Appropriate measures can be divided into two types: measures that document the extent of the problem (e.g., child maltreatment and/or its risk factors) and measures that document available services and service gaps.

The incidence of child maltreatment itself can be measured through official reporting sources such as state and local departments of social services. Either of these agencies should be able to provide aggregate data regarding the extent of abuse and neglect by reporting area (usually county or city). Other data sources can provide information regarding the incidence and prevalence of risk factors for maltreatment. Although the presence of risk factors does not guarantee that maltreatment is inevitable without intervention, it does provide reasonable support for preventive interventions. Table 1 lists several of these risk factors and identifies some common data sources among public, private, and nonprofit agencies.

The second type of needs evaluation measure documents the target group, available services, and service needs. Generally, describing the demographics of various community groups can establish a more accurate picture both of groups at risk and general community groups from which clients may be drawn. These sources help determine how many people in the community have the risk factors mentioned in Table 1 and how many of these people use exist-

Table 1.   Categories and sources of needs evaluation data

Data category	Potential sources
Incidence/prevalence of child abuse and neglect	State/local department of social services, child abuse treatment programs, parent support groups/advocacy groups
	Coalitions/councils targeting child abuse, family violence, state/local law enforcement
Poverty	State/local department of social services, state/local department of welfare
Unemployment	State/local department of labor, state/local department of employment
Substance abuse	State/local department of mental health, community mental health centers, treatment programs/support groups
Prenatal/infant health	State/local department of health, state/local department of social services, local hospitals/treatment facilities
Education/support services	State/local department of social services, state/local department of health, state department of education, local school board, nonprofit service organizations, advocacy groups
Group demographics	State/local census bureau, executive branch of local government

ing services. This statistical picture of service providers and clients may clarify which problems are being adequately addressed and may identify remaining service gaps and underserved groups.

These data source recommendations may not be necessary for every needs evaluation; rather, programs should determine which information can be helpful in developing a comprehensive understanding of a community's problems, strengths, and needs. Through work on substance abuse prevention and a "Communities that Care" model, Hawkins, Catalano, and Associates (1992) developed a community profile system that enabled them to compare a variety of risk and protective factors across localities. The differences between communities shape general service plans to respond uniquely to each community's needs. Similarly, individual prevention programs can draw from the recommendations in this chapter to develop their own unique community needs assessment.

Process Evaluation Data

Process evaluations focus on the manner in which a program is implemented. Data from these evaluations can be used to monitor how well a program remains true to its intended purpose and the impact of intentional changes in goals and objectives. This focus on the program process means that most of the data sources will be contained within the program, but community perspectives can be an important component. Table 2 describes each of the data types.

Data on clients who are recruited, agree to participate, and complete an intervention will provide a clear understanding of the service group. If a target group is not being reached, then recruitment information can clarify whether the target group remains unserved because of lack of contact or a failure to agree to participate. Client information also can shape how a program retains clients once they agree to participate. For example, if retention data suggest that it is *low-income* parents who have a hard time attending all education sessions, then staff members can work on ways to improve attendance for that group, such as provide transportation or hold meetings in local neighborhood centers.

Data on service delivery get to the heart of the program—*which* services are being provided and *how* they work. Maintaining comprehensive service delivery data does require a fair amount of record keeping. Although staff, understandably, may want and need to focus on the actual delivery of services, it is critical to maintain accurate documentation of educational curricula, instructional notes, and schedules. Once record keeping is integrated into daily operations, the administrative burden may lessen. Feedback from clients and staff can be obtained through interviews and surveys to highlight successful and unsuccessful program components.

Characteristics of program staff and volunteers also can affect program implementation. Background, training, and continuing education all can affect

Table 2. Categories and sources of process evaluation data

Data category	Potential sources
Clients	
Who is recruited	Monthly reports
Who agrees to participate	Logs/records
Attendance/extent of participation	Attendance sheets
Implementation/service delivery	
Substantive topic covered	Curricula/program/instructional information
Match between service delivery and goals/objectives	Policy/procedures manual, staff interviews, client feedback forms
Sessions: number, duration, time between sessions	Program schedule, program leader notes, program staff interviews
Staff/volunteers	
Background	Personnel records
Training	Policy and procedures manual, personnel records
Continuing education	Policy and procedures manual, personnel records
Job performance and satisfaction	Staff interviews and reports
Community integration	
Networking/interagency collaboration	Contact logs, records of interagency councils, collaborations, key informant interviews with other service providers, community leaders
Acceptance by general community	Public opinion surveys/feedback, media coverage

how well individual staff members are matched to clients and their ability to deliver services effectively. Job performance, description, and satisfaction feedback can highlight managerial and organizational aspects of a program that influence service delivery. For example, if home visitors receive little or no supervision through regular meetings, then it may be difficult to determine whether each visitor implements lesson plans consistently across time.

Finally, part of a process evaluation concerns the manner in which a program fits into the larger community. The degree of fit can be measured by the working relationship with other community service agencies. Are there turf issues or duplication of services? Or do several different programs maintain a consistent referral network and case consultation for shared clients? Interviews with other agency staff or members of interagency councils may be good information sources. Public opinion and media coverage can provide some indication of how a program is perceived by the general community.

Outcome Data

Outcome evaluations are used to measure changes that occur as the result of an intervention. As mentioned in the outcome evaluation section of Chapter 4, both short-term and long-term changes can be considered. One example of long-term change concerns rates of child abuse. Although reducing the incidence of child abuse is a laudable goal and actually can be used in carefully designed studies (see Chapter 8), most individual programs focus on risk factors for child abuse. Some of these communitywide risk factors—the information gathered during a needs evaluation—are listed in Table 1. Unless an intervention is implemented with the entire community, however, outcome evaluations usually focus on these types of risk factors in the group of participants who have completed the intervention, as well as, when possible, a comparison group that did not receive the same services. These critical concepts were mentioned in Chapter 4 and are listed again, with corresponding measurement instruments, in Table 3.

After reviewing the literature and talking with program staff and administrators about the types of outcomes that they would like to evaluate, we have developed a packet of measures that we believe would be useful for self-evaluation. We recommend these measures based on their acceptance in the literature and their simplicity in scoring and interpretation; however, we do not endorse these measures as the only possible ones that should be considered.

We must note that the benefit from these measures depends greatly on their accurate use and interpretation. Although most come with directions for scoring and interpreting where necessary, caution still should be exercised in extrapolating measure findings to parents themselves. We specifically note our

Table 3. Recommended measures for critical concepts in outcome evaluation

Administrative forms	Demographics Form
	Referral Form
	Termination Form
	Satisfaction Form
Stress inventory	Parenting Stress Index
Social support	Support Functions Scale (Short Form)
Abuse potential	Child Abuse Potential Inventory
Parenting skills	Adult-Adolescent Parenting Inventory
Knowledge of parenting	Nurturing Program Quiz
	Knowledge of Child Development Inventory
Home environment	HOME Inventory for Families Children
Self-esteem	Rosenberg Self-Esteem Scale

reservations in using the Child Abuse Potential (CAP) Inventory. Although it is the only measure that attempts to assess the potential to commit abusive acts, scores on the CAP do *not* indicate that an individual is indeed a child abuser, nor do they confirm that an individual will become an abuser. This is merely one tool that can document parenting attitudes and behaviors, and it must be used with caution. We include it here because some programs are using or have expressed interest in using the CAP, but we do not necessarily recommend its adoption as a standard assessment tool for parent education programs.

Although some of these measures are not copyrighted and are available to be duplicated, a number of them do entail one-time or repeated costs. In Appendix B, we summarize each measure, its characteristics, and, when possible, its availability. Because staff usually focus on service delivery, they may not have the time or the financial resources to gain access to research on current assessment tools. We, therefore, have included a comprehensive list of additional available relevant measures in Appendix C. This compendium also includes a synopsis of each measure, its characteristics, and, when possible, its availability.

The most common source of data in outcome evaluations is the self-report of participants about their attitudes and behaviors. The benefits of using unobtrusive self-report measures are that they can be easily integrated into service delivery, and they are completed by the very people who are experiencing the intervention. The measures can be used before, during, and after an intervention to track changes in risk factors across time. For example, measures of parenting stress and child-rearing strategies may be administered during an initial intake, screening, or program session to provide a baseline picture of parenting. The same or similar measures can be used at various points during the course of the educational program to track progress. Finally, similar measures can be used in a long-term follow up to determine whether the effects last after the program is over.

Using the same self-report measures repeatedly with program participants sometimes can cause problems. It is important to remember that most information obtained from clients can be corrupted by the effects of social desirability. Participants may get used to the measure and learn to report the "right" answers without really changing their attitudes or behaviors or to appear more favorable to program leaders. In one study, Milner and Robertson (1989) found that maltreating parents provide more inconsistent responses than nonmaltreating parents on a child abuse inventory. These types of effects are common to many types of testing, and they do not necessarily mean that participants are intentionally trying to create false impressions. It simply means that using more than one measure can keep evaluation from becoming too repetitious or boring. Similarly, adding alternative sources of information, such as staff observation, family reports, or other activities, can greatly improve the quality and reliability of the results. Multiple sources that consistently document change provide a stronger foundation for conclusions about program effectiveness.

SPECIAL ISSUES FOR CHILD MALTREATMENT PROGRAMS

Although these three types of evaluation and data types are common to most types of prevention programs, special issues arise for child maltreatment prevention programs. Specifically, data collection efforts for these programs should consider whether the clients are volunteers or are mandated to attend and confidentiality of sensitive data.

Parent education programs often serve both prevention and treatment functions for their clients. That is, many clients who have little or some risk for maltreatment volunteer to attend; some clients who already are involved in the justice system may be mandated by the court to attend or encouraged to attend as part of a court-recommended treatment plan. Mandatory and volunteer clients may bring markedly different attitudes, experiences, and motivations to parent education interventions. If an individual program does serve these two groups simultaneously, then data from each should be considered separately; what works for each group may differ in a process evaluation, or scores on outcome measures may not be equivalent. Staff should simply consider the implications of court-mandated and volunteer samples when designing and analyzing the evaluation data.

Because information about child maltreatment does have implications for children's safety and justice system procedures, programs should consider the implications of obtaining data about individual abuse incidents. Many states have mandatory reporting laws or possibilities of compelling the release of data in these situations. These issues should be considered when developing data instruments for process and outcome evaluations, particularly for client-specific measures. Confidentiality issues also may arise if outcome data on child abuse reports are obtained from a state abuse registry.

CONCLUSION

Data collection and analysis in child abuse prevention programs raise special issues regarding the nature of client participation and confidentiality of information. None of these issues is insurmountable, but they do require careful consideration and planning to address. Collecting data can be a time-consuming task when the process is set up initially; however, the information that evaluation data can provide usually has long-term benefits that outweigh the short-term costs. Sometimes the best information about the importance of evaluation and the methods of integrating data collection procedures into a program can come from programs themselves. Examples from existing programs can shed light on the practical side of evaluation so that new programs do not have to reinvent the wheel. The next chapter discusses a statewide process evaluation of parent education programs that served a variety of clients and collected various types of evaluation data.

Overview of Diverse
Parent Education Efforts

chapter

•

6

This chapter provides an overview of a process evaluation and a description of parent education efforts in Virginia. This process evaluation utilizes both a quantitative and a qualitative approach. We present an overview of the process evaluation strategy, describe the general approaches to parent education used in Virginia, describe the types of clients served, describe other program issues, and present criteria for evaluating the effectiveness of programs. Throughout the chapter, we use the names of only the five programs that we used as intensive study sites, although data from all 25 sites were used. (See Chapters 7 and 8 for case studies of the five intensive study sites.)

PROCESS EVALUATION STRATEGY

Recognizing the importance of working with grantees during the course of this evaluation, project staff initially met with representatives from 25 prevention programs from around the state. At this initial meeting, the project staff members were introduced, and the purpose and goals of the overall project were explained. Team members then met with small groups of program representatives to discuss in more detail program commonalities and unique characteristics of individual programs that should be considered in developing and implementing evaluation procedures. Because programs must meet the needs of their particular localities, variations in program design are inevitable. Broad-based commonalities, however, facilitate the use of evaluation approaches across programs. Shared characteristics include aspects of program design and community context.

Following this initial meeting with program participants, staff members reviewed issues raised by program participants, as well as all approved grant proposals, and then clarified goals and objectives for the initial round of site visits to all programs. Each program received an initial site visit by two members of the evaluation team during the first 4 months of the project. Team members interviewed program administrators and staff for several hours regarding program characteristics and implementation. The visits were designed to provide a more comprehensive picture of each program's design and implementation. Staff members developed an informal interview schedule to ensure complete coverage of important topics (see Table 1). In addition to the factual information collected, these visits provided staff with an opportunity to assess the likelihood of total cooperation if the program were selected for intensive study.

Based on these interviews, the evaluation team classified programs on a variety of dimensions and selected 5 programs that represented the group of 25 (see Figure 1). This subset was selected to be representative of the larger group on a number of criteria. Program designs represented in this subset include standard parent education classes, home-visiting programs, child care/parent education programs, and parent support groups, among other approaches.

Table 1. Interview topics

- Descriptions of all relevant programs, including standard curricula used and modifications made to existing programs
- Client referral sources and recruitment efforts
- Target client groups and groups actually served
- Existing barriers to and facilitators of program implementation and methods with which barriers were successfully eliminated
- Program relationships to local agencies including the Community Service Board, Department of Social Services, health department, school system, and court system
- Utilization and effectiveness of an advisory board
- Community perception and support of the program
- Use, training, and evaluation of volunteers
- Compilation and storage of client demographic information
- Use of standard assessment tools, measures unique to the program, and other methods of program and client evaluation
- Type of information that would be useful for program and client evaluation, as well as evaluation (e.g., questionnaire, observations) that would be appropriate

Program	Setting	Clients	Child activities	Education classes	Workshops	Support group	Home visiting
Parent–Child Center (Winchester)	Rural/ sub-urban	High risk		✔		✔	✔
Parents' Place (Roanoke)	Urban/ rural	Variety		✔	✔		
Good Beginnings (Portsmouth)	Urban	Teen moms	✔	✔			✔
Resource Mothers People, Inc. (Abingdon)	Rural	Teen moms	✔		✔		✔
Fellowship & Family Service (Goochland)	Rural/ sub-urban	Variety	✔	✔			

Figure 1.   Characteristics of five sites used for intensive study.

These programs serve a variety of clients, including pregnant and parenting teens, parents and families at high risk for child abuse and neglect, parents in the process of obtaining general educational training, and the general population. The programs reflect urban, suburban, and rural settings, although a majority are located in either rural or suburban settings.

The programs vary in the amount of data that they collect from clients. Some programs collect extensive demographic information that is computer coded; others collect basic information that is kept in files. Methods of collecting client evaluation data range from using a number of standard assessment tools gleaned from the psychology literature to using satisfaction forms developed for individual programs. Each program has the potential to collect additional information about program implementation and client progress, although the ease with which new assessments and procedures can be implemented differs across programs. An important goal was to identify procedures for data collection and evaluation that would help in assessing program effectiveness without creating unreasonable demands on the programs. Evaluation team members visited each of the five sites approximately once per month for 5 months to interview administrators, staff, volunteers, and clients; review case files; review educational curricula and materials; collect statistical data; interview community members and other service providers; and attend programs, planning sessions, and fund-raising events, if feasible.

GENERAL APPROACHES TO
PARENT EDUCATION USED IN VIRGINIA

Although many programs use a variety of approaches, four major types emerged (see Figure 2). The majority of programs use some form of education classes. Ongoing support groups often operate in conjunction with other educational efforts. Both stand-alone and series of workshops are offered by several programs. The fourth and perhaps most intensive approach is home visiting.

Education Classes

Programs most commonly provide parent education through courses composed of a series of classes that meet 2 hours each week for as few as 4 to as many as 15 weeks. Seventeen of the 25 programs offer formal parent education classes. The specific length of the class sessions and the number of weeks spanned vary from program to program because of curriculum specifications, staff limitations, and difficulty retaining clients, among other factors. One Department of Social Services, for example, offers a 9-week course every fall and spring. Classes meet weekly for 2 hours, with the first hour of the class devoted to a curriculum developed by the program and the second half reserved for discussion of specific problems that the participants in attendance face. Some parents from the fall sessions continue to attend in the spring. Unlike that program, several of the other programs offering weekly parent education

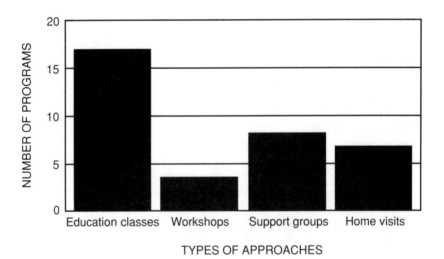

Figure 2. Program approaches.

courses conduct two or more of these courses concurrently. Three times each year, the Child and Family Service of Southwest Hampton Roads program in Portsmouth conducts a 12-week "Good Beginnings" course with three separate groups of teenage mothers. Class meeting times vary as well; evening sessions are common in order to accommodate work schedules, although daytime sessions are offered in many locations for at-home or nonworking mothers in particular (see Chapter 8 for the full case study).

Ten of the 17 programs offering parent education courses have a designated parent–child interaction activity or period during each class, necessitating child care or a child education component for the children while they are not with their parent(s). Some programs offer child care or adult education courses to hook parents into attending parent education classes. One program operates a developmental preschool 3 days per week. For children to be permitted to attend, parents must agree to participate in a series of weekly parenting classes, complete interactive activities in the home, and contribute 20 volunteer hours to the operation of the preschool. Another program attaches parent education to its high school equivalency degree classes, which are available to parents who attend the program's day care center. Holding the courses at the child care center during its hours of operation facilitates parent–child interaction activities and allows teachers the opportunity to model good caregiver–child interactions. During parenting education classes conducted by Winchester's Parent–Child Center in local churches, staff and volunteers provide child care for very young children but also offer structured education sessions for children in several age groups, which meet concurrently with parenting education sessions. During a break, staff members or volunteers lead a parent–child interaction task or program.

Programs use a variety of parent education curricula; some employ more than one (see Figure 3). Often programs choose their curriculum based on what they believe is most appropriate for parents with children of a specific age range, separating parents into different groups based on their children's ages. For example, one program uses Systematic Training for Effective Parenting (STEP) for parents with children ranging in age from 1 to 6 years and Pride in Parenting for parents with children under 1 year of age. The Parent–Child Center in Winchester offers separate Nurturing Program classes for parents with children from 4 to 7 years of age and those with children from 8 to 12. In addition, some programs, many of which have illiterate clients, select criteria and/or group parents based on their education level. One director found that her clients tended to have very low reading levels; she has sought standard curricula developed with this group in mind, and she continues to modify the material to parallel client ability.

Ten of the 17 programs that provide parent education classes have created their own unique curriculum; the remainder modify or rely heavily on existing curricula. Those programs that create their own curriculum often synthesize

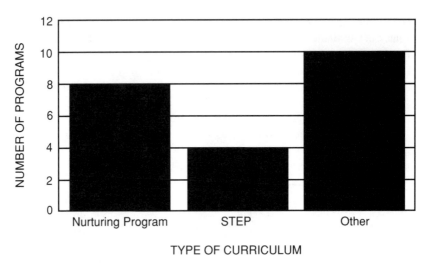

Figure 3. Educational curricula used.

materials from published parent education materials. The most widely used published curriculum among the programs is the Nurturing Program (eight programs draw heavily from the NP), followed by STEP (four programs draw significantly from STEP). A variety of other curricula were used by programs throughout the state. (See Chapter 3 for a review of various parent education curricula.)

No programs reported that they use a standard curriculum without modification. Interestingly, one program said that it plans to use the Nurturing Program without modification but has not yet attempted to do so. Another program, which strongly maintains that curricula should not be modified without permission of the author, nevertheless substitutes more simplistic handouts than those included in the STEP curriculum for its less-educated clients. Typically, programs modify the existing published curriculum that they select in order to make it more salient to the groups that they serve. Given the diversity of clients within and among sites, it should not be surprising that modification is common. Although such modifications make comparisons across programs difficult, they are beneficial in that they can make the curriculum more sensitive to the community context and more responsive to clients' needs.

Workshops

Four programs report using workshops as an educational strategy. Some of these programs design the workshops in response to parents' needs and do not intend for them to constitute a parent education curriculum. For example, a

YMCA-based program holds a seminar each month for parents of children who attend the YMCA's child care program. At this seminar, program staff present information on a relevant topic, such as attention-deficit/hyperactivity disorder. These seminars are designed in response to the parents' needs and do not follow a set curriculum. Other programs plan their monthly meetings according to an existing curriculum and/or expect parents to continue to attend each month for the predetermined length of the program. One child care program offers a 10-month course that meets the second Thursday evening of the month beginning each September. The first class provides information regarding developmentally appropriate expectations that parents should have of their children. The next seven meetings follow a published curriculum. In the next-to-last class, parents complete an on-site ropes challenge course, which is an outdoor obstacle course whereby a group of people must accomplish goals through teamwork and group problem solving. The final class consists of a wrap-up and evaluation of the year's activities. Although other programs may not use single workshops as an explicit educational strategy, most of the 25 programs offer speaking engagements that often serve as mini-workshops.

Support Groups

Eight programs offer parent support groups such as Parents Anonymous, often in addition to parent education classes. Many of these support groups have developed in response to parents' desire to continue to meet after completing parent education classes. The Parent–Child Center in Winchester organized a Parents Anonymous group at the request of "graduated" parents and now continuously offers a Parents Anonymous group during the day and another during the evening. The groups are run by volunteers and remain unstructured. Attendance soars during vacations and summers when Nurturing Program classes are not in session. Adopting an unusual strategy, another family service center begins with a support group for pregnant and parenting teenagers to spark their interest and put them at ease and then helps the teenagers make the transition to parent education courses. Support groups often have an educational component, such as raising alternative discipline techniques during a discussion of control issues. Conversely, educational classes often function as support groups as parents share their experiences and seek advice.

Two unique programs that focus on the needs of parents facing specific challenges—one dealing with divorce and custody issues and the other dealing with adoption of sexually abused children—build their programs around support groups that are designed to provide parent education specific to their parents' and children's needs. A rural social services agency runs an 8-week support/parent education group called New Chances for parents going through mediation for custody in divorce. One of the goals of the group is to reduce individual stress so that parents can focus more on their children's needs and feelings. An urban, private agency offers to postadoptive families a 9-month series of support/parent education groups in tandem with support groups for the children. Each monthly meeting concludes with an interactive activity between parents and children.

Home Visiting

Seven programs educate parents through home visits, which may be particularly beneficial to those living in rural, isolated areas without access to transportation and those needing more intensive, individualized service. Home visits range in frequency from weekly to monthly. People, Inc., of Southwest Virginia program in Abingdon, for example, visits teenage mothers for 90 minutes each week during pregnancy and until the child is 1 year old, whereas the Good Beginnings program in Portsmouth uses an initial home visit to assess the teenage mother's living situation and to recruit those most in need to attend parent education classes. Abingdon's home visitors also provide transportation to and from medical and other social services appointments for mothers and their babies. In-home therapists from Winchester's Parent–Child Center provide home visits to families who require more intensive, one-to-one services. These families may have a child or children of any age and often spend many hours each week with their home visitor.

A few programs augment their parent education classes with a mentoring component for those needing or desiring additional support. Usually these programs match trained volunteers with interested parents. Volunteer parent aides from one center spend 4–6 hours each week with a parent, providing companionship and assistance that includes connecting the parent to any needed community resources.

Other Approaches

Several programs house parenting information and/or toy-lending libraries. One resource program operates several Young Family Centers in the local public libraries where parents can read to and play with their children as well as check out parenting materials. Many programs publish newsletters or fliers containing parenting tips and information that they mail to their clients and other members of the community. For example, the program coordinator of one rural Parent Skill Center routinely composes a newsletter for the community, which covers parent issues; a local printing agency assumes the cost of printing the newsletter. A suburban program mails several times each year to elementary school guidance counselors, child care centers, pediatric offices, and health centers a one-page flier listing the signs of child abuse and neglect and specifying the legal duties to report such incidents. Several programs also host annual fairs to rally community support; publicize their programs' missions and offerings; disseminate information on child abuse and neglect to the general public; and provide a fun, wholesome function for the community to enjoy. The Parent–Child Center in Winchester hosts Doo Dah Day, an annual festival made possible through volunteer support and community donations. The festival features games and entertainment; information booths; a parade; and appearances by cartoon heroes, who address the crowd about the horror of child abuse and neglect and the right for all children to be safe from maltreatment.

TYPES OF CLIENTS SERVED

Client groups vary markedly between and within programs. The client composition is not necessarily reflective of the demographic makeup of the community; instead, it often is a result of the program's source of referrals and reputation in the community. For programs that routinely accept referrals, most come from other service agencies (e.g., health department, hospital, Department of Social Services [DSS], Community Service Board [CSB], the court system). Schools and churches also are common referral sources for many programs. Thus, those programs that have a wider network among local agencies and organizations may meet and serve a larger number and wider variety of clients. Some programs rely on advertisements and fliers to recruit participants.

Parents and Families at Risk

Fourteen programs specifically gear their efforts toward a group at risk for child abuse and neglect, such as teenage mothers; DSS-, CSB-, or court-referred parents; and parents with low incomes. Whereas DSS, CSB, and/or court-mandated referrals comprise part of most programs' client base, usually they intermix anonymously with other clients, although one program would like to separate referred parents who are known abusers from other parents in order to confront them directly about their abuse. Combining different groups of clients prevents programs from being labeled as a program only for "bad" parents and allows parents who may not parent well to observe more effective parenting techniques; it also is likely, however, that different groups of clients may have very different parenting education needs, necessitating careful planning on the part of programs attempting to meet all of these client concerns.

Parents and Families from the General Population

Not all programs target a specific client group or receive referrals from other agencies. Unless some type of specific client restriction exists (e.g., residency requirements), programs usually try to serve whatever clients come to them. Eight programs make specific efforts to draw from the general population, usually attracting low- and middle-income clients. Largely as a result of the location of the programs, the majority of them serve clients living in rural areas.

Children

Several programs target children primarily and provide them with skills that, it is hoped, will enable them to be good parents in the future. One school board uses the Nurturing Skills curriculum, which was designed by the author of the parent education Nurturing Program curriculum (Bavolek & Comstock, 1985) used by many of the Virginia programs, to foster self-esteem and impart knowledge to students about child development, AIDS/HIV, birth control, pregnancy, and other related topics. All students in grades 7–12 in the county will participate in the program for one semester each year. The YMCA-based program offers quality child care to many families in the community and teaches conflict resolution tactics to children in small groups to help them learn how to manage anger and resolve their differences peacefully. In addition to small group meetings with the children, one-to-one conferences are scheduled with parents whose children seem to be experiencing problems at home.

Clients Who Would Benefit from Programs

Because few programs evaluate the effectiveness of their interventions using standard measures, it is difficult to determine which "types" of clients have benefited from each program approach. Until further evaluation procedures are implemented and data are collected, it is feasible to suggest that clients would benefit the most from programs that match their needs. Teen mothers with little knowledge, skills, or support probably would benefit from more intensive classes or home visits. Parents who have adequate knowledge of parenting practices but are isolated and stressed probably would benefit from support groups. Risk status varies according to a number of factors, including age, income, and circumstance; however, it is clear that all parents face stress and unfamiliar situations simply by virtue of being parents. It is probable that all parents would benefit by having access to parenting resources and support.

OTHER PROGRAM ISSUES

In addition to parent education approaches, curricula, and clientele, several other important issues were addressed in the initial site visits to the Virginia programs. These include summer activities, volunteers, advisory boards, fundraising activities, relationship to state agencies and the courts, and community receptiveness.

Summer Activities

Many programs do not offer parenting classes during the summer, especially during the months of July and August. Instead, some programs concentrate on planning and recruiting. At programs that do continue to offer parent education classes, attendance typically suffers. Vacations, other summer activities, and special programs compete for enrollment. As one staff member from Good Beginnings in Portsmouth noted, the teen mothers in the program "are just kids themselves and need a summer break." Many programs also have had difficulty enlisting enough staff and volunteers and providing additional child care during the summer for children who are out of school. For these reasons, several programs that offered summer parent education courses in the past have abandoned them. Not all programs, however, have experienced these problems. In fact, a few increase their enrollment during the summer by providing additional services to children. One program, which concentrates its efforts primarily on children and quality child care, expands its outreach during the summer by organizing summer camps and offering other services, believing that it is important for families to have access to services and facilities during the summer months. Another program also expands its child care component, extending its period of operation to 10 hours each weekday to accommodate children who are out of school; this program, nevertheless, suspends its parenting education classes during July and August.

Volunteers

Volunteers play a valuable role in the operation of the majority of programs; their contributions are critical to many programs' success, especially the handful of those with only one paid staff person, some of whom work only part time. Many programs recruit volunteers from the professional community to conduct their parent education courses and workshops. At one family resource program, volunteers interested in facilitating the Nurturing Program participate in a 16-hour training program provided by the statewide advocacy group Prevent Child Abuse–Virginia (PCA–V) as well as program-sponsored in-service meetings. They then serve as co-facilitators and soon after make the transition to lead facilitators. After they have demonstrated their ability and interest in serving as lead facilitators, the program finds funds to pay them for their work. In addition, several programs have contracted with nearby colleges and universities for interns and work-study students, arranging for them to perform a range of duties from administrative tasks to direct services. A number of clients who have completed programs return to volunteer their services at some programs, and several programs require their participants to contribute volunteer hours as part of their service agreement. The Fellowship and Family Service program in Goochland requires parents placing their children in its developmental preschool to contribute 20 hours to its operation. Other community members also volunteer at many of the programs, assisting with child care, transportation, tutoring, mentoring, mailings, and annual fairs, among other activities.

Only a few of the programs have an established training/orientation program for volunteers. The training programs differ somewhat in their intensity and purpose according to how the volunteers will be utilized and the program's training resources. An urban family resource program asks volunteers to assist in preschool and adult classrooms, usually to read stories and tutor adults. In preparation, the volunteers participate in a 2-hour "Day in the Life" orientation to the clients and complete a "Celebrating Diversity" program. Because many volunteers come from the professional community, programs often do not need to provide orientations or training. For this reason and also because volunteers contribute an array of services and because programs lack adequate resources to provide formal supervision, the majority of programs believe that informal supervision is sufficient. A few of the programs that routinely utilize volunteers, however, have instituted more formal evaluation/supervision procedures. One family service agency, which enlists volunteers to help organize parent education classes and support groups, arrange transportation, and serve as mentors and peer counselors, holds a yearly progress meeting of all volunteers to review the year's activities and set goals for the coming year. Monthly reflection groups are scheduled for ongoing discussion of volunteer progress and activities. The Parent–Child Center in Winchester has created a staff position for a volunteer coordinator, who focuses on recruiting volunteers to facilitate parenting education classes, serve as in-home therapists, and run fundraising/educational events. Meetings are scheduled before and after each parenting series in order to evaluate volunteers' work and plan for future programs. The program director provides training and ongoing supervision of all program volunteers. Unfortunately, the understaffed programs may be unable to invest their precious time and resources into organizing and supervising volunteers; these programs potentially could benefit most from such assistance.

Advisory Boards

Not all programs have advisory boards, and several of those without a board expressed interest in creating one. Some programs utilize and/or report to the advisory board of their umbrella agency. Those that have their own advisory board differ in the stated importance and purpose that the board holds for the program. Two common primary roles of the board are fund-raising and policy direction, although many programs wish that their board would expand its policy direction role. Programs typically draw board members from area service agencies, schools, churches, and the business community. Several programs emphasize that business community representatives are essential for effective fund-raising. Service agency representatives often improve interagency collaboration. All board members potentially can facilitate community involvement and promote the program. An involved, supportive board can add stability to a program, especially during transitional periods. (See Appendix A for the topical brief "Working with an Advisory Board.") Some programs were founded by board members, and some boards have members who have been with their programs from the start.

Programs tended to express a few common problems regarding their boards. A few programs stressed that their boards needed a better appreciation of their clients; clients usually do not serve on the boards. If the board and staff conceptualize the board's role differently or if the board members do not identify easily with the clients, then serious problems can result. When the board members of one program refused to volunteer their assistance to the staff or parents directly by not attending program meetings or providing much needed transportation, several Parents Anonymous facilitators quit because of their frustration over a perceived lack of board support and interest. Programs also described boards that were ineffective fund-raising bodies; in most cases, this appeared to be the result of different fund-raising expectations on the part of staff and board members and the paucity of written "job descriptions" for board members. A lack of consensus regarding the board's purpose, unmet fund-raising needs, and unmotivated board members led one program to seek consulting advice from a professional fund-raising center. The information provided suggested a number of steps to take to remedy a crisis situation and provide a board plan for more long-term stability and leadership. At a very basic level, it is critically important that the mission of the board and expectations for board members (e.g., involvement in programming and fund-raising) be clearly defined and that the program and the board be mutually supportive. The following case study illustrates how an ineffective advisory board can contribute to the termination of a program.

• • •

The Parenting Project (PP) provides an informative example of the possible role that an advisory board can have—or fail to have—within a project. The local community action agency received funds for 2 consecutive years to operate the currently defunct PP. PP goals were to decrease stressors in the family environment of 30 teenage mothers; increase positive interactions between these parents and their children; and ameliorate the effects of social and emotional isolation, thereby reducing the incidence of child abuse and neglect. PP was developed to augment one of the community action agency's existing programs, the Teen Program (TP), which similarly targeted local teenage mothers and shared the same principal goals as PP.

The presiding TP director and an active member of the TP advisory council crafted and submitted, with advisory council's enthusiastic support, the grant proposal for PP in order to secure funds to hire a full-time staff member to provide long-term case management to teenage mothers through a minimum of two home visits per month. As originally proposed in the grant, PP families also would benefit from volunteer matches, a core component of TP: "The second component of the project will be linking each of the 30 teen families with a Parenting Partner. A Parenting Partner is a family who is willing to spend time monthly with a teen family. The goal of the Parenting Partner is to provide relief from emotional isolation and to provide a model of effective family life." The writers of the grant ascribed the task of recruiting Parenting Partners to the advisory council. Thus, the TP advisory council, which dually functioned as the advisory council for PP after the program received funding, had a fundamental role in establishing the program as well as explicit responsibility in operating a key program component. The grant proposal additionally lay plans for a multidisciplinary evaluation team to carefully assess process effectiveness, and many advisory council members submitted letters in support of the grant proposal in which they specifically mentioned their intent to serve as members of the evaluation team.

In the 2 years of the project's existence, plans for the formation of the evaluation team were never realized. In the application for a contract extension following the first year of operation, mention of the evaluation team was not made. The role of the advisory council also was undercut by the de-emphasis on the volunteer match component. According to the TP director, the addition of a full-time home visitor eliminated the need for Parenting Partners because she and the teenage mothers believed that the home visitor provided adequate attention. At the time of the statewide evaluation team's site visits, the TP director stated that the advisory council was in a period of restructuring because of lack of commitment and focus but that she perceived that its primary role had been and would continue to be fund-raising. A long-standing advisory council member, however, emphatically stated that the council no longer had any interest in fund-raising. Before the advisory council completed its restructuring process and clarified its role within the project, the community action agency and TP directors decided to discontinue both PP and TP.

The role of the advisory council may not have factored significantly into the decision to end the program, but, nevertheless, the advisory council did not have the opportunity to function as originally intended or effectively support the program. The volunteer matches were abandoned on the basis of anecdotal evidence, the project was never systematically evaluated to determine which programmatic elements were successful, and the purpose of the council was never clear. Although the advisory council adopted bylaws, the bylaws specified general, not specific, goals and responsibilities. The specific goals and responsibilities delineated in the grant were abandoned. Advisory council members served varied lengths of time according to their own prerogative, and priorities changed as new TP directors assumed control. In the 2 years of PP's existence, not less than three people held the position of TPSP director. The advisory council, in large part due to a lack of specific goals and undefined roles and expectations, was unable to provide stability or support to the project that it initially had endorsed very strongly.

• • •

Fund-Raising Activities

One of the most commonly expressed concerns among programs that qualify as legal nonprofit organizations was lack of time and/or knowledge to conduct effective fund-raising. Programs with one or two staff members, in particular, often seemed to find fund-raising an overwhelming task. A large number of programs rely on a small number of funding sources (e.g., the state, the United Way, an umbrella organization, special events) for annual support and do not have any strategic plan for seeking other sources of immediate or long-term funding. Many staff members have little experience or training in fund-raising, especially corporate and foundation grantwriting; they often do not know how or where to research potential funding sources, and they find the administrative requirements too time consuming. Other program staff simply do not view fund-raising as an important use of their time. As a result, most programs do not have a fund-raising plan to direct their efforts and tend to experience unstable funding that, in turn, affects their ability to provide quality programming.

Several programs have been successful in fund-raising efforts; Winchester's Parent–Child Center consistently solicits and receives funding from state agencies, private foundations, local corporations, and individuals (through special events, board member gifts, and direct-mail campaigns). Their success is due largely to the amount of effort directed to grantwriting, their ability to specify how funds will be used programmatically, and their use of standardized questionnaires and procedures to evaluate programming. (See Appendix A for the topical brief "Fund-Raising.")

Relationship with State Agencies

The overwhelming majority of programs, when asked specifically about their relationship with local Departments of Social Services (DSS) and Community Services Board/Mental Health (CSB) agencies, described that relationship as favorable. A few of the programs operate from within their local DSS or CSB agency, benefiting from that agency's resources. One program added that although its relationship with DSS is very good, it does not mention its association publicly because of the stigma attached to DSS within the community that it serves. Several programs report that collaboration has been enhanced by participating on each other's boards and/or through joint participation on other agencies' boards. Local DSS and CSB agencies provide referrals to many of the programs; this appears to be the most frequent source of contact that the programs have with these agencies. Some programs also enlist DSS or CSB personnel to speak at their parent education classes. Local CSB staff help one program with transportation. Only two programs reported difficulties with DSS and CSB, both citing territoriality problems. Surprisingly, in one of the communities, the local DSS and CSB agencies offer their own parenting education courses, competing with the state-funded program for enrollment.

The majority of programs receive court referrals, and, in return, many programs provide information to the courts. Reporting back to the courts does not seem to be problematic for the programs that do so, although the amount and type of information reported vary. Some report only the attendance of court-mandated clients. Others report scores on quizzes, class participation, and impressions of the parents and their interactions with their children. Programs with court referrals appear to be sensitive to confidentiality issues and are clear with clients and court staff about what types of information will be reported to the court.

Community Receptiveness

Nearly all of the programs report that they are well-received, at least by one community in which they serve, and present a multitude of evidence to support their claims. For example, in one community, enough funds were raised to finance a new complex to house the program. Another center, located in a high-crime area, has experienced few incidents of vandalism or robbery because of the neighborhood's acceptance of the center. Many programs receive donations from local churches and other organizations and members of the community. Local newspapers have published positive articles about many programs' activities. A hospital that has a collaborative relationship with one program features that program in its advertising, free of charge. The most commonly cited proof of community acceptance, though, is good interagency collaboration. The few programs that have experienced difficult community relations usually have had problems establishing positive interagency linkages. Turf problems occasionally hinder collaboration, and conservative community values make collaboration around the topic of child abuse and neglect and parent education for teenage parents a challenge. Communities vary greatly; several programs that are positively received in one county have experienced difficulty in another.

CRITERIA FOR EVALUATING
THE EFFECTIVENESS OF PROGRAMS

In a process evaluation, effectiveness is defined in terms of program design and implementation. A series of questions guided the intensive evaluation of the five sites.

Are Appropriate Groups Targeted and Effectively Recruited?

For the most part, the five sites do work with appropriate groups. These programs have identified specific groups that they want to serve and have targeted recruiting efforts toward them. The programs usually have full caseloads; if caseloads are down, it often is a function of personnel circumstances. For example, People, Inc., in Abingdon has had some difficulty with a home visitor maintaining a full caseload, but they are examining the circumstances and setting new goals to remedy the situation. Difficulties in effective recruiting also may result from moving into new areas. For example, the Parent–Child Center in Winchester successfully established programs in one county but has had difficulty developing client relationships in a second county. They are in the process of determining which characteristics of their approach and/or the region have led to difficulties in that area. At the Parents' Place in Roanoke, service to clients seems to follow demand in the sense that they offer classes to fill requests that come in (the number of which are rapidly expanding). Roanoke appears to be serving diverse clients, but staff still have the goal of increasing diversity, developing recruiting efforts, and expanding public awareness of their program as a resource center for all parents.

Are Participants Successfully Retained for the Duration of the Program?

Although the programs appear to do well, this question of whether participants are successfully retained for the duration of the program can be answered only by documenting attendance and participation. Most programs can answer anecdotally or calculate attendance but do not regularly look at client retention numbers. Retention has been identified by a majority of the 25 programs as a real concern. Within the intensive study subset, several programs actively address retention problems (see Chapters 7 and 8).

Are Program Goals and Objectives Clear, Concrete, and Measurable?

Each of the five programs has set relatively clear goals. The goals usually refer to specific programming activities and their implementation, such as how many education programs would be implemented or how many home visits each client would receive. Objectives regarding client progress are somewhat less clear. For example, the objectives may refer to client outcomes such as improved knowledge or decreased stress, but the degree of change is not quantified. This is, in part, a circular problem—most programs do not utilize outcome measures that could provide quantitative assessments of these concepts. Even so, those programs that do use assessment tools often do not use the scores to gauge whether objectives have been met successfully. When asked, the program staff and administrators believe that they have informal or anecdotal information that the goals and objectives are being met, but no systematic assessments are used. Therefore, it often is unclear whether the programs actually are meeting their goals and objectives.

Are Program Orientations Appropriately Matched to Participants?

In general, program orientations appear to be appropriately matched to participants. Programs working with teen parents offer more intensive services, either through home visiting or regular group meetings. The remaining programs offer educational classes and workshops to general groups and groups at risk, as well as support groups for clients at risk. Each program has some structured topics but remains flexible enough to allow clients to influence the agenda. Staff appear sensitive to clients' needs and adjust their services accordingly. Moreover, the programs that serve multiple client groups adjust their programming for each type of client.

Are Programs Implemented According to the Original Intent and Design? Are Modifications Appropriate?

Each of the five programs has remained true to its original program design with some modification. The Winchester program has remained fairly close to its original intent, although it has made modifications to the Nurturing Program curriculum in order to reflect parent needs (e.g., incorporating information on substance abuse and domestic violence). In general, it appears that program staff are aware of changes and that modifications are intended to respond to changing client needs.

Are Appropriately Trained Staff and/or Volunteers Utilized to Implement Programs?

Staff and volunteers appear to be appropriately trained in each of the five sites; however, the consistency and stability of the training program vary across sites. Programs, such as Winchester, that implement the Nurturing Program often have training that is specific to the curriculum, including official training from the state advocacy group PCA–V. For the most part, programs rely on in-house training programs. For home visitors and class leaders, "shadowing" veteran staff and co-facilitating classes are the most popular methods. It appears that most programs could benefit from more formal training opportunities, although cost is always a concern. Programs rely on community or regional workshops sponsored by other agencies. These opportunities are useful but are not under the control of the programs themselves, so they may not always cover topics that are needed.

CONCLUSION

Results of the process evaluation underscored the wide variety of ways that several common educational approaches can be implemented. Although most of the 25 programs used similar curricula, the unique needs of their communities as well as their fiscal and staff constraints meant that each program was unique. The process evaluation was not designed to report on whether programs were "working"; rather, it examined what types of interventions were being implemented and whether the implementation occurred in the intended manner. The in-depth study of the five intensive sites allowed the evaluation to focus on details of implementation and identify how the programs were meeting their goals and objectives. In order to provide a clearer picture of these programs, their successes, and their struggles, the next two chapters include case studies from each of the five sites.

Case Studies of Successful Parent Education Programs

Following the logic of Sarason and his colleagues (Sarason, 1972; Sarason, Zitnay, & Grossman, 1971), we were interested in assessing characteristics of the creation of human services settings. Sarason (1972) discussed how detailed descriptions of programs (e.g., the case studies of individuals used by clinicians) could provide insights for program developers. Looking at various human services programs, he detailed the institutions' historical contexts, pitfalls, staff, target groups, alternatives, and achievement of goals.

This chapter and the next provide brief case studies of the 5 (out of 25) sites that we selected for intensive study. Descriptions of (and anecdotes from) four of those programs are used in this chapter to illustrate different issues in creating and implementing parent education programs. The fifth, an excellent example of an opportunity for evaluating "effectiveness," is depicted in Chapter 8. The programs vary in terms of orientations, groups served, intensity, and a number of other dimensions. It is our hope that these case studies will provide assistance for practitioners who are, themselves, struggling with similar issues. Lessons learned from the case studies may allow practitioners to emulate procedures that have achieved successes and avoid the pitfalls encountered by others. Across the variety of case studies, stories from these real programs should, at the very least, raise issues about the choices inherent in creating, implementing, and evaluating human services programs (in general) and parent education programs for preventing child maltreatment (in particular). The five sites detailed in the cases are

Roanoke (Parents' Place)

- Urban, suburban, and rural (serving a mix of regions)
- Nurturing Program classes (6–8 weeks) and Surviving Motherhood classes (targets middle-class mothers)
- Variety of clientele (in terms of socioeconomic status [SES], ethnicity, mental health)
- Community resources (library, toy room, referrals)
- Excellent community relations

Goochland (Fellowship and Family Service)

- Suburban and rural
- STEP classes (run by a school psychologist)
- Variety of clientele (SES, ethnicity)
- Child component (High/Scope preschool program, tied to parent participation in parenting classes and program)

Abingdon (Resource Mothers of People, Inc.)

- Rural
- Teen mothers (and fathers)
- Home visiting (extensive)
- Comprehensive Support Program
- Extensive data

Winchester (Parent–Child Center)

- Rural and suburban
- Nurturing Program classes (15-week programs)
- High-risk target group (and identified abusers)
- Parents Anonymous group
- Home visiting (small component)

and, in Chapter 8,

Portsmouth (Good Beginnings)

- Urban
- Teen mothers (low-income, single, African American)
- Home visiting (for recruitment)
- Innovative education and support curriculum (12-week groups for teens and their infants)
- Extensive data
- Well-connected to other local services

THE PARENTS' PLACE: A RESOURCE CENTER FOR FAMILIES

with Peter A. Dillon

True to its name, the Parents' Place of Roanoke was initiated through the efforts of one of the city's parents. In 1988, during the course of researching a paper for a child development class, this parent spoke to social services agencies throughout the Roanoke Valley. She found that services for families in crisis were readily available and that several opportunities for education and support for typical, struggling parents could be sought out with effort. As a parent and stepparent dealing with the ordinary stresses of family life, she perceived a need in the community for someone to coordinate support and education services and to help make them more accessible to and approachable by "regular" parents. What she envisioned was a center for parenting resources that would be available to families at all levels of education, income, and parental distress. This parents' place would serve those in crisis and those who simply wanted to do a better job with the extremely difficult task of raising children.

The local Child Abuse Prevention Council (CAPC) seemed a logical place to turn because, at the time, it served as closely as possible the role of service coordinator for parents. It was a referral source, but it was perceived by the community as being for parents in distress. The parent presented her ideas to the female head of CAPC and received an enthusiastic response; however, the two acknowledged the limited ability of CAPC to initiate such a program on its own. Experience had taught them that most parents found the council's name to be threatening. Parents in their community seemed to reason that programs designed to prevent child abuse must have been created for "bad" parents. If the center was going to attract "regular" parents who wanted to become better parents, then the role of CAPC could not be a visible one. Nonetheless, the two women recruited a volunteer committee to work toward establishing the center for parenting resources, particularly solving the problem of finding an agency that could support and house it. After researching parenting resource centers in other Virginia communities, the CAPC committee members decided that their organization should have a physical location that was both convenient and approachable.

An executive director of the Roanoke YMCA was hired in 1987, at a time of transition in the philosophy of the YMCA organization. This change in the "Y movement" consisted of a shift in emphasis toward serving the needs of families rather than of young, single men. The new executive director and the YMCA board considered it their goal to reposition the public image of the Y

Peter A. Dillon is a Ph.D. candidate in clinical psychology at the University of Virginia, Charlottesville.

as providing resources for women, children, and families. Residential housing for young men had been phased out years before, leaving vacant two stories of the Y's central branch in downtown Roanoke. As the organizers were assembling their committee of volunteers, the YMCA board was brainstorming for ideas about how to utilize its space and achieve its goal of becoming an active provider of family services.

Due in part to the fact that the Y's executive director and CAPC's head were already friends, CAPC eventually approached the Y with the idea. Both CAPC and the Y board immediately realized that the collaboration served their goals very well. The Y would be perceived as nonthreatening and approachable to parents, and the Parents' Place would certainly help reposition the public image of the Y. Dedicated supporters and space were important components in getting the center started, but the committee realized that a paid staff would be necessary for operations. The Y and CAPC collaborated in applying for Department of Social Services (DSS) state family violence prevention grant money for 1989 but were turned down. By the next year, they succeeded in getting the DSS funds to pay the salary for a part-time director for the Parents' Place.

The decision of whom to hire for the director position was not a difficult one for the committee. One person's 15 years of experience as coordinator for special services for Head Start in the Roanoke community made her well-known professionally and personally to most of the Parents' Place committee members. The combination of her service delivery experience; her knowledge of the Roanoke social services community; and her warm, enthusiastic approach to working with parents and children made her ideally suited for the position. By September of 1990, one parent's idea for a parenting resource center in her community had taken form, and the Parents' Place was in operation.

MISSION STATEMENT

According to its mission statement, the Parents' Place was founded on the concept that both parents and their children continue to grow, develop, and require nurturing. The goal is to offer support and services in a positive light so that all parents, regardless of risk level, will feel comfortable seeking help. Although the term *at risk* is, among human services professionals, a buzzword that generally is used to describe individuals experiencing significant distress, it is the belief of the founders and staff that all parents are at risk for adverse outcomes. The stressful nature of the job of parenting and the uncertainty of economic standing, marital status, and social support make it impossible to state with confidence that an individual parent is not at some risk for future severe family distress. The center espouses a truly primary prevention model in making services available for all Roanoke parents. The services are designed to help parents improve their parenting skills by providing

- Education and information on child development and behavior management
- Emotional support and companionship
- Information and referral to others in the community who can help

PARENTS' PLACE SERVICES

Parent Education and Support

Interviews with Roanoke community agencies reveal that the Parents' Place is most readily associated with parenting classes. The Parents' Place either runs or co-sponsors classes to suit the needs of any parent in the community who seeks help. Between its Nurturing Program courses, "Surviving Motherhood" classes, and Transitional Living Center programs, parents across the entire gamut of economic level and risk status can find opportunities to improve their parenting skills.

Nurturing Program   The Nurturing Program (reviewed in Chapter 3) is a 15-session, group format, parent education curriculum designed to improve family functioning by teaching parents about child development, behavior management, and coping skills and by teaching children about emotional awareness through age-appropriate, expressive group activities. The course is based on the premise that parenting skills are learned rather than innate and that mutually respectful interactions between parents and children can lessen family stress.

The Parents' Place was approached by the head of Roanoke's Human Development Office to run modified parenting classes for families with children in the school system. The Nurturing Program curriculum was chosen because it was made available to DSS-funded programs and because the staff were attracted to the program's involvement of children. The director and the city reached an agreement to collaborate on resources. The city would recruit families through the schools, find suitable locations to house the classes, provide dinner for the families attending, arrange child care for children too young to participate, and offer door prizes to encourage continuing attendance. The Parents' Place would take care of teaching the curriculum. The programs have been offered twice per year, free of charge, alternating locations to make each one more accessible to a different geographic area of the city. The groups meet once per week for 6 weeks. They begin in the early evening, and families share a dinner before parents and children divide into their separate groups. The curriculum is appropriate to a wide range of educational levels. Printed handouts are commonly used; but for parents with reading difficulties, the information can be conveyed orally in class. Whereas most families who attend are recruited through the schools, judges in the region who want to mandate attendance at parent education have referred parents to these programs as well.

Although the collaboration between the Parents' Place and the city has been successful, it has not been without conflict. Given the city's larger stake in providing resources, the director sometimes finds herself wishing for greater control over the programs. For example, the curriculum is designed to consist of 15 sessions; however, for families with young children, such a time commitment can be excessive; and for the city, providing dinners, child care, and classroom space for 15 weeks can be prohibitively expensive. The city decided to offer six classes, leaving to the director the task of condensing the curriculum, without diminishing its effectiveness. Obviously, what can be taught in 15 sessions cannot be covered in only 6 (in order to do so, she calls upon her extensive experience with parent education to choose those parts of the curriculum that she believes to be most useful for parents and those that address the primary concerns of each group as expressed during the course). Also, the director prefers to place an upper limit of 20 parents for each program, but the city has occasionally allowed larger numbers to enroll, assuming attrition will decrease the class sizes over time. Ideally, the Parents' Place staff would like to have more control in running the Nurturing Programs but lacks the resources to run them independently.

Surviving Motherhood   The Surviving Motherhood educational support curriculum was created by its instructor, a local professional with an M.S.W. degree, who had been running the groups for years at the women's center of a nearby college. It was designed for more highly educated mothers who could benefit from assigned readings and thoughtful discussions without finding a classroom format intimidating. Participants pay a $20 donation for the class itself and an additional $20 if they want child care (which is provided in the Parents' Place playroom or the YMCA's child care facilities). Groups meet weekday mornings at the Parents' Place at the YMCA and consist of a maximum of 15 mothers.

Surviving Motherhood targets mothers of children in similar developmental stages to ensure the relevance of the often age-specific discussion topics. The 10-week curriculum consists of assigned readings, usually articles that argue opposite sides of controversial issues, after which mothers discuss their opinions and share experiences. The groups almost uniformly experience a high degree of cohesion. The mothers report contacting each other for support outside of class and attend any postclass reunions that are held. Classes were so successful that the instructor compiled different sets of readings for Surviving Motherhood II and III. After one recent Surviving II class, all mothers were invited back, and all returned for Surviving III. Though the class is not designed for everyone, it seems to serve its targeted group extremely well. Even with its middle- to upper-class clientele, mothers from these parenting classes have been referred for additional outside counseling, which reinforces the position of the Parents' Place that *at risk* is a term that should not be reserved for those experiencing obvious economic, social, or psychological distress.

Transitional Living Center The Parents' Place was approached by the case manager of a local shelter for women to conduct parenting classes for its residents. Local churches donate the space for the classes and for child care, and the Parents' Place and the Transitional Living Center (TLC) collaborate in providing transportation and baby sitters. The eight-session course consists of a fairly flexible curriculum, as the director modifies it to meet the special concerns of the group. Some TLC course materials are borrowed directly from the Nurturing Program, including discussions of developmental expectations, discipline techniques, and stress management. Outside speakers from the community are brought in whenever possible, including family counselors, nutrition experts, and fitness instructors demonstrating massage and relaxation techniques. These speakers donate their time because they view it as a worthy cause and because of the director's personal and professional connections.

Although parenting information is disseminated at these classes, it is not forgotten that these mothers are experiencing significant distress and often have long histories of physical abuse and substance abuse. Therefore, close attention is paid to the participants' own needs for nurturing and social support as well as their children's. Because learning new skills and information in a classroom format may be intimidating to these mothers and because they sometimes are too overwhelmed to take in new information, the value of these classes may lie as much in the social support that they provide as in the knowledge that they disseminate.

Other Services

The physical location of the Parents' Place consists of the director's office; a parenting resource library; a playroom; the YMCA board room, which doubles as classroom space; and the very popular toy library. Originally a joint venture of the Junior League and the Parents' Place, the Toy Room now has more than 100 members. Junior League members had the idea to begin the Toy Room and were looking for a suitable location when they heard about the center. Families pay a $5 annual fee for membership. The more than 400 donated toys are categorized by developmental appropriateness. Members can check out two toys and two puzzles at a time and may keep them for 2 weeks. The Toy Room is ideally suited for parents who find that their children quickly become bored with new toys; for those with grandchildren, nieces, or nephews who visit infrequently; or for parents with limited income. Community parents of all socioeconomic levels can feel comfortable coming to the Y to use the Toy Room and in doing so can learn of classes, support groups, or volunteer opportunities offered by the Parents' Place.

Another successful activity of the center is the annual Parenting Fair. Held at a local civic center, the event has been attracting more than 1,000 people each year. The fair provides interested parents an opportunity to meet with child care providers, school personnel, health professionals, and others who set up displays. Vendors, such as diaper services, toy stores, financial planners, and dance studios, set up booths to advertise their products and services. Donations pay for space and advertisement of the fair, and a raffle is held for a donated playhouse or swing set. A local hospital and a chapter of the Kiwanis have been closely involved with the fair. The popularity of the event makes the Parenting Fair an excellent public relations instrument in marketing the Parents' Place to Roanoke families.

The Parents' Place has had success sponsoring occasional one-time activities, such as workshops and fairs. Family enrichment activities, such as kite flying, infant stimulation classes, and a "First Night" New Year's Eve Festival provide enjoyable outings for community families. Some of their services have met with less success and were either abandoned or never started. A newsletter for the center was abandoned because of the lack of computer resources and volunteer writers. Support groups for blended families and stepfamilies were discontinued because of low enrollment. A proposed community "Warm-Line," intended to provide parenting information and emotional support by telephone, was repeatedly turned down for funding. Parenting support groups targeting fathers is another good idea that awaits funding and resources to get off the ground. A number of Roanoke judges have approached the Parents' Place to become a site for court-ordered supervised parental visits, and the board is considering whether their resources and mission are suited to providing such services. Still a relatively young organization, the Parents' Place has struggled to find its niche despite strong commitment from both the staff and the advisory board.

STAFF AND ORGANIZATIONAL STRUCTURE

In the center's 6 years of existence, the director has remained the sole paid staff person. Although her job description calls for 20 hours per week, she actually devotes much more time than that. The director coordinates, trains, and supervises the volunteers who staff the Toy Room and assist in running parenting groups. The director speaks at parenting workshops and sets up booths at local fairs or festivals. She enjoys teaching parenting classes herself, including the Nurturing Program for the city and the TLC program, and she is involved in the logistical aspects such as child care, transportation, and recruiting speakers. She organizes and runs steering committee and advisory board meetings. Coordinating the Parenting Fair by setting up vendors, sites, and funding consumes a significant portion of her time once a year. Filling out reports for her funding agency and answering telephone calls related to service referrals consistently require the director's attention.

The executive director of the YMCA works closely with the Parents' Place's director. Because it provides so much support for the Parents' Place, the

Y's board of directors has final authority over its operation, but the executive director is very quick to downplay this fact. In his view, collaboration among community agencies is critical to the existence of the Parents' Place. Many organizations, including CAPC, the Junior League, and the Kiwanis, have been instrumental in creating and supporting the Parents' Place. These organizations and the parents of the community need to feel a strong degree of ownership in the Parents' Place, and any perception that it is strictly a YMCA program threatens this vital collaboration. For this reason, the executive director and the Y board of directors are comfortable in taking a hands-off role and giving decision-making authority to the advisory board and the steering committee.

The Parents' Place advisory board meets twice annually to receive updates on the overall operations and to advise in planning general program goals. The board is made up of 20 volunteers, most of whom are key players in the service community or have other valuable expertise or resources. The advisory board serves to provide a network for a broad base of resources and ideas. The steering committee is a smaller group that is very much involved in the center's day-to-day operations. These seven volunteers meet monthly to receive updates on the progress of the programs and to make policy decisions. Some members of the original committee to create the center are still involved in the steering committee. It is through these advisory and steering committees that community collaboration and multiple organization ownership are maintained. Members of the committees are counselors, attorneys, or business leaders, most of whom are also Roanoke parents. Connections with CAPC, the Junior League, and the Kiwanis are preserved by having members of these groups on the Parents' Place committees, and the director sits on the boards for these and other organizations. (See Appendix A for the topical brief "Interagency Collaboration.") The success of the Parents' Place in avoiding turf conflicts with other service providers and in staying afloat with a minimum of funding has been in large part due to its efforts to maintain this collaboration.

Volunteers have played a vital role in the functioning of the Parents' Place. From serving as board members to staffing the Toy Room to running the parenting classes, the operation of the center has depended on volunteers. At least one member of the steering committee works closely with the director to run parenting classes, train other facilitators, and compile monthly report data. The Junior League and the Kiwanis have provided some funds and some tangible resources, such as Toy Room toys and assistance in renovating the YMCA offices, but they also have been helpful in supplying volunteers. Although the recruitment of volunteers has been identified by the board as a weakness overall, the Parents' Place has been very successful in reinvesting its resources by recruiting former program participants to become volunteers. For example, several Surviving Motherhood graduates have become volunteers. One Nurturing Program graduate has become a Nurturing Program facilitator and also sits on the Parents' Place board. The use of such volunteers requires that a smaller time commitment be invested in training; the director has little time to spare. Although recruiting, training, and coordinating large numbers of new volunteers is difficult for the center, the contributions of those volunteers who are active are high enough in quality to compensate partially for their low quantity. The wide gap between the accomplishments of the Parents' Place and the job description of its director has been spanned by the efforts of its dedicated volunteers, but recruiting and training larger numbers of volunteers is an area in need of improvement.

FUNDING

The Parents' Place is funded by a grant from the Virginia Department of Social Services Family Violence Prevention Program. The Department of Social Services has provided a consistent amount of support over the program's 4-year history. Most of this grant money pays the director's salary. The YMCA provides the office space and absorbs the majority of the overhead expenses for the center. A handful of local businesses and foundations have donated money, particularly in support of the Parenting Fair, and most of the fees generated by Surviving Motherhood classes pay for the instructor's time. Over its first 4 years, the funding from the DSS decreased, yet donations increased only slightly. Clearly, increasing funding for the center is a priority, and the search for additional funding sources remains high on the list of challenges that the board faces.

LONG-RANGE PLANNING WORKSHOP

In the summer of 1994, the advisory board arranged a day-long retreat for board members and other individuals strongly invested in the operation of the Parents' Place. The goal was to take a critical look at the success of the center's mission and to set down a plan for its next 3–5 years. An advisory board member experienced in facilitating such seminars volunteered to guide the discussion. In preparation for the workshop, the director sent out surveys to consumers asking them to evaluate their experiences with the Parents' Place and to describe their perceptions of its mission and purpose. Prior to the retreat, the workshop participants were given the results of this survey, a brief summary of the history and mission of the center, a financial summary of its 4 years of funding, and a paper reviewing the empirical literature related to parent education. Fifteen people took time off from work or otherwise arranged to make themselves available for the day.

In introducing the day's activities, the Y's executive director emphasized that the workshop participants should feel free to rebuild the center from the ground up if necessary. Any changes, including the center's leaving the Y if it were in the center's best interest, would be open for discussion. His suggestion served to reinforce the notion that multiple agency ownership superseded the concerns of the Y but was later dismissed because of the success of the collaboration between the center and the Y. Each of the participants stated their reasons for collaborating in the task of shaping the mission of the Parents' Place. This served both as an introduction of group members and as a verbal renewal of the individuals' commitment to the center. The facilitator then showed a videotape that illustrated the value of evaluating one's current modes of thinking, or paradigms; examining the limitations of these thought processes; and eventually freeing oneself to think creatively about the future. The narrator provided historical examples of missed opportunities caused by short-sighted thinking and innovations brought about by shifts in paradigms. The video set the stage for brainstorming about future ideas without the assumption that current constraints are fixed or permanent (e.g., waiting until after resources become available to plan for their use is shortsighted).

Participants discussed the strengths and needs of the center. Among the strengths listed were the broad target group, the nonthreatening image that makes the center approachable to all parents, the ability to provide parenting classes as a prevention measure rather than only as a resource for parents in crisis, the innovation of the programs, the reinvestment of volunteer resources, and the extensive interagency collaboration and community support. Next, the workshop participants were asked to identify and discuss the key strategic issues or challenges that the Parents' Place will face over the next 5 years. Three strategic issues were identified: defining an identity, marketing, and measuring outcomes.

Defining an Identity

Defining an identity for the Parents' Place was central. The task of defining the vague concept of "parenting" was sufficiently difficult to cause confusion among the board members as to the overall goal of the center. The group deliberated whether the mission should be to provide services for families or to function as a referral service in coordinating parent education in the Roanoke Valley. Although the original vision for the center called for the provision of both types of services, the board reasoned that it may be in the center's best interest to focus on one or the other because of the conflict of interest in referring parents to the center's own services and because the director's limited time was being divided between the two activities. Moreover, putting greater emphasis on service delivery would enable the center to compete for funding more successfully, and Roanoke parents generally continued to turn to CAPC rather than to the Parents' Place for referral information. Thus, they decided that the Parents' Place should focus its efforts on service delivery rather than on service coordination. With this clarification of goals and mission, the board moved to the next issue of advertising them more effectively.

Marketing

The second key issue identified was marketing. Some of the challenges discussed were closely related to strengths of the Parents' Place, the other side of the proverbial coin. For example, although the focus on providing services for every type of family can be considered a strength of the program, the general target of "Roanoke parents" represents somewhat of an obstacle in seeking funding. Many funding streams that are target specific (e.g., set aside for teen mothers or for families living in poverty) are not attracted to the Parents' Place because of its broad definition of clients who are at risk. Also, although the affiliation with the Y has been overwhelmingly positive, some confusion has arisen in that parents sometimes hesitate to use the center, erroneously thinking that it is for Y members only. Although the survey of past consumers of the centers' services showed that they overwhelmingly identified the mission correctly, the Parents' Place clearly would benefit from advertising its mission to the general public, thereby correcting any misperceptions. Developing an ambitious marketing plan for educating both funding agencies and community parents about the services and mission of the center was identified as a goal for the near future.

Measuring Outcomes

The final area for improvement concerned collecting data to measure program outcomes, a critical issue given the trend that DSS, the main funder of the program, is increasingly requiring such data from grantees. The center would need to demonstrate, for example, that its programs improve parenting skills, increase parents' knowledge of child development, or decrease parental stress before it could convincingly argue that it is preventing family distress or family violence. The literature review of parent education research highlighted for the workshop participants the obvious lack of empirical support to demonstrate the effectiveness of parenting education for preventing child abuse. For both of these reasons, the group decided to place high on its list of priorities the development of their programs as models for outcome evaluation.

The evaluation that has been conducted consists of open-ended questionnaires asking program participants for feedback and two questionnaires that are standard components of the Nurturing Program, assessing knowledge of child development, parental empathy, and attitudes concerning discipline. Considering the director's job description and multiple time demands, it comes as no surprise that these data rarely are collected, stored, or analyzed in a consistent manner. Like many mental health professionals, the director's preference is to devote her time to service delivery rather than to data collection. (See Appendix A for the topical brief "Evaluation: Making It Work for You.") In deciding to place serious emphasis on outcome evaluation, the board acknowledged that the director did not have either the time or the expertise to manage it alone. Although specific logistical difficulties were left to another time, it was generally suggested that interested graduate students from a nearby university could be recruited to put the outcomes measures into place and analyze the data.

THE FUTURE

In talking to those involved in the Parents' Place and in reading annual progress reports, the phrase "working toward finding our niche" comes up repeatedly. During the workshop, suggestions were raised about expanding the center to locations beyond the downtown area, such as branch offices in schools. Also suggested were expanding services to include home-visiting programs and collaborating with hospitals to direct parents of newborns toward the Parents' Place services. Enthusiasm about new ideas seems to characterize those involved with the center.

In the months following the workshop, the steering committee began to take a new shape. It designated a chairperson and restructured itself into smaller subcommittees to address the specific strategic issues identified in the workshop. Because committee meeting attendance tends to decline during summer months and because volunteer recruitment remains a problem, the director expressed a concern that changes were taking place at a pace slower than what she had expected. Given that the issues identified had been discussed by the board in at least a vague form throughout the center's history, perhaps skepticism about the changes occurring in the near future is warranted. The Parents' Place is indeed an asset to the Roanoke community, but the center still faces obstacles of improving donations and funding and enlisting volunteers. The steering committee is aware of the need for support in its mission, and the efforts of the subcommittee members will be geared toward improving this situation.

Like all social services agencies, the center has faced serious challenges in getting started. Limited funding, a shortage of personnel, and shifting demands for services have presented difficulties for the Parents' Place in its few years of existence. These have not been viewed as insurmountable problems that have led to stagnation, however. Rather, the dedication of the board members, the director, and the volunteers has made the center a positive force in the community and has provided a setting for personal growth among the staff. The long-range planning workshop illustrates the ability of the board to evaluate its weaknesses and approach them with commitment to improvement. In large part, this level of commitment and the flexibility of the staff in providing services to meet the needs of all Roanoke parents have been responsible for its success thus far. Its continued success will represent an important achievement in primary prevention of family distress by providing nonthreatening opportunities for parents to learn more effective means of handling the always-difficult job of being a parent.

FELLOWSHIP AND FAMILY SERVICE:
CHILD CARE AS A "HOOK"

with Deborah Schutte

HISTORY

In October of 1952, a group of Goochland County citizens founded an organization called the Goochland Family Service Society. This organization was created to promote the welfare of the community, particularly those people whose needs were not being met by the government. The society's first corresponding secretary claimed that the organization was "for people who fell through the cracks." The society's objective was to provide struggling members of the county with the skills and materials necessary to maintain a healthy, autonomous, and productive lifestyle. Through donations of food, clothing, and medicine, the Goochland Family Service Society hoped to create opportunities for these residents to become flourishing and contributing members of the community. Residents throughout the county immediately espoused the goals and efforts of the program. They contributed money, time, and personal belongings ranging from firewood to groceries. One man even donated two "good Guernsey cows to deserving families." A neighbor-helping-neighbor atmosphere began to emerge, and the society adopted the slogan "Helping People."

Throughout its history of "helping people," a constant focus has been placed on improving medical care in the community. This can be observed even in the society's earliest activities, which included providing free milk and vitamins to school children. By 1971, the society had raised funds sufficient to construct the Goochland Medical Center, which would house both a physician and a dentist. In addition, in 1977, the society purchased a van to provide county residents with transportation to and from medical appointments. In later years, the society continued to expand and evolve, but the emphasis placed on health care persisted and is reflected in its objectives even today.

As the population of the county grew during the 1980s, the needs of the residents expanded, and new programs emerged to meet those demands. One such program, the Goochland Fellowship, was established in 1985 by three women from a local Episcopal church. While possessing a similar ideal of "enhancing the quality of life of people in Goochland County," these women concentrated on new areas of need surfacing in the community. The founders contacted the Department of Social Services for assistance in identifying the county's most salient needs. As a result of this collaboration, the Goochland Fellowship set its priorities on reducing the incidence of child maltreatment

---

Deborah Schutte is a graduate student in psychology at William & Mary College, Williamsburg, Virginia.

and providing assistance for older adults. They attempted to combat child abuse by offering free parenting education programs to county residents.

MERGER AND CHANGE

The Goochland Fellowship began to serve an increasingly larger number of people as awareness of their services spread throughout the county. In order to meet increasing demands, the founders realized that they would need their own facility. Their location at the time, an Episcopal church, did not provide adequate space and was located in a remote end of the county, making it inaccessible to many residents. A two-story house near the center of the county soon became available. A fund-drive was initiated, with a capital campaign spearheaded by the organization's board of directors.

While new opportunities were transpiring for the Goochland Fellowship, one of the founders was concurrently serving as a board member for the Goochland Family Service Society. She realized that both organizations shared a common goal of improving the welfare of the county. She suggested that the two agencies merge in order to consolidate their efforts and to prevent a duplication of services. Largely by her efforts, the organizations merged in the summer of 1987, and the name was changed to Goochland Fellowship and Family Service (GFFS).

The merger, although successful in improving the services to the community, initially created problems for the organizations involved. Each organization was concerned that it would not be equally represented on the board. Members of the Goochland Fellowship, the smaller agency, were particularly concerned that they would lose control over the direction and emphases of the organization. These issues were resolved by allowing the society's three founders to compose the programs committee of the new GFFS. This committee possessed the broad power to direct the focus of the organization and to determine which of the county's needs would be addressed. The Goochland Fellowship, therefore, retained the power to make genuine contributions to the future role of the organization.

As GFFS evolved throughout subsequent years, the desire for each of the former programs to retain its independence diminished. In 1993, the bylaws to the merger were revised. The new bylaws no longer assign particular duties to a specific program, thus reflecting a more complete integration of the organizations. GFFS has a rich history of service to the county's residents. This commitment to fellow community members has been a guiding force throughout its many years of existence and is highly visible in the organization today.

CURRENT ORGANIZATION

Many of the problems afflicting Goochland County in the 1950s are still salient in the 1990s. The predominately rural composition of the county fosters conditions of loneliness and isolation, sustaining the need for outreach services for older adults. The prevalence of child abuse also has remained alarmingly high (Goochland has been ranked as the eighth worst county in the state for the number of child abuse reports per capita). The county further battles widespread problems of illiteracy, poverty, and unemployment. GFFS responds to a number of the needs of the county by running five programs serving approximately 900 individuals each year. Its diverse array of services includes an older-adult outreach program, emergency appeals, a literacy program, van transportation for various services, and a parenting education and child care program. It is evident that the parenting and older-adult outreach programs, although remaining prominent components within the organization and the community, are placed within a context of multiple programs serving a variety of the community's needs.

PARENTING EDUCATION AND CHILD CARE

Resources and programs for the prevention of child abuse are sparse in the county. The Department of Social Services (DSS) offers one-time classes on specific aspects of parenting and sponsors speakers. These are provided only when "the need arises," however, as determined by various groups or people in the community (e.g., Parent–Teacher Association, social workers). Consequently, GFFS consistently has remained the primary resource for preventing child abuse in the county; it has attempted to achieve this by educating parents on proper parenting techniques.

The parenting program at GFFS, like the organization as a whole, has undergone numerous changes since it began in the fall of 1986. Originating under the Goochland Fellowship, the program initially consisted of eight weekly sessions. This format was followed until 1989, serving a total of 91 parents. Although the program provided parents with useful information and techniques, the executive director of GFFS believed that 8 weeks was not sufficient to create permanent and genuine changes in parenting behavior. She believed that "it is time to move on to focus more on the developmental needs of the children and to facilitate more basic changes in lifestyle for the mothers. These things cannot be done in 8 weeks." Those beliefs laid the groundwork for future parenting education and child care programs at GFFS.

With funding secured through the Virginia Family Violence Prevention Program, the U.S. Department of Agriculture (USDA), and two local private foundations, GFFS was able to open the Family Development Center (FDC) in 1990. This center houses both a developmental preschool and an 8-month parenting education program. The two programs are interactive, as parents with children in the preschool are encouraged to volunteer in the classrooms and are required to attend the weekly parenting classes. In addition, both programs share a common objective of reducing the incidence of child abuse.

STAFF

GFFS is operated by an executive director, the only full-time staff member, and nine part-time employees and numerous volunteers. The executive director joined the organization as the part-time program coordinator shortly after the merger in 1987, bringing with her a rich and extensive background in early childhood and parenting education. Her experiences have strongly influenced the existing format of the child care and parenting programs at GFFS and have enabled her to possess the leadership, innovation, and foresight necessary to operate these programs successfully. The executive director is responsible for hiring and training the program coordinator; managing the vast network of volunteer activity; planning and directing the preparation of budgets and grants; determining organizational and staffing needs; and, broadly, ensuring that the organization's goals, as determined by the board of directors, are being implemented and evaluated.

The program coordinator joined GFFS in 1989. She, too, arrived with expertise and experience in child care programs; she was a Head Start director for 10 years and received a master's degree in education. She is responsible for the overall implementation of the programs (preschool and parenting classes) in the Family Development Center. Her responsibilities specific to the preschool include hiring, training, and evaluating four preschool teachers. She also provides the teachers with guidance in developing curricula and ensures that the preschool meets the National Academy of Early Childhood Programs and government regulations. The project coordinator's responsibilities for the parenting program include developing and implementing the parenting curriculum. In addition, she spends a large portion of her time offering assistance and support to parents. Her responsibilities for the overall center include ensuring that the FDC is serving the targeted group and providing an orientation for parents interested in the program. Finally, she supervises the other staff involved with the FDC: the parent education facilitator, two infant care providers, two van drivers, and a cook.

The immense responsibilities assumed by the program coordinator are handled efficiently and competently. She is firm and consistent with parents and staff yet displays an endless amount of patience and compassion. She possesses a genuine concern and interest in the parents and children at GFFS and a wonderful enthusiasm as she discusses "success stories" of the program.

VOLUNTEERS

Although the staff at GFFS perform numerous and varied tasks, the range of services offered at this organization would not be possible without the assistance of volunteers. Approximately 125 people volunteer at GFFS each year in a variety of capacities. Volunteers serve in positions ranging from clerical assistants to literacy tutors to child care providers. Because of this extensive range of opportunity, GFFS is perceived throughout the county as *the* place to volunteer. (See Appendix A for the topical brief "Managing Staff and Volunteers.")

Volunteers are recruited through a variety of methods, the most successful of which is an annual newsletter that is distributed to every household in the county. The newsletter describes recent activities of each program and requests that members of the community donate their time and/or money. GFFS further recruits volunteers through fliers sent to local groups and clubs and through talks given at churches. Once recruited, volunteers are matched to jobs according to their interests and abilities. Most volunteer a few hours per month; however, one full-time volunteer assists with training and evaluating other volunteers, publishes the annual newsletter, and maintains the GFFS library. Historically, there has been no formal screening process. The executive director found it unnecessary, as Goochland is a small county, and she is familiar with most members of the community; however, GFFS received a large grant to install a Central Volunteer System. This computer program will serve as a central "bank" for the entire county, matching volunteers' requests and interests with the needs of the community. The program also contains a screening device capable of detecting prior criminal records and child abuse or molestation convictions.

In an effort to retain the services of volunteers and to uphold a high level of morale and motivation, the executive director provides GFFS volunteers with service awards and recognition in the community. She creatively utilizes local and organizational events to commend GFFS volunteers and to publicize their activities. The executive director identifies businesses and other organizations that reward volunteers for outstanding service. Through these established awards, she is able to promote both her volunteers and GFFS itself. One such award is the Golden Rule award offered annually by the JCPenney Corporation. Last year, a GFFS volunteer received this award for her work as an adult literacy tutor. GFFS volunteers received five such awards for a variety of activities in 1994 alone. The efforts of GFFS volunteers are further recognized during the annual county parade and celebration. Finally, the executive director honors GFFS volunteers by hosting a Volunteer Recognition Tea. Volunteers throughout the county are invited to attend this event to recognize their service and commitment to the community.

FUNDING

GFFS is supported by a variety of private foundation and government grants and individual donations. The largest contributions typically are secured through the United Way Development Fund, the Virginia Family Violence Prevention Program (VFVPP), and an annual public fund-raising drive.

Additional support has come from Medicaid, the USDA, and various foundations. GFFS is a good example of a program that started with seed money and was then able to secure other, more permanent, sources of funding and build up community support, including financial support. (See Appendix A for the topical brief "Fund-Raising.")

PRESCHOOL COMPONENT

The preschool operates 3 days per week from 9 A.M. to 1 P.M. It serves approximately 26 children each year, approximately half African American and half Caucasian. There typically exists a waiting list to get into the preschool, which enables the program director to select a diverse mixture of children. There is no tuition charge for the preschool, but parents are required to participate in the parenting program and to annually contribute 20 hours of volunteer service to the organization.

The preschool strives to reduce and prevent developmental delays in children and to offer social, emotional, physical, and intellectual opportunities for them. It achieves these goals by fostering an atmosphere in which children are encouraged to explore and to become actively involved in the learning process. The classrooms are divided into learning corners for art, computer, music, natural science, fine and gross motor development, language arts, and dramatic play activities. The multiple centers enable children to pursue their own interests and curiosities while building self-esteem and independence.

Children are evaluated three times per year to ensure that they are continuously progressing toward the center's goals. The Stepping Stones Checklist is used to assess children's developmental progress and to identify areas on which the curriculum should be focused. The checklist assesses a child's cognitive development, communication skills, motor skills, and social development. In addition, a Parent Questionnaire developed by the National Academy of Early Childhood Programs is used at the end of each year to assess parents' satisfaction with the preschool and to identify areas needing improvement.

Parent Involvement

The success of the preschool is largely dependent on parental involvement. Parents are commonly seen assisting their children in the computer center or watching intently as their children participate in large-group activities. These opportunities for parent–child interaction enhance the efficacy not only of the preschool but also of the parenting program. Many parents also report that the preschool, teachers, and other parents serve as sources of social support. The notion of support is an interesting one, especially with respect to the child care setting. In a study of child care centers and family day care homes, Britner and Phillips (1995) found that parents' perceived social support from the care arrangement was the best predictor of satisfaction with child care.

In this program, the primary emphasis is on quality child care, parent–child interactions, and support. Nonetheless, there is strong emphasis on parent training. The Parenting Program seeks to reduce the incidence of child abuse by "instilling age-appropriate expectations in parents and reducing family dysfunction and isolation." To attain these goals, the parenting program uses a traditional, education-based program in addition to developing strong support systems among the parents and strengthening literacy skills within the families.

The parenting program serves approximately 25 parents each year. Fifty percent of the participants are African American women, and 50% are Caucasian women, all of whom are from low- and middle-income families. Although a majority of the women are single mothers, the program also serves married mothers, grandmothers, and an occasional father. Approximately half of the parents are referred from community agencies such as the Health Department and the Department of Social Services. In addition, a majority of the parents have children in the GFFS preschool. The parenting program is not limited to these parents, however, and periodically serves parents with infants or older children. The parenting program is held only on Tuesday mornings (starting each September); thus, it inherently attracts a large proportion of parents who are unemployed or employed only part time. Originally, the program director diligently recruited parents from the health department and Head Start. As awareness of the program spread through community agencies and members of the county, however, participation increased, and recruitment became unnecessary.

The first three sessions are spent discovering how these parents were parented. Specialists from the local Community Services Board work with the class to reveal how their parenting behaviors may be a reflection of techniques that they were exposed to in their childhood. Issues of codependency, substance abuse, and stress management also are addressed at this time. Parents must identify and resolve their own problems, it is believed, before they can effectively manage the difficulties of parenthood.

The parenting classes follow a consistent routine, which can be broken down into four sections: coffee hour; education and support, literacy development, and lunch. The day begins with a coffee hour during which the program coordinator for the FDC helps parents make activities that they can share with their children at home. These activities, which include making homemade playdough and creating jigsaw puzzles out of cereal boxes, are chosen for their accessibility to families of all income levels. The coffee hour also offers parents an opportunity to build and strengthen relationships with other parents.

The educational component of the program begins at 10 A.M. with a school psychologist from the public school system. She uses concepts from the Systematic Training for Effective Parenting (STEP) curriculum but does not follow the program rigidly. She feels that the parenting program must have flexibility in order to accommodate the specific needs of the parents. Another key factor of successful parenting programs, she believes, is to actively involve parents in the learning process. The facilitator encourages problem-solving and brainstorming activities and often gives the parents homework assignments. In addition, she tries to take the role of facilitator rather than of "expert." When discussing specific parenting problems, for example, she often solicits opinions from several parents before reaching a solution. Over the course of 1year, the facilitator has helped parents confront problems including spousal abuse, child abuse, and divorce.

During the next stage of the class, the program coordinator teaches parents how to develop and strengthen literacy skills in the family. She uses a development-based book that provides materials for in-home activities. She demonstrates these activities and encourages parents to try them at home. The class also takes an annual trip to the library to ensure that all parents and children have library cards and are familiar with the procedures, rules, and contents of the library. The goal of this family literacy component is to foster interaction between parents and their children in their mutual education. Parents end the day by eating lunch with their children in the preschool. This allows staff to observe parent–child interactions and to offer guidance when needed.

EVALUATION

Parents are assessed continuously throughout the year, both formally and informally, to ensure progress toward the program's goals. The Adult-Adolescent Parenting Inventory (AAPI) (Bavolek, 1984) is used as a pretest and a posttest to evaluate parents' knowledge of appropriate parenting techniques. GFFS uses this information to determine which areas should be targeted and emphasized throughout the year and in future programs. Although the AAPI is administered regularly, its function is limited to directing the curriculum and emphases of the program. This test is not used to systematically measure improvement in parenting.

Parents also are evaluated informally through observation. Throughout the year, staff at FDC become intimately knowledgeable about participating families. Parents share personal experiences and feelings during the parenting classes, and teachers learn extensively about the lives of the children during preschool. In addition, lunch and parent–child activities provide opportunities for staff to observe the interactions between parents and their children.

This close association between the families and staff enables the staff to observe each family's progress and pitfalls as they advance through the program. Administrators at GFFS depend heavily on this informal feedback to inform them of the program's success. Unfortunately, this heavy reliance on observation further limits their ability to produce the hard data necessary to verify the effectiveness of the program.

CHILD CARE AS A "HOOK"

The success of the parenting program largely is dependent on other services that GFFS provides in order to hook the parent into attending the parenting class as well. Often parents initially attend the parenting program merely to fulfill the requirements of the preschool. Indeed, a survey distributed to parents during a recent parenting class revealed that 83% of the parents originally participated in the program so that their child could attend the preschool. Another important feature of this program is the transportation provided for parents in need. In an effort to be more accessible to lower-income families, GFFS offers free van transportation to and from the parenting classes (in addition to other services). Nearly half of the parents utilize this service.

Once a parent is "hooked," however, the program must offer other benefits to ensure the parent's continued participation. The parenting program at GFFS accomplishes this by creating strong bonds among staff members and parents. Parents look to other participants as well as to staff for advice, friendship, and support not only during the course of the program but also for many years afterward. The survey distributed to parents indicated that 75% of the parents continued to attend the program because of the friendships formed there.

Parents also have a strong influence over the direction and foci of the parenting classes. As parents encounter personal problems throughout the year, the program often accommodates the individual by centering the daily topic around his or her issue. A large proportion of the class may be devoted to discussing the problem, developing solutions, and offering support. Ninety-two percent of the parents surveyed said that they participated in the program because it offered them an opportunity to talk about personal feelings and problems. Parents reported a sense of ownership in the program, and they make genuine contributions to the curriculum and the procedures of both the preschool and the parenting program.

DIFFICULTIES

Although the successes of the parenting program are numerous, it also has experienced its share of failure. In 1992 and 1993, GFFS attempted to offer an additional parenting program in the evening for members of the community who worked full time. The evening program was soon eliminated, however, because of difficulties with finding teachers and low parent participation.

In addition, parents in the initial parenting programs were uncooperative and unwilling to fulfill the obligations required of parents who have children in the preschool. The program coordinator recalled an episode when she dismissed the parents during the parenting class for a 10-minute break. Following this break, however, none of the parents returned to the class. She attributes these initial problems to the parents' lack of understanding of the seriousness of the organization's policies. She believes that the climate improved as county members became more familiar with the type of program existing at GFFS. Parents then unwilling to give such a commitment looked elsewhere for child care. The program coordinator readily admits that the program at GFFS is not for everyone. She believes, however, that those who are willing to make the commitment obtain enormous personal and social benefits.

RESOURCE MOTHERS: PARENT EDUCATION
THROUGH RURAL HOME VISITING

People, Inc., a nonprofit community action agency, was established in 1966 to serve low-income families and children at risk for maltreatment through multiple programs. Over the years, it had become a salient and well-regarded part of the sparse health care and social services network that served rural southwest Virginia. By 1986, when Virginia First Lady Linda Robb focused statewide attention on the importance of prenatal and support services for healthy babies, approximately 120 teenagers were becoming pregnant in the catchment area annually, resulting in about 80 births to single adolescent mothers. Recognizing that Robb's initiative strengthened efforts to obtain funding for medical and support services for this group, People, Inc., identified two major barriers that had to be overcome in order to improve infant mortality and life outcomes: inadequate medical care and lack of support services.

First, adequate medical care was unavailable to a number of women. Before 1986, no comprehensive prenatal services were available in the region because no OB/GYN doctor served the area. To improve the availability of adequate prenatal care, staff worked with local government to write a grant to help bring an OB/GYN to the area; however, availability did not always result in accessibility. The local hospital refused to take Medicaid patients. Furthermore, those doctors who did provide OB/GYN services were reluctant to serve low-income and teen mothers because they were "difficult" patients— they often missed appointments, they didn't follow the doctor's instructions, and they were expensive to serve. Regardless of their accuracy, these perceptions prevented many clients from utilizing much-needed health services.

The second barrier to improving infant outcomes was the lack of support services for parents at risk, primarily teen mothers. The expansive geography (hundreds of square miles) of the rural service area and lack of public transportation highlighted the need to bring services to teen mothers rather than to centralize services and expect pregnant and parenting teens to find a way into town. As a result, staff wrote a grant to fund a small home-visiting program to serve Washington County and Bristol City with two resource mothers. In subsequent years, the original grant was expanded to serve an adjoining county, and a separate grant was written to provide services for two additional counties. With these initial funding efforts, the Resource Mothers program was created in 1986.

THE RESOURCE MOTHERS PROGRAM

The name "People, Incorporated," truly reflects the mission of this private, nonprofit community action agency: to assist and empower low-income residents to achieve a better quality of life. The empowerment philosophy permeates all aspects of the agency from the programming choices to the administration. One third of the 30-member board of directors is elected from low-income communities. The agency works with low-income residents through education services, emergency assistance, and employment programs. Education services utilize a variety of delivery models, including center-, school-, and home-based services. These efforts are designed to eliminate and/or reduce the contributions of personal and community or situational factors to negative life outcomes. As one of the many programs administered by People, Inc., the six home visitors and project coordinator of the Resource Mothers program (see Robinson, 1992) provide education and support services to pregnant and parenting teenagers, primarily through home-based education.

The goals of the Resource Mothers program for its teenage clients are

- To reduce the number of preterm and low birth weight infants
- To prevent school dropout
- To delay second pregnancies
- To help teens become more knowledgeable, nurturing parents

Serving Clients in a Large Rural Area

The Resource Mothers service provision operates on several premises about teen mothers in rural southwest Virginia. First, many of the problems that place teen mothers and their babies at risk for negative outcomes are the result of a lack of knowledge in two main areas—appropriate child rearing and methods of gaining access to social resources. This premise translates into a large educational component that focuses on parenting strategies as well as available resources in the larger community.

Second, the geographic isolation of teen mothers places them at risk for negative outcomes in two ways. Because they may be isolated in rural areas without access to transportation services, teen mothers are not inclined or able to take advantage of center-based services. Three of the counties served by the Resource Mothers program do not have any Medicaid medical providers; clients are required to travel 80–90 miles one way for a single visit to a doctor. Therefore, a large component of Resource Mothers services are delivered to the clients in their own homes, and transportation is provided to other community-based services. Also, the geographic isolation prevents many mothers from developing social support networks of other young mothers as well as parenting mentors or role models. An additional service component facilitates these peer and mentoring relationships through group activities.

Recruiting Clients and the Participation Contract

The Resource Mothers program identifies clients through interagency referrals and word of mouth, depending on the location. In some counties, guidance counselors, social workers, and health department workers automatically refer pregnant and parenting teens to the Resource Mothers program. Once referrals are made, these professionals stay in close contact with the home visitors to encourage participation, share information, and work together to reinforce educational information.

The first contact with potential clients often is made through a visit to the teen's home. Visitors talk a little about the program and try to use the free transportation as a key to bringing the young women into the program. When talking with a teen mother about participating in the program, however, staff are clear that they expect a certain level of responsibility from the teens. The teens must sign a participation contract when they enter the program, which acknowledges the expectations for both the teen mother and the home visitor. The home visitor agrees to help the teen make appointments, assist with transportation, keep appointments, and develop effective skills. The teen mother agrees to go for regular medical checkups, keep appointments, be prepared for the visits, carry out the home lesson, follow through with referrals to other social services agencies, and understand that she is capable of being an effective teacher for her child. If possible, the home visitor may try to talk with other family members and get them interested in the program too.

For those teens who choose not to participate, pressure from other family members often is the culprit (see Birkel & Reppucci, 1983, regarding negative and positive aspects of social networks). Home visitors suggest that the strong tradition of family privacy in this region sometimes leads to perceptions of the program as "interference" rather than as support. Alternatively, some married teens may not need the support services offered by the program. Thus, the program tries to target specifically the very young parent without financial resources and those teens without adequate social or emotional support. (See Appendix A for the topical brief "Targeting and Recruiting Clients.")

Poverty, social isolation, and lack of knowledge, combined with early childbearing, are risk factors for a variety of negative health and mental health outcomes, including abuse and neglect. These risk factors are targeted by the three components of the Resource Mothers service delivery—home visiting, transportation to community services, and peer group sessions.

SERVICES

Home Visiting

Staff of People, Inc., and other community services providers agree that the Resource Mothers program is best known for its educational home-visiting services. These visits provide the foundation for up to 2 years of support and involvement with teen mothers.

Educational Curriculum   Several years after the original grant supporting Resource Mothers was obtained, the staff and program director realized that there were no readily available prenatal or postnatal curricula developed for weekly educational sessions. In 1989, People, Inc., obtained a 1-year grant to develop two linked curricula, 1 year prenatal and 1 year postnatal. The resulting curricula are quite comprehensive in scope, relying on material gathered from a variety of sources. The flexibility in the curricula allows lesson plans to be tailored to individual clients. It is not clear, however, whether there is a common minimal amount of information that is to be conveyed in each lesson plan. The balance between consistency and flexibility can be difficult for a program to manage.

Weekly Visits   At the beginning of the program, the resource mother works with the client to develop a long-term lesson plan. The weekly visits are designed to cover the scheduled curriculum topic, but they are flexible enough to allow the home visitor to tailor each lesson to individual clients' needs. During the 60- to 90-minute visit, a majority of time is spent on the structural lesson focusing on parenting, child development, safety, and health. At least 15 minutes of each weekly visit are spent on setting personal and professional goals. These discussions focus on future planning regarding issues such as education, additional births, family finances, and child-rearing strategies. A copy of the home-visit plan is left with the teen to remind her about weekly assignments and appointments.

Another important goal of the weekly meetings is to empower the teens to identify and utilize community services. These services include education, health care, social services, child care, and welfare, among others. The home visitor provides contact information for the teen and demonstrates how to interact with service agencies and obtain information. Initially, home visitors may travel to appointments with their clients and show them how to register, make an appointment, and fill out necessary forms. The home visitor will advocate for the teen with other service agencies, but during the course of the year, the teen takes increasing amounts of responsibility. This technique is designed to improve the teen's confidence and motivation to negotiate service systems for herself and for her child.

The home visitors encourage continuing education by connecting the teens to home-based services, facilitating communication with guidance counselors, and motivating those teens who have dropped out of school to pursue a GED. The home visitors also try to reinforce the recommendations of medical and nutritional professionals who are working with the teen mothers.

It is clear from conversations with medical, educational, and social services providers in the surrounding areas that they each try to coordinate their efforts and messages to the teen clients whom they share. In some counties, once the social services personnel get a teen mother onto Medicaid, they automatically refer them to Resource Mothers because it helps keep them connected to services. As one social worker explained, "I know the Resource Mother will stay with her teen client. Because my Medicaid caseload is so large, I can't follow up with every teen mother, but I know the home visitor will be there." Normally reluctant to accept Medicaid clients, the few local doctors say that they will accept teen mothers as long as they are enrolled in the Resource Mothers program. When asked why the link to Resource Mothers is critical, doctors respond that they know that the clients will follow advice and show up for appointments when they are linked to a home visitor.

Peer Group Meetings

The peer group meetings serve both social support and educational functions. Bimonthly group meetings held in each county afford teen mothers the opportunity to meet with other teenagers who share similar circumstances. Teens share their concerns and experiences with pregnancy and child rearing. As a group, the teens select educational topics for the group sessions. Outside leaders are brought in to cover topics such as child abuse and neglect and domestic violence. Beyond formal educational information, the group facilitates mother–child interaction and the modeling of appropriate behaviors by group leaders and other teen mothers.

The enrollment contract does not require the teen clients to participate in the peer group meetings, however; they are strictly voluntary. Once again, the program tries to make attendance as easy as possible by providing food, transportation, and child care during the meetings. In the more rural counties, participation can drop to as low as 30%–40%, suggesting that social isolation may remain an issue for some of these teens.

STAFF AND ORGANIZATIONAL STRUCTURE

The home-visitor positions are hourly wage, paraprofessional jobs requiring a minimum of a GED or high school diploma. Six visitors working approximately 40 hours per week serve 80 teens in an average year. Program administrators and home visitors emphasize that, more important than educational background, the effective home visitor must have a knowledge of the community and an ability to communicate with adolescents. Most of the home visitors are residents of the counties that they serve. There is no "typical" home visitor; they range in age from 20 to 50 and have varying degrees of experience raising children. From group and individual discussions, it is clear that most home visitors become involved in every aspect of their clients' lives. The key to success, according to most home visitors, is a nonjudgmental involvement with the teens. Many develop a close, personal relationship with the clients and view the formal "teaching" part of the interaction as secondary to the social support, empowerment, and teaching by example that occurs throughout the program.

The project coordinator works with each of the visitors to monitor caseloads, strategize about individual clients, and keep the program running smoothly. The original project coordinator took over the Resource Mothers program in addition to her supervisory duties with the Head Start and other early education interventions. In 1993, a recent college graduate from the southwest area was hired as a full-time coordinator of the Resource Mothers project. She serves as the link between the Resource Mothers program and the rest of the programs and staff in the People, Inc., administration.

Much of the training for home visitors occurs on the job through a 2- to 3-week "shadowing" period. Visitors are required to complete 40 hours of training per year, but continuing education and training are not formally structured. Most visitors take advantage of training sponsored by other agencies, such as perinatal and early childhood education conferences. Again, cost and distance to training sites often limit training opportunities.

Likewise, there is no formal evaluation of job performance. Monthly staff meetings and paperwork keep administrators apprised of caseloads and client progress, but the amount of traveling required and the flexibility of individual client education plans does make monitoring and evaluating difficult. Home visitors only spend 1 day per month in the office. The program administrator tracks client case notes and statistics; otherwise, job performance usually is addressed only when difficulties arise. (See Appendix A for the topical brief "Managing Staff and Volunteers.") There have been individual situations in which home visitors were terminated or resigned for poor performance, but turnover seems relatively low.

FUNDING

The financial viability of Resource Mothers depends on creative, active funding efforts assembled from a variety of grant and nonprofit sources. About 40% of the program's funding comes from federal resources; the rest comes from state and local contributions. Because the positive health outcomes potentially reduce the likelihood of abuse and neglect, the program obtains some financial support from the state's family violence prevention funding stream.

Because the home-visiting work is time intensive, each visitor maintains an annual caseload of approximately 10–15 clients. Although this may appear expensive on the surface, the annual cost per client served is approximately $1,400. The cost to hospitalize just one infant for 1 day in the region is estimated at $800. If the extensive involvement of support services (including medical) prevent even 2 days of hospitalization, then the program is economically sound.

Although creative funding allows the program to serve a large geographic area, relying on multiple funding sources does have negative aspects. Unique reporting mechanisms are required by each funder, keeping program administrators busy with paperwork and grant renewals. The multicounty service area also complicates matters because some grants stipulate residency requirements. So, for example, two counties could not be served by a particular funding source because People, Inc., is not the designated Head Start grantee for those counties; therefore, separate grants were developed to serve those counties.

LINKING SERVICES THROUGHOUT CHILDHOOD

Because People, Inc., operates the Resource Mothers program as well as several other programs serving parents and families, the agency has potential to link families at risk to support programs throughout children's early development. This continuity of involvement could extend from prenatal to school age. The agency's advisory board wanted to develop a program that could bridge the gap between the Resource Mothers program, which ends when the child is 1 year old, and the Head Start program, which begins serving children at age 3. The agency received a demonstration grant to provide services to income-eligible parents with children from ages 1 to 3. This program is implemented in several counties, and People, Inc., is trying to obtain funding to expand into their entire service area. If this expansion is accomplished, then Resource Mothers, the demonstration program (PCC), and Head Start can be linked in each county. Such a linkage would allow the agency some administrative efficiency by allowing the same staff person to serve families in each of the programs. For example, one home visitor could serve Buchanan County families in Resource Mothers, PCC, and Head Start. The continuity of staff involvement could be maintained throughout a child's development and across programs, providing individual families with a stable, personal connection to social and educational support.

Empowering families at risk to meet parenting challenges throughout early development is a critical task for the Resource Mothers program. The home-visiting model appears suited to the expansive geographic service area and the young, isolated teen mothers. The program has expanded since the mid-1980s from serving two counties to serving five counties and a city. As it grows, the program continues to search for the balance between the flexibility to tailor services to individual needs and the consistency necessary to deliver a common education curriculum to all clients. It is clear, however, that the home-visiting model is a valuable method for providing teen mothers with the educational and social support that they need to become effective parents.

THE PARENT–CHILD CENTER:
EXPANSION AND GROWING PAINS

with Heather O'Beirne Kelly

Winchester is a city of 22,000 (Bureau of the Census, 1992) in the northwest corner of Virginia, surrounded by mountains and rural counties. It supports a fair amount of local industry, mostly manufacturing and food distribution, in addition to farming. People living in the community say that it feels like a small town, and its citizens appear to be very involved in religious and civic activities. In the mid-1980s, a local citizen who was a member of the Winchester chapter of the Exchange Club (the Exchange Club is a national civic group with local chapters, much like the Rotary or Lions Clubs) wanted to become more active in spreading the mission of the Exchange Club locally. At that time, the Exchange Club's new national mission was preventing child maltreatment, and to this end it sponsored the creation of local parenting centers to be staffed primarily by trained volunteers.

Apparently, the member began talking to other members and friends in town about creating such a center, the focus of which would be reducing child abuse and neglect in the city and two surrounding counties. Some of the specific sources of financial support for the creation of the Parent–Child Center came from the Exchange Club and a number of individual and small corporate donations. A volunteer board was set up, members of which were to include prominent local business people, social services professionals, and experienced nonprofit staff members and volunteers. Expectations for board participation and financial obligations were clearly established. It is striking that this planning period, during which funds were solicited and the basic mission and programming were sketched out, lasted approximately 4 years; one of the ongoing strengths of the Parent–Child Center has been its emphasis on carefully planned development. (See Appendix A for the topical brief "Working with an Advisory Board.")

The major focus of this Parent–Child Center was child maltreatment prevention, and a multifaceted, comprehensive approach was designed to accomplish this goal. This included providing parenting education classes; parent support groups; home visits; and more time-intensive, home-based family therapy. This original mission of the center has changed only slightly since its inception as the center has grown, with paid employees assuming more responsibility (this also reflects a shift in the Exchange Club's mission toward incorporating more full-time employees) and with the addition in the fall of 1993 of two new counties served by the center. The geographic area now served by the center is called the Northern Shenandoah Valley. In addition to

---

Heather O'Beirne Kelly is a Ph.D. candidate in clinical psychology at the University of Virginia, Charlottesville.

the center, which is located in an office building in the heart of downtown Winchester, two satellite offices have been set up, one in each of the two new counties.

STAFF

The first paid employee hired was the executive director, a local woman with an M.S.W, who remains in the position. She was the only paid staff member for a full year until she hired a part-time secretary. Shortly thereafter, she added a prevention coordinator, who now has the title of case manager, for the original geographic area (consisting of the city and the first two counties, which use the city location for services). That same year, the executive director wrote her first grant requesting funds from the Virginia Family Violence Prevention Program to provide for additional staff salaries as well as a host of substantive services. In addition to the three initial staff members, now there are case managers for the two new counties: two women who serve as home-based therapists (they carry a caseload of several families at a time and cover a large geographic area), a woman in a newly created volunteer coordinator position, and an additional secretary. Volunteers are highly valued by the center and are key to ensuring that all of the proposed programs can be offered and sustained throughout the year. There is a structured process for training and supervising volunteers, and at any given time, the volunteer pool ranges in size from 20 to 40 people.

PROGRAMS

In terms of programming, the center offers parenting education classes, using slightly modified versions of the Nurturing Program curriculum. The center runs two sets of the parenting class twice each year in the city—one 15-week group in the evening and one during the day in both the fall/winter and the spring. The daytime group often has fewer consistent attendees (sometimes as few as five parents), which the center attributes to higher daytime employment. The evening groups tend to be more successful, with higher parent enrollments. Classes are offered in community churches, which often already are established sites for neighborhood programs and involvement. Each Nurturing Program class is co-led by a staff member and a trained volunteer; the center also uses another paid staff member and a volunteer for each age group of the child session that runs concurrent with the parenting classes. Referrals for parents to join the city groups have come from a variety of sources over the years, including the local social services agencies, schools, courts, churches, and self-referrals. In one of the original counties, the center has started offering a modified version of the Nurturing Program in two local high schools by linking with a program designed to help keep teenage parents in school.

In one of the new counties, the center's case manager started offering one Nurturing Program and reports that 12–13 parents consistently come to the sessions. The case manager, who also lives in that county, began by talking about the potential services of the center with her church, which then offered to sponsor the parenting education program by providing space for weekly meetings, food, and volunteers to handle child care. The case manager also maintains an office in the church. In the second new county, the center has been unable to get any referrals for a Nurturing Program, so no services have been provided. Despite the county's initial support for expansion, it is possible that the county did not want to divert services from DSS; other possibilities include underreporting of maltreatment in the county and that linkages between the program and existing services in the county have not yet become well-established.

In terms of parent support, the center runs two Parents Anonymous groups in the city (one in the evening, run totally by volunteers, and one in the daytime, co-facilitated by a paid, home-based therapist and a volunteer), each of which attracts 7–10 parents each week. Parents Anonymous (see Fritz, 1989) is run largely as an unstructured, support-based (rather than education-based) group, open to parents with any combination of needs, stresses, and supports. The center plans to start one Parents Anonymous group in each of the two new counties. Because parents who have completed city Nurturing Program groups in the past often have gone on to join the parent support groups, the center will wait to start the new Parents Anonymous groups until parenting education classes are fully in place in the new areas.

CONTINUUM OF CARE

One of the executive director's programming priorities has been creating and maintaining an effective continuum of care for the center's targeted clients, who primarily are parents at increased risk for child maltreatment (e.g., teen parents, parents whose children have been placed in temporary foster care as a result of abuse or neglect). To this end, the Parent–Child Center's services also include a home-visiting component for families that may benefit from individual services in addition to parenting classes and support groups. Home visitors assess referred parents' specific needs and then provide weekly home visits. At any given time, the center has approximately 10–12 volunteers trained as home visitors; each is responsible for one family and makes a visit to the home once or twice each week to provide basic parenting information and/or support. The executive director believes that this is a very stressful job for volunteers and that it is difficult to recruit, train, and retain good people; she would prefer to hire employees with master's degrees for these positions and increase the caseloads and perhaps work together with the local community mental health workers, who provide similar services in the city. The center uses its two paid home therapists to provide home-based family therapy for those families who need even more intensive intervention by trained, master's-level clinicians. The home-visiting and home therapy programs have not been initiated in either of the new counties yet. The director attributes this, in part, to a lack of volunteers in the new areas and to fewer referrals requiring this level of involvement.

From the staff's point of view, which appears to be shared by a number of other professionals, service agencies, and families in town, the Parent–Child Center is the primary place for city residents (and those who live in the original two counties) to obtain parenting services. A number of factors may contribute to the apparent success and popularity of the center in its original service area. First, the executive director herself is a very dynamic leader with a rare combination of strong interpersonal and clinical skills and extremely savvy fund-raising, networking, and organizational talents. She manages her staff and volunteers well, allowing them to work independently while providing sufficient training and structure to ensure a standard of service delivery and professionalism. Staff and volunteers admit that working with families' issues of abuse and neglect can be very stressful at times, but the strain, or "burnout," appears to be an issue that is openly discussed and handled directly. One of the results of the friendly and hardworking atmosphere created has been a very low staff turnover rate, especially for a nonprofit organization of this kind.

The executive director also has integrated the center extremely well into the community and into the local network of service agencies by placing a priority on interagency collaboration and by voluntarily serving on a number of other community boards and projects. The center has a written memorandum of agreement with the Departments of Social Services for the city and the original two counties, stating that the departments will provide referrals to the center. There seems to be quite a lot of informal collaboration as well with the executive director serving on other related committees; attending and presenting at various community meetings; and using her connections with people whom she meets through these activities to develop new referral sources, attract monetary and in-kind donations, and recruit volunteers. Other agency representatives concur that the center is their first-choice site to refer parents for education and support. Board members and center volunteers also appear to maintain a high level of personal commitment to the center, which has contributed to the center's success in becoming and remaining a vital part of the community's social services network.

More substantive, the center has been successful in defining goals, targeting clientele, and creating a package of services to meet defined needs in the original geographic area. Since its inception, the center has continuously offered parent education classes, support groups, and home visiting/therapy. Staff consistently evaluate how well their programs are being received by keeping track of referral numbers and parent involvement and by making follow-up contacts with their participants. The center also has attempted to identify factors that appear to have hindered a given program's success in order to reassess and readjust the format if necessary. For example, when the city Nurturing Program class was having problems with parent attrition (i.e., parents would attend inconsistently or drop out after a few meetings), the center found that parents were more likely to attend evening classes and stay in the program when dinner and child care were provided; staff solicited in-kind donations and volunteers to provide these services, and the percentage of parents completing the program rose substantially. By being attuned to possible issues that might affect a program's success, allowing staff to be flexible in delivering services, and finding creative ways to support programs, the center is able to tailor its offerings to a given community's needs.

EXPANSION

In order to provide this continuum of services, the center has become very proficient in obtaining financial support from a variety of sources, including individual and corporate donations, annual community fund-raising events, and foundation/government grant programs. The executive director has been a large part of the center's financial success by seeking outside training in fundraising and grant writing; balancing service delivery and fund-raising as center priorities; and maintaining detailed records of service provision and evaluation, which can be provided to potential funders. As a result, the center received a state Trust Fund Grant of more than $200,000, its largest single funding source by far.

One of the major requirements to be eligible for the state grant was that the center be seen as a resource for parenting programs in the region (not just in the city). This was one of the primary reasons behind the center's decision to expand into two new counties several years ago, a process that has been decidedly more mixed in its success than the creation and growth of the center in its original geographic area. The executive director noted that assessing possible factors that may have affected the expansion and readjusting the current plan for service delivery in these two new counties were her main goals for 1996.

Several factors may help explain why the expansion process was more difficult than originally expected: quality of connection to established agencies and community resources, unexpected professional "turf" issues, possible differences in client groups, and logistical issues. The center's expansion into the first new county has been much more successful than its move into the second; one reason may be that the case manager in the first county was a woman native to that county who already had established ties to the community (much like the original founder of the center in the city). She was able to use personal relationships and connections to gain access to a site for parenting classes as well as initial referrals. Even though the center's executive director met with

DSS workers in both new counties to assess the need for additional services and the likelihood of referrals, the lack of a case manager who came with established community ties in the second new county may have substantially affected the speed, if not the likely success, of the center's entry. Similarly, few existing board members or volunteers were from the new counties and thus were unable to provide alternative links to agencies and clients.

Although the center's executive director conducted informal needs assessments (see Appendix A for the topical brief "The First Step: A Needs Evaluation") in each new county, during which potential referral agencies expressed a need for parenting programs like the center's in their communities, the reality of how willing these agencies would be in providing referrals to the parenting classes appears to have been quite different, at least in the second county. The executive director noted that no referrals had been received in this community, and one of her hypotheses was that agencies and clinicians there became more protective of their client base in the face of additional services (which the center considers nonduplicative of existing services). Because the center came with its own existing financial support, the executive director did not envision that competition over funding resources would be a major reason for lack of interagency collaboration. A related factor possibly affecting the lack of referrals to the center's programs may have been a different perspective on prevention of and intervention with possible abuse and neglect; the executive director described the second county's social services department as much less likely to investigate and intervene in possible abuse situations and thus suggested that the agency may be similarly less likely to refer families for education and support in these instances.

Differences in client groups also may have been a factor in the successful transfer of services to the first new county and the more problematic development in the second. The executive director described the demographic make-up of the first county as similar to that of the original geographic area, whereas the second county is substantially more rural, with families more physically isolated from a town center and each other. Social workers in the county report that they place a high premium on family privacy. Staff report that there also are potential clients in isolated, hard-to-reach locations and that there may, in some cases, be hesitation to visit clients because of safety concerns. Furthermore, the center may not have accurately predicted what the parenting needs were in this second area; logistical factors such as increased need for transportation and lack of established neighborhood centers also may have affected the effective start-up of programs there.

The real challenge that this otherwise successful organization appears to face is reassessing and managing its expansion into the two new counties, which may have been motivated more by the attraction of a large grant and its requirements than by a request for services that came from within the new areas. Although their needs assessment indicated a niche for their services, the center was not explicitly invited to expand within the county. Whereas the center's executive director was able to plan for and very effectively manage the initial growth of the center in the city, she, her staff, and board members will need to evaluate the process of recent expansion carefully and determine how best to readjust their programming and relationships with the communities in order to more effectively reach their target clientele and become integrated into the social services networks in the new areas. The mixed success of the center's expansion provides important information for other programs seeking to grow effectively because even though the process was approached with a good deal of prior planning and advance work (e.g., community needs assessments, planning for only one start-up group initially), there still were unexpected obstacles. Programs may benefit by first carefully assessing their own motivation for growth and then by choosing staff from within new communities or those who have established links to the area, identifying not only other agencies' impressions of service need but also potential "turf" issues that may affect referrals and accounting for different kinds of clients who may require alternative approaches and programs.

Even with slow, careful planning of geographical or program expansion, some obstacles will become obvious only after the process has begun; the eventual success of a program's development will depend on the willingness of staff to constantly review the growth and readjust in ways that make programming more attractive and effective. One of the Parent–Child Center's greatest strengths has been the ability to monitor growth and respond to problems quickly and creatively.

CONCLUSION

Whereas the four cases presented in this chapter represent diverse program orientations with a variety of client groups, there are some commonalities that begin to emerge (as well as a number of issues unique to each setting). We attempted to paint a picture of the history/creation, evolution, and issues confronting each of the sites.

Some of the crucial issues raised included the importance of the history and community context of the program creation; the type of leadership and the organizational structure; long-term planning, especially with the cooperation of an advisory board (the Parents' Place in Roanoke); including a child component as well as an adult component at some programs (the Goochland Fellowship and Family Service); providing inclusive, comprehensive services for families in need (the Resource Mothers program of People, Inc., in Abingdon); and identifying characteristics of successful and unsuccessful expansion efforts (the Parent–Child Center in Winchester). In the next chapter, we use our last case study to illustrate how evaluating a prevention program can be feasible, informative, and vital for its (financial) survival.

Portsmouth's Good Beginnings

Chapter 8

A Case Study in Outcome Evaluation

Good Beginnings is an intervention program that provides comprehensive parent education, support, and agency referrals for new teenage mothers. This program operates under the auspices of Child and Family Service of Southwest Hampton Roads in Portsmouth, Virginia, a nonprofit agency providing a range of educational, counseling, and advocacy services to the community, and serves parts of the Tidewater area. The intervention is a 12-week, on-site parent education program for teen mothers and their infants and also serves as a support group and referral point for other community and social services in its low-income, urban community. The program is an example of a well-designed, practical curriculum (involving disseminating parenting knowledge and providing informal social and formal community-based supports) that is matched to the needs of its clientele and is implemented effectively by a small, organized, committed staff that is flexible enough to market the program and make it work. It is the only continuous parenting program in the community.

Good Beginnings is an example of a prevention program that has made the effort to self-evaluate. On a week-to-week basis, the staff employ standardized measures that tap constructs such as social support and parenting stress. These data remain in the clients' files for long-term follow-up, but the information from the measures also is used for immediate feedback to teen

This chapter is based in part on an article, "Prevention of child maltreatment: Evaluation of a parent education program for teen mothers," by P.A. Britner & N.D. Reppucci, to be published in the *Journal of Child and Family Studies* (1997), Vol. 6(2). For more analytic details, please see the article. We especially thank Bessie Abner and Ed Welp of Child and Family Service of Southwest Hampton Roads, Inc., for their co-operation and assistance with this evaluation.

mothers in the parenting group, serving both educational and supportive functions. This is an important point for encouraging data collection among programs—the information can be useful to staff and participants as a short-term marker of change or as a basis of discussion. Of course, these data also can be analyzed to show changes in knowledge, attitudes, or behavior over the course of the program (using pretest and posttest measures) and to help program staff determine whether they are effectively recruiting the target group (e.g., by comparing individuals' risk status with matched controls or stress levels with standardized norms).

The goal of this chapter is to show how the community research team was able to use existing data from this ongoing program to help evaluate process and outcome in terms of long-term behavior changes, including reduced instances of child maltreatment, greater maternal educational attainment, and the delay of subsequent pregnancies. The evaluation gave the program a better idea of the long-term effects of its intervention (to go with its own data on short-term knowledge and attitude change). The results of the evaluation also paid quick dividends for the program, enabling staff to apply for (and receive) increased funding to expand the program.

An outcome study was possible in Portsmouth because of the program's systematic data collection over several years and the information obtained from participants and nonparticipants, which allow for evaluations of targeting, recruitment, retention, and outcome. The program's success in collecting and using data underscores the main point of this chapter: Evaluation can and should become an integral part of every prevention program. In most programs, there are numerous ways in which the use of evaluative techniques can be improved. It also is important to remember that programs vary in their capacities to incorporate levels of evaluation. Even so, we strongly believe that the benefits of evaluation far outweigh the costs and should become a standard component of every program.

TEEN MOTHERS

Much attention has been given by the media and in academic circles to the issue of teen pregnancy and the associated negative outcomes of child abuse and neglect, poor parenting, high stress, school dropout with concomitant limited educational opportunities, and multiple pregnancies at a young age. Although we have gained some insight into the importance of the issue and many of the correlates of teen pregnancy, little outcome evaluation exists for maltreatment prevention programs in general or for parent education and support programs that have been designed to address teens in particular (see Chapters 2 and 3). Only a few exceptions, in the form of well-designed evaluations of prevention programs for teens, exist (e.g., Allen, Kuperminc, Philliber, & Herre, 1994; Olds & Henderson, 1989; see Moore, Sugland, Blumenthal, Glei, & Snyder, 1995, for a comprehensive review). The paucity of published evaluations of parent education and family support programs severely limits our ability to discuss the efficacy of such programs as intervention and prevention tools.

Intervention with teen mothers to prevent child maltreatment has been a high priority because of legitimate concern about risk to their children and the (relative) ease of identifying the teens and encouraging their involvement (e.g., Mulvey & Britner, 1996; Osofsky, Hann, & Peebles, 1993). There are some indications that young mothers lack knowledge of child development and that this may influence their behavior toward their children (Newberger & White, 1989). The transition to parenthood is a difficult and stressful period for most new parents and may be especially so for teens, who often are unmarried and exposed to greater risks for poverty, lesser supports, and (to the extent that the father is involved) strains on the romantic relationship (Belsky & Vondra, 1989; Furstenberg, Brooks-Gunn, & Chase-Lansdale, 1989). It is possible that young mothers will not respond sensitively (consistently, quickly, and appropriately) to their infants' needs, thus elevating the risk of insecure attachment of the child to the parent and subsequent neglect, abuse, or disorganization in the relationship (e.g., Crittenden & Ainsworth, 1989; Pianta, Egeland, & Erickson, 1989). Parent education programs, designed to reduce the risk of child maltreatment by teen parents, vary in their curricula but often seek to change parents' attitudes about parenting and expectations and increase their knowledge of child development and their formal and informal supports in order to influence short-term and long-term behavior.

In addition to the elevated risk of maltreatment, there is a great deal of concern expressed in the popular press and academic literature about additional pregnancies and educational attainment by young parents. Subsequent pregnancies occur at alarming rates among teens; age at first pregnancy is one of the best predictors of additional childbearing as a minor (see Moore et al., 1995). Efforts to prevent teen pregnancies, first or subsequent, have met with mixed success (e.g., Allen et al., 1994; Furstenberg et al., 1989). Teen mothers are more likely to drop out of high school, and few go on to college after having a child (Furstenberg et al., 1989; Moore et al., 1995; Osofsky et al., 1993). The outcomes of maltreatment, multiple pregnancies, and poor educational attainment may exist as interdependent risk factors (especially with poverty). As such, many parent education interventions attempt to change teens' behaviors in all of these domains. Prevention and intervention efforts designed to ameliorate one or more of these risks may indeed show their effects across a range of outcomes.

ISSUES IN EVALUATING PREVENTION AND INTERVENTION EFFORTS

Researchers have called for service providers to respond to parents' perceptions of what they need and balance the needs of child, parent(s), and the family as a system (Britner, Morog, Pianta, & Marvin, 1997), though such individualization of services makes evaluation in a traditional experimental design that much more difficult (Garbarino & Long, 1992; Powell, 1988). Different parents need different services, and all parents respond better to services (of any type) that are matched to their needs, values, culture, and expectations (Powell, 1988). Parents should be viewed as active participants, not as passive recipients of what is deemed "correct." Often, families' needs and the effectiveness of services offered to them differ by racial and ethnic group, due, in part, to economic hardship and differences in family structure and cultural differences in the use of "supports" (Davis & Rhodes, 1994; Wilson, 1986).

Recruiting and retaining poor, stressed parents are problems that confront most intervention projects, and it is always a concern as to whether those parents who are most in need actually are served (Powell, 1988). Issues of accessibility of services to the target group; identifying concrete goals and objectives; and documenting targeting, recruiting, and retaining of those most in need of services rather than those who simply show up are important to address when evaluating the efficacy of any human services program (Garbarino & Long, 1992).

THE GOOD BEGINNINGS PROGRAM

Good Beginnings was initiated with funds from a local children's foundation and a local hospital auxiliary and has been funded by the Department of Social Services (DSS) since 1984. In recent years, its primary funding has come from the United Way. In-kind donations of food, meeting space, and printing are received annually from a variety of sources. Child and Family Service of Southwest Hampton Roads has been around for 40 years, doing "typical Family Services stuff," according to the executive director. The Good Beginnings program has its roots in a request for proposals for parenting programs from the Virginia DSS. The former executive director and a former director of social work in the area DSS were a part of a multidisciplinary local team, the forerunner to current prevention coalitions for teen pregnancy and family violence, that recognized the need for a parenting program for teen mothers in order to prevent child abuse and neglect and future pregnancies. Thus, from the beginning, this program had the support and endorsement of multiple community agencies. Staff continue to participate in these coalitions; this keeps them well-connected to all local human services personnel. As part of the program, staff try to link mothers to as many local resources as possible in order to increase the supports available to the teens.

The Good Beginnings program has continued to utilize outside community resources effectively. Red Cross volunteers teach infant CPR as part of the parenting course. The program refers clients to a health department program that provides transportation and medical services for Medicaid clients; the

Women, Infants, and Children (WIC) program; and the Food Bank. The program also has used facilities of community agencies such as the city recreation centers and a hospital as meeting sites. One local hospital provides snacks for group meetings, and another provides printing of brochures. Through the coalitions, the program has a cooperative network of community agencies and individuals for making referrals, such as schools, community service boards, parks and recreation departments, health nurses, school psychologists, and guidance counselors.

Staffing

Initially, the program was a one-person production, and the classes were held in a nearby church. The program got most of its referrals from the health departments. Within a year, however, the program moved to Child and Family Services, and the current staffing pattern was developed. Staff consist of two full-time employees: the program director, who directs and oversees the program and is active in community coalitions, and the program assistant, who helps with the classes and recruitment. In addition, the executive director of the agency does the grant writing and assists with long-term planning and evaluation.

The transition to a new executive director in 1990 generally was smooth, but it came at a time of deficit; the executive director continues to see funding as his major concern. The program director was hired in 1992 as the program assistant. She had previously facilitated program development in the community, and she came from a health education background. When she was hired, the curriculum materials existed but were in piles. After her former boss left (less than a year after she arrived), she was promoted to program director, and she put together more formal and organized "lesson plans." The program assistant position has had several occupants during the time that the program has been in operation. Typical of human services programs, staff wages are low relative to the required hours, commitment, and experience (and, in many cases, education). The program director and program assistant both are African American women who have lived in the program's catchment area for some time; observations of their interactions with clients suggest that they have excellent rapport with (and respect from) the teens.

Community Response and Needs

Religious backgrounds and political ideologies can, sometimes, influence community attitudes toward prevention, especially with teen mothers and issues of pregnancy prevention. Staff have found this program to be an "easy sell" in the community, however, and the program has expanded to a three-city area. The community, as a whole, has been very receptive to the needs for a program for parenting teens who are viewed as at risk.

Despite the support, the staff believe that the community is lacking several major resources: 1) a place to refer teens for child care, as there are few places that teens can afford, and the demand is great; 2) funding for a separate prenatal group; and 3) a strong program for parents of older children to which Good Beginnings can refer some of its graduates (a Parents as Teachers [PAT] program for parents of children from ages 1 to 3 has started up, and the Program Director is hopeful that it will be a good tie-in).

Goals and Objectives

The goals and objectives of the program have remained fairly constant since the programs inception, with an additional focus on the educational attainment of the teen mothers. The manner in which the program has been implemented also has been remarkably constant. (See Appendix A for the topical brief "Using Goals and Objectives to Improve Programming.") What has changed over the years has been the content of given "classes" and the instrumentation used to document change. With respect to retention, efforts to minimize dropout rates have been successful. The program director and assistant make reminder calls and offer transportation to each client before every class, give incentives (e.g., food, prizes, books) for attendance, and make the meetings fun (as well as informative). (See Appendix A for the topical brief "How to Improve Client Retention.") In terms of recruitment, the risk-based targeting of teens has already been addressed. See Table 1 for a description of the program's self-stated primary goals and objectives.

Table 1.   Identified goals and objectives of the program

Goal: Identify high-risk teen parents.

Objective: Screen all teen mothers with live births at three local hospitals for program participation. Identify all high-risk parents in catchment area for program participation.

Goal: Encourage participation through support and incentives.

Objectives: Offer socialization and peer support through weekly group sessions; link clients to community resources for individual needs; provide transportation to and from group meetings; and offer infant stimulation toys, books, and other tangible items.

Goal: Develop and promote good parenting skills and foster positive parenting attitudes.

Objectives: Increase knowledge of age-appropriate developmental capabilities (and ultimately prevent abuse and neglect), enable mothers to communicate their needs and recognize their children's needs, enhance knowledge and value of appropriate methods of behavior management, expand parents' awareness of appropriate parent–child roles, provide career development workshops for program graduates, and provide clients with concrete parenting skills.

Curriculum

The content of the program's specific curriculum continues to evolve as staff identify parent and child needs and improve methods of teaching. The curriculum is their own rather than one of the popular published curriculum packages (e.g., STEP [Dinkmeyer & McKay, 1976]). Topics include bonding, communication, child development, and substance abuse. Discipline is a major issue because of the prevalence of corporal punishment among the teen mothers whom the program serves. The staff encourage mothers to continue with their own education (in order to increase self-esteem and earning potential), and staff also connect teens with several jobs programs. Classes are structured, but there is always time for open-ended discussion. Staff arrange for free infant car safety seats, and Infant Cardiopulmonary Resuscitation (CPR) and safety measures are taught; staff members believe that these are "concrete" incentives for enrolling. Topics usually are the same over the 12-week program, although the program director emphasizes the need for flexibility. A guest speaker occasionally will cover the section on substance abuse. For example, during one session, a police officer talked to the teen mothers about the relevant laws and problems of getting caught up with drug dealers, effects of drug use, and so forth. (See Appendix D for an outline of the curriculum topics, a list of the evaluation materials kept in clients' files, and a list of the risk factors used to screen potential participants.)

Parent–child interaction is a key component of the classes. Each week, infants are in the meeting room with mothers throughout the class, giving staff time to observe interactions, intervene, model sensitive interactions, and document changes. Descriptions of interactions are recorded weekly, and mothers are required about midway through the program to keep a 7-day diary of their interactions with their child. These and other activities are used to work on "bonding" of mother to child and establishing the security of child attachment to mother (see Crittenden & Ainsworth, 1989). In addition, staff keep records of attendance, outside resource utilization and referrals, and weekly content "quizzes" in each individual's case record. These records are used on a week-to-week basis to evaluate individuals' progress and topical needs for the class, as well as in year-to-year changes in course content and implementation. As such, the program represents a rare example of an effort to self-evaluate.

Outcome Evaluation

Participants   Participants in the program are young (ages 11–20 years at the time of the birth of their first child; mean age of 15); unmarried; predominantly African American (over 95%); and living in a mid-Atlantic urban community with a 1990 population of 156,000, 46.4% of whom were African American (Bureau of the Census, 1992). In 1991, African Americans represented 74% of the teenage pregnancies (live births, induced terminations of pregnancy, and natural fetal deaths) and 81% of the out-of-wedlock pregnancies in the community (Virginia Vital Statistics, 1993).

Mothers were recruited in each of the three hospitals serving the community within 36 hours after they gave birth. In the hospitals, program staff are considered employees (with badges) for purposes of recruitment. Mothers sign a consent form for release of information. With each new mother, staff complete an intake sheet, ask for concerns, discuss education and knowledge about infants and care, and interview nurses about the mother and her family. Teen mothers who were unmarried, were from low-income families, and had limited social support networks and/or limited knowledge of important child development milestones were deemed at risk.

Two weeks later, staff try to set up a home visit with those mothers who showed the greatest number of risk factors in the hospital interview. A staff member brings a gift (e.g., a blanket, formula, baby clothes), discusses infant care and any problems that have arisen, talks with involved family members, administers a measure of parenting attitudes (Adult-Adolescent Parenting Inventory [AAPI] [Bavolek, 1984]) to the mother, and offers to enroll the mother in the classes. Although staff especially target for the parenting class those teens with the most risk factors and difficult home situations, other teens with fewer risk factors are allowed to enroll at their request.

Classes run on a 12-week cycle, three times annually, with multiple groups concurrently; the average group size is 10 mothers (and their babies). Two months after the course is finished, the mothers are called to check on the child's physical condition (including hospital admissions) and the mother's school status and to answer any questions that they might have.

Over a 3-year period, the staff reported that they actively recruited participants who were most at risk in terms of their hospital assessment of 25 potential early indicators (e.g., income below poverty level, depression, family discord) (for reliability and validity data, see Bolton, 1990; risk factors are listed in Appendix D) and their administration in the home of the 32-item AAPI. The AAPI provides an assessment of inappropriate parent characteristics, including lack of empathic awareness of children's needs, use of physical punishment with young children, and parent–child role reversal; the AAPI has shown adequate reliability and validity (see Bavolek, 1984).

These assertions of targeting were tested by statistically comparing the hospital control group (those interviewed in the hospital but not home visited or enrolled in the program [$N = 314$]), the home-visit control group (those home visited once after the hospital interview but not enrolled in the program [$N = 96$]), and the program group (those interviewed in the hospital, home visited once, and enrolled in the program [$N = 125$]) on the number of identified risk factors (0–25) and the home-visit control group and the program group on AAPI scores (ranging from unrealistic to realistic expectations). Retention in the program was high; 85% of the teens attended at least 9 of 12 sessions, and over 90% (113/125) completed the AAPI at the pre- and post-program admin-istrations. Given the high retention, the program group consisted of all teens enrolled in the program—even if they did not attend all classes or complete the program. Program participants possessed significantly more risk factors than the home-visit controls, who were in turn at greater risk than were the hospital controls (F [2, 532] = 40.03, p <.0001). Program participants scored lower on the AAPI (indicating less realistic expectations), although they were not sig-nificantly different from home-visit controls on the AAPI. The program's re-cruitment strategy was, in fact, successful in that program participants were at greater risk than were nonparticipants (see Table 2).

Procedure   Although the staff routinely follows up with program grad-uates 2 months after program completion (and documents the results of the call in their files), the evaluation presented in this chapter is the first systematic at-tempt to document program effects beyond the short term. As such, the state's computer database on documented abuse and neglect was searched for posi-tive matches using the name and date of birth of the child and the name of the mother (as perpetrator or co-perpetrator). At the time that the search was con-ducted of the 535 mother–child dyads, the children ranged in age from 3 to 5 years. The state's Department of Social Services conducted the search and pro-vided (anonymous) information from all founded reports, separately for each of the three groups (hospital, home visit, and program). At the time of the study, the procedure in the state was that all child protective reports were in-vestigated and classified as 1) unfounded for lack of evidence, 2) reason to sus-pect (but without proof), or 3) founded (in cases of documented maltreatment). Only the stringent founded category was used as an outcome variable in this study. Descriptively, the search revealed a variety of types and severity of abuse (physical and sexual) and neglect, timing of maltreatment, and sources of reports. Physical neglect, followed by physical abuse, were the most fre-quent types of maltreatment in the sample, as is the case nationwide (U.S. Department of Health and Human Services, National Center on Child Abuse and Neglect [NCCAN], 1996).

Table 2.   Risk status means and standard deviations of controls and partici-pants

Group	Number of risk factors (mean [standard deviation])		AAPI score (mean [standard deviation])	
Hospital control	3.33	(2.90)	n/a	
Home-visit control	4.35	(2.61)	97.14	(29.27)
Program participant	6.24	(3.76)	91.99	(30.08)

Note: Risk factors (listed in Appendix D) range from 0 to 25. AAPI scores range from 32 (unrealistic expectations and poor parenting knowledge) to 160 (realistic expectations and good parenting knowledge).

Follow-up telephone calls were made to a random subset of 40 mothers who were home visited once and 80 mothers who completed the program in their child's first year. The calls were made from 3 to 5 years after the birth of their child. The mothers reported on whether they had graduated from high school (or were still enrolled), completed any college course work, and had any other children (or were currently pregnant) prior to age 21. Unsuccessful attempts were made to contact an additional 20 home-visited women and 20 program participants.

Results

Founded Abuse Report Rates   The search of the state's maltreatment database yielded rates of founded reports: 21 of 314 (6.69%) in the group of teen mothers who were recruited in the hospital control group; 7 of 96 (7.29%) in the home-visit control group; and 2 of 125 (1.60%) in the program group (see Figure 1).

A one-way analysis of variance comparing identified maltreatment and group (hospital control, home-visit control, and program [$N = 535$]) was significant (F [2, 532] = 2.39; $p < .10$; and crosstabs Likelihood Ratio Chi-Square [2 df] = 6.34, $p < .05$). Post-hoc tests indicated a significant difference (at the $p < .05$ level) between the rates of maltreatment for the program and hospital control groups but not for the program and home-visit control groups, due to the small sample size and base rates of the behavior. In sum, mothers who were enrolled in the 12-week parent education program, despite demonstrating a

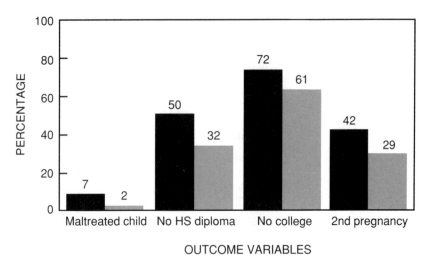

Figure 1. A comparison of outcomes for controls and participants. (■ = controls, ▨ = participants.)

higher number of risk factors than did controls, were less likely to have any founded reports of abusing or neglecting their children.

Educational Attainment and Delay of Subsequent Pregnancies A series of three statistical tests were conducted to compare program ($N = 80$) and home-visit ($N = 40$) mothers, who were contacted by telephone, on the dichotomous outcomes of high school graduation (or continued enrollment), the completion of some college course work, and additional childbearing (after the target child) before the age of 21. For the outcome of high school graduation, there was a trend for group membership such that program graduates (68%) were more likely than were home-visited mothers (50%) to have completed high school or to be currently enrolled in a GED program ($t[118] = 3.50, p < .10$). Only 29% of the program graduates had a second child before age 21 (in contrast to 43% of the home-visited controls), and a full 39% of the graduates took at least some college or vocational school courses after graduating from high school (in comparison with 28% of the controls). All trends were in the direction of more favorable outcomes for the program group (see Figure 1). The effect sizes are good, and significant differences should emerge with a larger sample size; the program will continue to follow up participants and controls over the next few years in order to build up a larger sample for future comparisons.

Attitude Change Administration of the AAPI (Bavolek, 1984) to participants in the last meeting of the 12-week program offered an opportunity for a pre- and post-intervention comparison of parenting attitudes. Of the 125 program participants, 113 completed the AAPI both before and after the program. These 113 program participants gained an average of 22.3 points on the AAPI, climbing from a mean of 92.0 on the administration in their home prior to the program to a mean of 114.3 at the conclusion of the program (paired differences $t[112] = 17.17, p < .001$). Roughly translated, participants moved from a mean of 2.9 to 3.6 on a scale from 1 (unrealistic) to 5 (realistic) of child expectations and parenting attitudes. Consistent with other studies of parent education programs (e.g., Weinman, Schreiber, & Robinson, 1992), the intervention produced short-term gains in parenting attitudes and knowledge of child development milestones, in addition to overwhelmingly positive post-intervention responses to a "satisfaction" survey. This satisfaction also is reflected in anecdotal staff reports of teens who occasionally return as volunteers, just to "check in," or to go on an annual alumni trip to an amusement park (usually about 50 attend).

Discussion

The results of the program evaluation are both interesting and important because the evaluation represents a rare attempt to systematically examine the efficacy of a service program in effecting the intended outcomes. Although the limitations of sample size and possibilities of selection biases prohibit definitive conclusions, it appears as though the prevention program showed its intended effect of preventing child maltreatment. In addition, related positive outcomes for the teen mothers included trends toward delaying subsequent pregnancies until after age 21, staying in school, and even increasing enrollment in post–high school courses.

Program staff utilized a combination of strategies to influence the behavior of the teen mothers whom they served. First, they were able to increase parents' knowledge about child development milestones and favorable parenting practices (i.e., reasonable expectations, less harsh or traditional disciplinary practices) on pretest and posttest comparisons. Second, they addressed the daily stresses of the teen parents—most of whom entered the program with a number of risk factors and stressors—by providing formal referrals to other community agencies and informal support through discussions in the program group (which was part didactic parent education and part interactive support group). Finally, by including both teen mother and infant child, opportunities to observe the dyads and to model good caregiver–infant interactions were possible (and, by avoiding the need for child care, retention was high). Which components of the program influenced which outcomes for which participants? That question cannot, of course, be answered by this evaluation, but the multiple components of the program probably are best viewed as a strength (with chances to effect change on multiple levels [Belsky & Vondra, 1989]) rather than as a weakness.

In addition to the encouraging results, the relative ease of documenting change, above and beyond typical questionnaires of client satisfaction or pre- versus post-intervention measures of parenting knowledge, using information from naturally occurring comparison groups and program files represents an important lesson both for researchers and for practitioners. Careful record keeping and basic research designs can aid service programs in answering critical questions about their targeting (and recruiting) and short- and long-term effectiveness (with clearly defined objectives).

One of the difficult hurdles in persuading programs to self-evaluate is convincing the program staff that evaluation is helpful (in the short-term and the long-term) rather than a necessary evil or wasted time that could be spent on service delivery. This is an important point for encouraging data collection among programs; information (in the form of weekly quizzes or attendance records) can be useful to staff and participants as a short-term marker of change or as a basis for discussion. Of course, these data also can be analyzed to show changes in knowledge, attitudes, or behavior over the course of the program (using pretest and posttest measures) and to help the program staff determine whether they are effectively recruiting and retaining their target group (in addition to long-term behavior outcomes, such as the follow-ups in the present evaluation).

Limitations of this evaluation bear additional mention. They include the small sample size (especially in the telephone-call follow-up but also in the maltreatment search, given the low base rate of maltreatment), possible selection bias in the telephone-call follow-up, and other potential selection biases in recruiting program participants (though our data would suggest that participants actually were those *most* in need of services). Despite the fact that all teen mothers were from a rather homogeneous group and that all were labeled as being at risk in terms of factors such as poverty, lack of social supports, and traditional or unrealistic parenting attitudes and expectations, it is possible that teen mothers who entered the program were more motivated to learn and change their behavior than were those who did not. Future attempts at such comparisons could take a "waiting list" approach (comparing those who go through the program with those who request the program but cannot be served) to help tease out motivational differences.

Despite these possible limitations, the outcomes for the program group were striking. Relative to many larger and more expensive prevention programs (e.g., see Dubowitz, 1990; Moore et al., 1995), the community-oriented intervention program seems effective in both short-term parenting knowledge and attitude change and in effecting favorable behavior outcomes for child and mother several years beyond the intervention. The program was rewarded for its efforts to evaluate (and, presumably, for the strength of its effects) with increased funding from its primary grant source. In sum, it represents an example of how a comprehensive, flexible, well-constructed, and well-executed program can be effective and—perhaps just as important—document its effectiveness.

CONCLUSION

Although we emphasized different issues in each of the case studies (the four reviewed in Chapter 7 and the one detailed in this chapter), more often than not similar issues came up across our visits to all 25 programs throughout the state. In Chapter 9, we abstract some key components for replicating successful programs gleaned from our review of academic literature, our visits to the 25 sites, and—perhaps most important—our intensive studies of these 5 representative (but also "model") sites. Thus, examples from these case studies will be used to demonstrate critical development and implementation issues involved in program creation and change.

Key Components of
Successful Programs

What lessons have we learned from the literature reviews and the Virginia multisite assessment project that would allow for the replication of successful approaches? Foremost, on a practical level, programs need not "reinvent the wheel," as they can make use of the efforts of existing programs; however, modifications inevitably will have to be made in order to meet the unique needs of communities. In selecting programs to emulate, preference should be given to approaches that have empirical data in support of their effectiveness. Programs that are standardized and systematically evaluated are few in number but should be given priority for replication. Networking with other organizations and using existing resources allow programs to learn from the successes and failures of others in all aspects of operation, including implementing programs, establishing funding goals, and using evaluation procedures.

On a theoretical level, we agree with previous reviewers (e.g., Wekerle & Wolfe, 1993; Wolfe, Reppucci, & Hart, 1995) that maltreatment is best conceptualized along a continuum ranging from typical and acceptable forms of parenting at one end to more extreme and violent forms at the other end. Such a view places child maltreatment clearly within the context of socialization practices rather than of deviant and criminal behavior and, thus, emphasizes building and strengthening appropriate child-rearing methods aimed at enhancing the parent–child relationship (Wolfe, 1991). It also suggests that parent education and family support are the preventive interventions of choice. Rather than focus on the misdeeds of parents, a family support prevention strategy provides the least intrusive, earliest assistance possible by promoting an optimal balance among the needs of the child, the abilities of the parent, and the extent and type of stress experienced by family members. As Wolfe et al. (1995) have suggested,

> The advantage of a family support strategy (i.e., enhancement), in contrast to an interception approach, is that it provides a blend of services in a family-centered format. Moreover, primary services (e.g., education on infant care and stimulation) can be provided to all parents, without identifying particular groups. A major advantage of this approach lies in the emphasis on providing services to families before child maltreatment is detected and labeled, which concurrently provides a more positive and successful entry into the child welfare and health-care system. (p. 7)

Keeping this in mind, we delineate five characteristics of the leadership and staff of successful parent education programs; reiterate that evaluation of these programs is *essential*; and discuss elements necessary for replicating successful approaches, emphasizing that program design should match community needs.

FIVE CHARACTERISTICS OF SUCCESSFUL PROGRAMS

During the round of intensive visits to the five sites, commonalities emerged that appeared to contribute to the stability and viability of the programs. Using examples from these programs, we point out the characteristics that contribute to the development of successful programs: 1) dynamic leadership, 2) community involvement and interagency collaboration, 3) fund-raising savvy, 4) long-term planning, and 5) recognizing the importance of credibility and acceptance by clients.

Dynamic Leadership

A key characteristic of successful programs appears to be a dynamic, dedicated leader. Although most administrators of prevention programs are dedicated to program success, these directors, in particular, share an energy and enthusiasm that is easily apparent. They project the commitment to primary prevention to their staff, other service agencies, and funders. They seem to serve as the force that keeps an underfunded, understaffed program running, and they do this in large part by paying attention to their staff. They cultivate positive staff attitudes and have a commitment to creating a growth-producing and motivating organizational environment. Dynamic leaders can be important at several levels within an organization, each position emphasizing different characteristics. For example, The Parents' Place in Roanoke benefits from an administrator within the YMCA (which houses the program) who is fully committed to supporting local parents and actively works within the YMCA and in the community to garner support for the program. In addition, the program director has a very warm, caring personality that immediately connects with clients and other service providers. Similarly, program administrators in the People, Inc., project of Abingdon are very confident, dynamic leaders who are able to actively seek out new forms of support for the project. This is exemplified by the Resource Mothers supervisor, who is a recent college graduate without much experience but who grew up in the area, is familiar with local needs and issues, and has the energy to invest in the project. It is a potential problem if responsibility for the program is diffuse, or no one leader advocates for the program within the setting (as well as to others in the community). Especially if a program is located within a larger organization, there needs to be a person involved at an administrative level who can keep institutional attention and interest in the program; this also means that there is accountability to others.

Community Involvement and Interagency Collaboration

Each successful program appears to be integrated into the existing network of service agencies. The administrator and staff are committed to this integration. Interviews with other professionals at several sites confirm that referral networks and interagency collaboration flourish where personal contacts between providers are made. Each of the agencies is viewed as a "player," or significant resource, in that community's service delivery network. Each of the five intensively assessed programs is well-established and has had time to develop and nurture these contacts, but in each a commitment to collaboration was made in the early stages of program development. The collaboration and involvement often occurs through participation in interagency service planning teams; issue-oriented councils and coalitions; community-oriented activities, such as parent fairs and open houses; or membership in local service organizations, such as Kiwanis.

Interagency collaboration also includes coordinating clients' services. Because service providers often deal with similar issues for the same clients, case managers and educators should talk to members of other agencies, such as health department nurses, social services, and school services, to ensure that the client receives all available services. This coordination often is translated into better communication with clients and enables each service provider to provide consistent information to the client and to use time with the client more efficiently by preventing duplication of services.

It is important to recognize that the community context plays a large part in determining the success of collaborative efforts. Prevention-oriented communities have a precedent for accepting and promoting various prevention services; however, some communities can raise barriers that effectively preclude collaboration and the delivery of certain services. For example, in a politically and religiously conservative town, implementing teen pregnancy prevention services was much more difficult than in a town dominated by a large public university.

Fund-Raising Savvy

Successful administrators are or become savvy about the funding process. This knowledge may come from previous experience with other projects. Some administrators devote a significant amount of time to learning about potential funding sources and writing grants. The scope can be local or national. For example, Portsmouth's Good Beginnings program has been successful in obtaining grants from the United Way but looked to a local hospital for its initial grant and to local businesses for donations of goods and services. The Resource Mothers program in Abingdon has received several federal grants to develop its curriculum. The ability to obtain and manage grants successfully requires some level of resources—most at least document their services and clientele well. They also usually have some measure of outcome, such as the number of subsequent pregnancies, active Child Protective Services (CPS) cases, or changes in parenting attitudes and behaviors.

Long-Term Planning

Sometimes programs evolve from a series of unforeseen events, such as media attention and new funding sources, and program administrators do take advantage of these circumstances. Administrators also maintain a long-term vision of where they would like the program to go. The leaders in each of the five sites are able to describe in some detail the next steps that they would like to see their programs take. Although many of these steps are dependent on funding levels, a sense of direction and purpose emerges from discussions with these administrators. It also appears that these leaders are able to manage the growth of their programs successfully and look to outside sources for funding, recognizing that dependence on any single source of money ultimately is not helpful for their program. Long-term planning appears to go hand in hand with efficient utilization of resources. These leaders are cognizant of their programs' parameters and are sensitive to their limits. They do not overextend to the point that their efforts are unable to make a difference, yet they make maximum use of the resources that are available, including volunteers.

**Recognizing the Importance of
Credibility and Acceptance by Clients**

Successful program administrators recognize that their ability to facilitate positive change in their clients depends to a large extent on clients' perceptions of credibility and acceptance of the parent educators. Several programs make an effort to match their educators with clients on key characteristics such as gender, race, ethnicity, or place of residence. Of course, success as a program leader depends on a number of qualities beyond demographics, but qualified people who share similar backgrounds with clients may be able to establish rapport and trust more quickly and more effectively. For example, the

Resource Mothers program in Abingdon employs home visitors who live in the same counties as their clients. Good Beginnings in Portsmouth has two African American women working with its sample of (predominantly) inner-city African American teen mothers.

Although it is not necessary for each program administrator to exhibit all of these characteristics in abundance, successful programs do appear to have staff who fit these characteristics. In addition, as already noted, the leader is committed to having her or his program be a positive environment for the staff. The staff are valued, and their active involvement and commitment is solicited and rewarded with praise and attitude even if no tangible financial resources are available.

EVALUATION

As we have pointed out in previous chapters, evaluation (needs, process, and outcome) can and should be integrated into the everyday operations of prevention programs. Although resources are always limited, and most administrators have real or perceived pressures to focus them on direct services, we believe that the lack of evaluation truly does a disservice in the long run.

Although evaluation of primary prevention programs can be difficult, the benefits far outweigh the costs. Issues of resource allocation, measure integration, and resistance can be overcome through the commitment of program staff to the utility of information generated by an evaluation. Existing child abuse prevention programs can integrate process and outcome evaluations into current practices to determine whether the program is being implemented as intended and is having the desired impact. The design of future prevention programs can begin with a needs evaluation, which will guide the development of concrete goals and objectives. In turn, these goals and objectives will focus and integrate process and outcome evaluation procedures into the service delivery process. Parenting education as a form of family support is a promising strategy for preventing child abuse and neglect, and incorporating evaluation into all phases of program design and implementation will help ensure that programs are efficient and competitive for scarce prevention dollars. Ultimately, of course, evaluation processes benefit the clients by helping program staff provide useful, responsive, and effective prevention services. In addition, process evaluations help to provide guidelines to others who may want to replicate a successful program.

REPLICATING SUCCESSFUL PROGRAMS

After completing a needs assessment and establishing reasonable program goals and objectives, an organization can seek out existing programs with similar goals and objectives. Identifying the key ingredients for success allows new programs to choose those components of the programming that should be replicated. Especially in replicating more standardized programs, organizations should be careful about adapting the successful approach to their own needs; however, community needs, program staff and resources, and clientele are likely to differ significantly between the community of the established program and that of the new program. Therefore, attempts to transplant successful programs to new communities with no modifications are not likely to succeed. Also, practical limitations often necessitate that only components of successful approaches be replicated.

Conversely, organizations should be cautious in adapting an approach and should ensure that the key ingredients for success are not eliminated. For example, if it becomes necessary to shorten the length of a parent education program, then it is less likely that an abbreviated program will be as effective in increasing parenting knowledge or changing parent behavior. Also, if a program works primarily because of the particular skills of its individual staff members, then using similar curricula with a new staff may not succeed. If an established approach is replicated, then it is important to continue to use similar evaluation procedures in order to determine whether the approach works as effectively in a new community and whether adjustments to programming have eliminated critical components. Because the assumption that an evaluated program will be successful in a new community is probably not valid, continued evaluation of outcomes is essential.

Efforts to replicate successful approaches can be facilitated by efforts to network between programs. For example, we organized a workshop for representatives of the 25 programs. Such workshops allow for programs to compare notes about successes, failures, and special challenges in implementing programs, seeking funding, and documenting outcomes. The program personnel benefit from both the information shared and the social support of peers.

In a process evaluation, successful programs are defined by several characteristics that describe the development and implementation of the intended services. The degree to which individual programs exhibit these characteristics is related to the stage of program development, stability, and longevity, among other considerations. Successful programs are defined by a number of characteristics: 1) that the program design matches community needs; 2) that concrete goals and objectives are identified, and a long-range plan is developed; and 3) that key elements of the approach are incorporated.

Program Design Matches Community Needs

Given the variation among communities, it is clear that multiple models of prevention services are required. Successful programs have tailored their service delivery format to meet the needs of their communities. The services offered, the incentives necessary to recruit participants, and the complexity of the programming must be matched to the target group's needs, setting (e.g., urban, suburban, rural), and educational or reading level. The information conveyed and the approach taken by the staff must be sensitive to cultural differences and relevant for the target group. The focus of the information conveyed and services provided also depends on whether the target group for the prevention of maltreatment is the general public, a group labeled as at risk, or a number of known abusers.

Understanding the Community's Needs Successful programs appreciate that a comprehensive understanding of the community is vital to the development of appropriate prevention services. State and local statistics virtually guarantee that child abuse is a social problem in every community. It is not immediately clear, however, which type of preventive intervention is appropriate for a particular community. Therefore, a necessary component of successful intervention is assessing the current state of the community regarding an issue or problem and documenting the extent to which services are needed for particular groups. This process can occur formally or informally. For example, a local DSS program conducted a door-to-door survey on parenting techniques and child abuse issues to learn about the community's parenting strategies. The Parent's Place program in Roanoke benefited from a description of existing services for parents in the Roanoke Valley before designing its program. Programs use the information regarding client needs and service gaps to direct program development.

Format and Approach Match Clients' Needs Parent education programs' orientation and implementation may need to vary greatly according to the group being targeted and served. A "classroom" format designed to educate parents about child development and discipline techniques might be adequate for adults but seem less interesting to teen mothers, who may be more successfully recruited and retained by a "club" format program that offers food and recreation in addition to the education component.

Parent education classes assume that parents are capable of appropriate parenting when they have the proper education and support to do so; thus, these programs strive to meet the needs of children by meeting the needs of parents. Parent education programs attempt to benefit participants by increasing parents' knowledge of child development and effective nonviolent discipline and by decreasing parental distress through expanding social support networks. The assumption underlying the basic parent education orientation is that knowledge of child developmental milestones will minimize inappropriate expectations and thus reduce the incidence of child maltreatment. Thus, parent education classes are appropriately targeted to parents who, for a variety of reasons, lack knowledge or have inappropriate or false knowledge about childrearing and development. This lack of knowledge can be at a variety of levels. For example, The Parents' Place "Surviving Motherhood" class serves middle- and upper-class mothers who already have basic knowledge, so the class emphasizes high-literacy readings and advanced topics. Other classes serve parents with more limited knowledge, so they focus on more basic parenting skills.

Social support models assume that parents can respond positively and effectively to their children when they are given the knowledge, skills, and support necessary and when their own emotional and physical needs are met. Parent support groups thus emphasize the importance of informal conversations and a network of support to help individuals discuss the difficult and stressful demands of parenting. One local DSS program in the eastern part of the state runs an 8-week support group for parents going through mediation for custody in divorce, one of the goals of which is to reduce individual stress so that parents can focus more on their children's needs and feelings. Home-visiting programs provide parent education, social support, and individual crisis intervention to promote healthy infants and mothers and to prevent child maltreatment. Because services are offered in the home, visitors may be able to reach families who are unable to gain access to other family support programs. People, Inc., in Abingdon serves teen mothers who lack transportation in several rural counties—it is unlikely that the teen mothers could attend a center-based program as often as they meet with their home visitor (weekly).

Regardless of approach, successful programs attempt to respond sensitively to the practical demands of participants (e.g., offer services at times that accommodate work schedules) and minimize any stigma associated with the prevention program (focusing on "strengths" rather than on "weaknesses").

Curricula Are Sensitive to Clients' Needs Copyrighted curricula have been used extensively throughout the nation and have been endorsed by child abuse councils and task forces, despite the limited amount of process and outcome evaluation data on these programs. Using these curricula and the evaluation tools provided is an important step in evaluating the programs. In some programs, however, curricula have been developed over the years, or modifications of existing curricula have occurred to meet the needs of the individual program. For example, several funded programs have modified the Nurturing Program curriculum by adding a substance abuse component in order to address a problem that they deemed significant for their target groups. Many projects have illiterate or low-literacy clients and therefore must adopt curricula and/or form groups according to parents' level of education. In addition, project staff often design and/or select a curriculum based on what they believe is most appropriate for parents with children within a certain age range, separating the parents into different groups based on their children's ages. Such modifications are necessary but must be documented in order to evaluate the implementation of the program.

Concrete Goals and Objectives Are Identified, and a Long-Range Plan Is Developed

Successful programs have clear ideas about what changes their intervention should make. Clear goals and objectives make explicit the program's purpose and intended impact. Project goals are general statements that specify the end condition that should occur as a function of the program; objectives are more specific statements of outcomes that reflect progress toward or achievement of a goal within a specific time frame. A periodic review of the stated goals and objectives during the period of service delivery can help identify when a program has either strayed unnecessarily from its purpose or has intentionally adapted in response to new situations or information, perhaps signaling the need to reformulate goals and objectives. Specific goals and objectives also enable staff to communicate more effectively about program accountability in terms of identifying particular strengths and weaknesses.

Developing a long-range plan, which includes identifying service goals and objectives, predicted budgetary needs, and evaluation methods, is crucial for programs to undertake. Planning for the next 1-year, 5-year, and even 10-year period can help focus a program's mission, shape its service activities, and provide information that is helpful to outside funding sources as well. In addition, a cost–benefit analysis can be critically important. Calculating the dollars saved by family support programs is one sound way to measure their efficacy. Participants in these programs are using and probably will continue to use few social services, thereby saving tax dollars.

Key Elements of the Approach Are Incorporated

Intensity, Duration, and Format Successful programs tailor the format, intensity, and duration of their programming in order to meet the needs of a specific group; identifying the level of services appropriate for any given group of parents or a specific family is one goal of effective planning. For example, the Parent–Child Center in Winchester schedules a home visit to a family as a first step; they may determine that this initial visit is sufficient and invite the parents to attend weekly parenting classes to increase skill and support levels. A family in need of more intensive services, however, might be more appropriately served by weekly, one-to-one home visits by a therapist or paraprofessional.

Programs providing weekly parenting education classes vary in the number of classes that they offer; some offer as few as 4 sessions per series, whereas most provide between 9 and 15. Most programs tend to need at least one or two class periods to get started and one or two at the end of the series to synthesize what has been learned. The number of sessions devoted to substantive presentations varies, but more successful programs tend to spend at least four or five sessions on parenting skills, knowledge, and behavior. This suggests that a minimum of six to eight classes is preferable if a parent education program is to be successful. Reviews of research on programs that serve families at risk suggest that sustained contacts of at least several months are necessary to achieve meaningful and lasting effects on family functioning (see Chapter 2).

Recruitment and Retention Effective programs clearly identify the group(s) that they want to recruit and outline plans for successful recruiting; for example, Good Beginnings in Portsmouth targets teen mothers for its programs and has an arrangement with local hospitals that allows them to visit every new teen mother before she leaves the hospital. Interagency collaboration often is a crucial factor in obtaining referrals for programs. Similarly, programs need to address ways to retain clients once they are recruited; Good Beginnings offers incentives to its teen mothers for joining and staying in the program, including free transportation to and from classes and opportunities to socialize with other teen mothers at a variety of events. Other tangible rewards that programs offer to keep parents involved in classes and to combat barriers to participation include free child care and/or meals during sessions and material goods such as car seats and infant clothing.

Keeping clients interested in staying with prevention programs is an important issue, and it represents a very significant problem for most programs. After a program has been initiated, staff often run the parent education program only to find that attendance begins to trail off rapidly from week to week. Some suggestions to reduce drop-out rates follow.

Why worry about client retention? Is client attrition important, beyond the fact that programs are serving fewer people than they had hoped to serve? Yes, in that those individuals who "drop out" may be different from those who stay with the program. For instance, the five young mothers who stopped coming to a parent support group may have been at greater risk for abusing their children than the nine who kept coming, in terms of being more isolated, less knowledgeable about child development and disciplinary techniques, more stressed by poor marital relationships and lack of stable incomes, and so forth. In this case, the program not only is serving fewer individuals but also is failing to retain those individuals who may need the most help. In addition, staff may not know that these clients are, in fact, at greater risk if they drop out early in the program. Thus, it becomes important to work at retaining the clients who have been diligently targeted and recruited.

As a first step to improving retention, the initial meeting is the key to getting parents interested in a program. Programs should keep it simple, perhaps short, and let the group get to know the facilitator and one another. After a rapport-building first meeting, the facilitator can move on to more of the "meat" of the program. Staff should be as dynamic, warm, open, and flexible as possible. Staff should show the parents that the staff are there to share some information and facilitate discussion but that the group will be both helpful and interesting, not boring and didactic.

If possible, participants should be offered something in return. Tangible items such as a door prize, a free dinner at each class, or perhaps an incentive to finish or "pass" the program (e.g., a graduation party) may assist in retention. Some programs try to make the class a "fun" social experience for participants so that they get to know one another and expand their social network. Participants can be encouraged to exchange telephone numbers and car-pool/bus/walk together to the program if transportation is not provided. Participants in the Surviving Motherhood class formed their own play group, which continued after the class itself ended.

Arranging transportation to and from the program is an essential element to successful recruitment and retention. Quite simply, people might not attend if the program does not pick them up or arrange for transportation. Participants may not have the means to get to the program, or it may be "too much of a has-sle" unless arrangements are made for them. People rarely will stand someone up if they know that they are being picked up. Goochland, for instance, offers participants rides to the doctor or the grocery store. The van or car ride to the program also can be a great time to get to know one another in a less formal setting than that of the class.

The location of the meeting place is important in terms of convenience for the participants. Participants are more likely to get to know one another if the program meets in their own community. Meetings in community settings may be more convenient and less stigmatizing than those held in government or so-cial services offices. Location also may solve the transportation problem if the program is on a city bus line or meets in several places close to clients' neigh-borhoods.

Child care is another consideration. Without a nursery or a few volunteers to take care of children while their parents are in the group, it may not be fea-sible for parents to attend. Some programs, like Portsmouth's Good Beginnings, have parents and their infants attend in order to observe their in-teractions and alleviate the issue of child care.

Programs should consider the literacy or educational level of the partici-pants and tailor their materials to parents' needs. Some participants may stop coming to the program if they feel "dumb" or embarrassed about their inabil-ity to read, write, or understand the curriculum. Several programs combat this problem by scaling down written handouts to a simpler level or presenting pic-tures. If many in the class do not read or if they have a low reading level, then staff can try to convey materials and administer evaluation instruments orally.

Programs should help participants link to other services, toward a goal of continuity of services. This will enable clients to receive all of the services available to them without unnecessary duplications and confusion. Most im-portant and most basic (though most frequently overlooked), staff should ask the participants what they want from the program. Once their needs and hopes for the program are known, staff can more effectively help and retain the par-ents in the program.

Of course, no program can be expected to address all of these issues, and for some, these issues may not exist. Rather, programs should utilize these sug-gestions in meeting the needs of their particular clients. Some of the specifics about how program staff think about and work toward client retention may vary somewhat across program orientations (home visiting or class), urban or rural settings, or target groups (teen parents or adults). At a more general level, however, attention to the needs and wishes of participants will help staff improve their program's retention of clients and make it easier to serve the needs of clients in an effective manner.

Interagency Collaboration   Programs often must face the continual challenge of a scarcity of resources. In addition, the problems handled by programs often are too complex and far-reaching for any individual agency to resolve alone. In order to maximize resources and increase the effectiveness of their work, many programs rely on interagency collaboration. Organizations united for a common cause may constitute a "critical mass," allowing them to accomplish goals beyond the reach of any individual agency (Brown, 1984). Gray (1985) defined collaboration as "(1) the pooling of appreciations and/or tangible resources, e.g., information, money, labor, etc., (2) by two or more stakeholders, (3) to solve a set of problems that neither can solve individually" (p. 912). The efforts of one agency may reinforce and magnify those of another. More comprehensive services may be made available, a greater number and diversity of clients may be reached, and a better understanding of these clients may be achieved. In this regard, the work of the whole may be greater than the sum of the individual agencies. Another incentive for interagency collaboration is provided by granting agencies, especially government, which, with limited funds to award, generally look favorably on interagency collaboration while scowling at duplication of services.

According to Price and Smith (1985), the following questions can be used to guide interagency collaboration efforts when a structure for collaboration has not yet been established:

1. What are the other agencies and groups in the community that are involved with the target group and/or share similar goals?
2. How do these agencies interact with each other?
3. Are there planning councils or other coordinating agencies that can facilitate collaboration?
4. What steps need to be taken to secure the interest and cooperation of the other agencies and groups?

The first three questions can be addressed within the context of a community needs assessment. In conducting a needs assessment, programs can educate other agencies and groups about the services that they will offer, highlight common goals, and begin to build an informal network of service providers. Interagency collaboration also can be encouraged through the formation of an advisory board for the program composed of personnel, including administrators and front-line staff, from other organizations. Participation by program staff on other agencies' advisory boards, planning councils, and coordinating agencies likewise can facilitate interagency collaboration. Many communities already have established service boards to oversee the activities of all social services agencies in the area.

Gray (1985) divided the planning necessary for successful interagency collaboration into three stages:

1. Problem setting—identifying the collaborating agencies and acknowledging a common guiding purpose
2. Direction setting—articulating the values held by the participating agencies and agreeing on shared goals
3. Structuring—creating a structure to support long-term collaboration allowing for ongoing contact and negotiation between agencies

Power and responsibility do not necessarily need to be divided equally between/among collaborating agencies, but they must be shared in order for true collaboration to occur (Gray, 1985). A formal agreement or contract specifying the goals and responsibilities of each collaborating agency can enable programs and agencies to work together more easily. Regular follow-up, through direct contact, telephone, or written report, of clients referred from one agency to another for service(s) can ensure comprehensive, integrated service delivery in addition to helping agencies remain informed of each other's activities.

Staff   Small programs in particular often are challenged to provide direct services while also handling administrative and fund-raising responsibilities with few staff members and very little time. In order to make good use of staff, programs must identify their staffing needs for projected services and devise plans for training and evaluating staff on a regular basis.

Establishing clear, specific written job descriptions is helpful for several reasons. Doing so gives all members of the organization a knowledge of what is expected of them and what they can expect of others. Good job descriptions can eliminate confusion as to who is expected to perform which tasks and can be helpful in evaluating individual job performance. It is important to recognize that, of course, descriptions need to maintain flexibility and cannot cover everything, especially if the jobs are as complex as they typically are in social services agencies. In writing job descriptions, it should be clear that all of the program's goals and objectives are broken down into tasks for which someone within the organization is responsible. If an evaluation of overall program goals suggests that a problem exists, then job descriptions can be useful in assessing the problem's cause.

Although most members of social services organizations are devoted to their work and perform it competently, monitoring job performance is an important component to ensuring the quality of service delivery. Methods for individual job performance evaluation vary from organization to organization. Many find that annual or more frequent evaluations are useful and follow a fairly structured format for doing so. Others are less formal. Many administrators find that sitting in on programs, even those run by experienced staff, is helpful, both for supervising staff members and for maintaining contact with the clients. It is not uncommon for social services programs to use staff members who are officially employed by other community agencies. It is important that even when personnel are "borrowed," their roles should be well-defined and evaluated.

Although rewarding, the demanding, interpersonal nature of human services work often can lead to high levels of stress or job burnout. It is important for organizations to monitor the job satisfaction and job-related stress of employees. Individuals typically are attracted to social services fields because of the intrinsic rewards of the work. The high rates of job turnover in these agencies, however, suggest that such rewards are not great enough to keep people motivated for long periods of time in the absence of extrinsic rewards. Assessing job satisfaction and stress is particularly important in fields in which burnout and high turnover are so common. Organizations can evaluate satisfaction and stress through questionnaires with established reliability and validity; through informal, open-ended questionnaires; or through unstructured interviews with individuals or groups of staff members.

Social services agencies are likely to find that extrinsic rewards are inadequate, especially the typically low salaries, but an accurate assessment of the sources of dissatisfaction and stress is crucial in preventing burnout and high turnover among workers (Cherniss, 1981). For example, many workers report that educational opportunities that are made available to staff are valuable in meeting future career goals. Even if extrinsic rewards are not an issue or cannot be improved, job satisfaction is likely to be increased if employees sense that the organization is taking care of them. For example, staff-only workshops or retreats, periodic group evaluation, and goal setting can be helpful. When possible, debriefing and stress-reducing activities should be explored and implemented.

Volunteers Volunteers can play a valuable role in the operation of the majority of social services programs; their contributions are critical to many projects' success, especially those that are understaffed. Strategic use of volunteers can greatly enhance the number and range of services available, the quality of those services, and the number of clients who can be served. In addition, volunteers can assist projects to operate more efficiently and prevent paid staff from being overburdened and/or overwhelmed with job-related responsibilities. Volunteers can be recruited from a variety of sources, including the professional community, the students and faculty of local colleges and universities, the general population, current and past clients, and the business community.

For volunteers to be most effective, attention must be directed toward their training and evaluation, and expectations must be specified clearly.

Training and evaluation programs will differ in their intensity and purpose according to 1) the volunteers' previous training, 2) how the volunteers are to be utilized, 3) the project's commitment to training, and 4) the program's resources. At the very least, volunteers working directly with clients can benefit from being familiarized with the common stresses and challenges facing those clients, particularly if the volunteers and clients do not share a similar background and/or have not worked together previously. Furthermore, minimal supervision is necessary, even of skilled professionals, to ensure that project goals are being achieved and that quality services are being delivered.

Some programs have become very sophisticated in their use of volunteers, employing a full- or part-time volunteer coordinator and/or maintaining a database of past, current, and potential volunteers. Unfortunately, understaffed programs may not be able easily to organize, utilize, and oversee the activities of volunteers; however, these programs could benefit most from such assistance. Establishing a volunteer component should be viewed as a long-term investment requiring substantial commitment up front. As for most program activities, the planning stage is critical to later success. Programs should carefully decide 1) how volunteers can most effectively be utilized, 2) who these volunteers should be and how to recruit them, and 3) what type of training and evaluation is necessary to enable volunteers to contribute quality services to the program.

CONCLUSION

The following points encapsulate what lessons we have learned:

1. Programs should determine which groups they will serve and identify which program approach would be most effective in reaching them. We suggest that programs provide a rationale for the format of services that they propose to offer a given group (e.g., a program should describe when and why home visits will be conducted rather than or in addition to parenting education classes).
2. If standard curricula are modified, then modifications should be appropriate and documented.
3. Programs should explicitly address issues of client needs and capacities and how the program format will correspond. For example, responses could include modifying curriculum content or topics covered, providing different types of services to varying client groups, or using a didactic versus a discussion-oriented approach in class.
4. Programs should delineate how they plan to identify clients' needs and respond to them within the context of the educational curriculum. Needs can encompass literacy levels, background knowledge, skill level, and topical issues (e.g., substance abuse).

5. Programs should be encouraged to make their goals and objectives specific and concrete. Programs should provide guidelines regarding creating and implementing program goals and objectives. Projects also should identify mechanisms for long-range planning.

6. Parent education programs should consist of a minimum of six class periods. Shorter-term programs are not likely to engage participants in the education or provide enough time to review and practice new concepts.

7. Programs should be comprehensive enough, and contacts with families should be sustained long enough to make a substantive difference in the program's specified goals and objectives. Programs should be able to explain how their program, given duration and intensity of services and linkages to other programs, could be expected to make a difference in their stated objectives.

8. Programs should develop a specific recruiting plan that targets the appropriate groups.

9. Issues of attrition and how to combat it should be addressed in the program plan.

10. Programs should be able to make explicit how they plan to handle issues of successful recruitment (e.g., by offering tangible incentives to attend, connections to desired services, a welcome social/peer experience), arrangements for transportation, the stigma and/or convenience of the location of the services, child care, literacy of clients and curriculum delivery, linkage to other services, and use of client input in the program.

11. Programs should demonstrate that they have the appropriate number of trained staff and/or volunteers to administer projected programs.

12. Programs should detail what constitutes training, supervision, and evaluation of staff and volunteers to prepare them for their respective tasks.

13. Programs should develop an evaluation plan in which measures (beyond client satisfaction) corresponding to the goals and objectives are identified and utilized. If possible, standardized measures should be used in addition to any adapted or specialized measures.

14. Data from the measures should be examined by the administrators and used to provide feedback to program staff and suggest changes in program implementation.

If parent education programs attempt to deal with or, at the very least, are aware of these goals, then the likelihood of successfully implementing viable and effective programs should be greatly enhanced.

A Policy Agenda for Child Maltreatment Prevention

For most of this century, parent education has been a middle-class self-improvement movement. By the late 1960s and 1970s, however, parent education, as a result of the federal government's public policy incorporated under the rubric of the "War on Poverty," became focused on those at an economic disadvantage. Under this policy, many comprehensive programs that emphasized parent education of various types were funded (Wandersman, 1987). In spite of questions regarding the effectiveness of parent education (e.g., Rosenberg & Reppucci, 1985), interest intensified because of societal changes, not the least of which were the increased stress on parents brought on by the increasing proportions of single, working, and teenage mothers and the developing public awareness of the problems of child maltreatment and juvenile delinquency. Even as the divorce rate expanded and the traditional family was having evermore problems surviving, families were recognized by policy makers as the linchpin of society. Thus, by the 1980s, public policy became one of strengthening families, and parent education was viewed as a central component of "family support" (Kagan, Powell, Weissbourd, & Zigler, 1987).

The family support programs that have emerged nationwide share several basic assumptions even as they are reflected in a variety of approaches and methods. Weissbourd (1987) listed these assumptions:

- All families need support, regardless of economic status or specific concerns. Most parents want to be good parents no matter what their resources are. The varying kinds of support provided by family resource programs are determined by the needs of the parents and are responsive to the cultural and social characteristics of the communities in which families live.

147

- The availability of social networks, mutual aid, and peer groups is essential to the family's ability to enhance the child's development.
- Information on child development, obtained both formally and informally, assists families in their child-rearing role.
- Support programs increase the family's ability to cope rather than provide a system on which families become dependent. Support should build on strengths that whole families and individual family members already have. The confidence that family support helps parents build enables families to manage their own lives and participate in shaping the environment in which they live.
- Providing support during the first years of a child's life serves a preventive function. Early and continuing support is aimed at strengthening the family unit and preventing dysfunction.
- Because families are part of a community, their needs cannot be met in isolation from it. Support is provided in the context of community life and through links with community resources. (p. 53)

These assumptions clearly underlie the various parent education programs that we have discussed in this book. It is because of these assumptions that many parent educators believe that parent education programs have the potential to be major contributors to the prevention of child maltreatment. Obviously, they may, and we have presented some evidence that, at least in a few cases, they do! Some cautions exist, however, regarding the use of parent education as a vehicle for preventing child maltreatment. First, Garbarino (1987) emphasized that prevention goals and their limitations need to be stated as precisely as possible. Parent education may have more of an impact on some forms of abuse than others, and these prevention efforts may be effective only under specified conditions. For example, some family support programs may work only for unmarried young mothers, whereas others may work only for families with adequate economic resources (Garbarino, 1987). If this is the case, then it suggests that realistic interventions may involve matching programs to targeted groups, as many of the programs that we have investigated have done. The Good Beginnings intervention, which we presented in detail in Chapter 8, may well have been less effective if it had been focused on older rather than teenage mothers or if it had not limited the participants to first-time mothers. Second, Garbarino (1987) suggested that evaluation of both generalized primary prevention and targeted programs for groups at high risk should be based on comparisons of similar groups randomly assigned to different types of interventions and that "the need for such prospective evaluation studies is critical" (p. 108). Wandersman (1987) reinforced this need: "Analysis of the efficacy of parent education is greatly hampered by the paucity of published documentation and evaluations of parent education programs" (p. 208).

With these cautions in mind, we present the following major recommendations as a framework for a public policy agenda for using parent education to help prevent child maltreatment: 1) take a systems approach to helping families, 2) make a commitment to effective parenting education, 3) develop methods for monitoring program effectiveness, and 4) develop general funding considerations.

TAKE A SYSTEMS APPROACH TO HELPING FAMILIES

Policy makers and prevention advocates alike share an understanding that families do not live in isolation; the community context can either facilitate or prevent families from helping themselves. A comprehensive systems approach emphasizes that families live in ecological contexts, and the interaction between family and context is critical for prevention efforts.

Identify Strengths and Barriers in the Community as Well as in the Individual

Emphasis should be on the strengths of a family, along with identifying structural and individual barriers to healthy and productive childrearing. Focusing on strengths will lead to interventions that are meaningful and productive for the families, whereas focusing on individual deficits frequently makes families more dependent on service providers. Certainly, some families have serious problems that require in-depth intervention. Whenever possible, a deficit model focused on fixing "broken" people should be avoided.

Promote Interagency and Client Collaboration

A number of different public, private, and nonprofit agencies can serve families in a single community. True collaboration requires that representatives of these agencies sit down with other key community leaders, including clients themselves, to evaluate a community's needs and design effective interventions. Collaboration can occur in funding streams as well as in service provision; in order to remain financially viable, a number of Virginia programs solicited funds from multiple sources and spent a significant amount of time on grant paperwork. Collaboration at the state and local levels can help identify funding sources for parent education and child maltreatment prevention, perhaps streamlining application processes and improving coordination.

MAKE A COMMITMENT TO EFFECTIVE PARENTING EDUCATION

Research, although limited, supports the efficacy of parent education as a strategy for prevention. Therefore, we advocate that parent education be encouraged by public, private, and nonprofit agencies as one of the components of the child maltreatment prevention effort and that funding priorities encourage regular, reasonable evaluations of program implementation and effectiveness. Ongoing research is essential for effective programming!

Include Parent Education in a Policy Agenda to Support Families

Parent education represents one essential component of general policy to support and strengthen families. In a time when policy making often is reactive, short term, and crisis driven, few legislators invest time in developing a comprehensive prevention agenda. Advocacy and scientific organizations often are relied on to synthesize experience and research to bring a broad focus to the larger issues affecting the health and welfare of children and families (e.g., Allen, Brown, & Finlay, 1992; National Institute of Mental Health, 1994; Virginia Department of Mental Health, Mental Retardation, and Substance Abuse Services [DMHMRSAS], 1988). Although crisis intervention and treatment services are key components of an effective response to troubled families, it is clear that intervention after the fact cannot be the sole solution to child maltreatment. Parent education must be viewed as an intervention that is a long-term investment in the well-being of children and families.

Enable All Families to Gain Access to Primary Prevention Services

Primary prevention must be *the* major component of a comprehensive policy to prevent child maltreatment. All families deserve access to education and support; those under stress and/or subject to other factors that increase their risk may need more support. Universal access does not mean mandated or coercive intervention; rather, it addresses the structural barriers that label families who utilize services as at risk or "troubled." Educational support that is offered to all parents, regardless of risk status, represents a communitywide commitment to families and an acknowledgment of the larger responsibility to support families when they feel that they need it.

These recommendations represent a policy agenda, grounded in research and experience, that promotes parent education as one component of a comprehensive child maltreatment strategy. In an effort to become more specific, we focus the remainder of this chapter on program effectiveness and funding priorities. These two areas were identified as being the most critical to the implementation of successful programs by service providers, the funding agency, and the research team. These recommendations can guide state and local administrators who want to fund effective parent education programs, as well as individual programs that want to improve services and strengthen their ability to gain access to funds.

DEVELOP METHODS FOR MONITORING PROGRAM EFFECTIVENESS

Several chapters of this book have been devoted directly or indirectly to discussions of program effectiveness and issues of measurement. Large public agencies, such as state departments of social services, often provide language in their requests for proposals to implementing agencies about the importance of monitoring program effectiveness. Each proposal is required to include a discussion of evaluation issues and how they will be implemented. Thus, the language for monitoring program effectiveness is present, but it is apparent from our literature reviews and from our process evaluation of the 25 Virginia programs that the language seldom is translated into program activity. Previous chapters have discussed the variety of reasons that most programs will not incorporate evaluation techniques on their own. We believe that external motivation and practical assistance are required for any evaluation to take place and that they must start with the funding agency. To do this, stated commitments to evaluation must be translated into actual evaluation activity among its programs. These activities include but are not limited to the following: 1) define effectiveness, 2) encourage linkages between programs and local colleges and universities, 3) provide structural and technical support for creating and implementing evaluation activities, 4) provide written materials regarding evaluation issues, 5) sponsor meetings/workshops on evaluation design and implementation, and 6) provide assistance with record keeping and database management.

Define Effectiveness

It is essential that effectiveness be defined in meaningful terms that can be measured. It often means that base rates of certain activities (e.g., the incidence of child maltreatment in a community) must be determined before the intervention and then at varying lengths of time after the intervention is concluded. It also may mean that information (e.g., knowledge of child development or patterns of mother–child interactions) must be obtained before the intervention and then explicitly measured following the intervention. What measures are decided on should be determined before the intervention begins and should be guided by the goals of the intervention.

Encourage Linkages Between
Programs and Local Colleges and Universities

Often, local college faculty will include people with expertise in the human services field and/or evaluation. Given the renewed nationwide interest in promoting partnerships between state agencies and public/private universities, evaluation assistance for child abuse prevention programs is a natural link. The universities will benefit from participating in evaluation projects with their students; and the programs will benefit from expertise on the development, implementation, and analysis of evaluation. Such linkages entail the expenditure of funds, but using the resources of person power and expertise available at most colleges and universities, these arrangements often can be accomplished at minimal expense.

Provide Structural and Technical Support
for Creating and Implementing Evaluation Activities

Structural and technical support can come in a variety of forms. The most desirable would be the designation of a central office staff position(s) devoted full or part time to evaluating prevention programs. This position would not be designed to evaluate the programs themselves but rather to travel to the program sites and assist the individual programs in developing ways to self-evaluate. For smaller programs with fewer resources, this staff person could assist in analysis once the data have been collected. If a staff position could not be devoted to this task, then perhaps one of the duties of a member of the funding agency's evaluation unit could be to provide some form of technical support to these sites for self-evaluation.

Provide Written Materials Regarding Evaluation Issues

Because most programs operate under serious time and resource constraints, staff do not have the opportunity to research the evaluation process and gather appropriate materials. The funding agency could provide practical written materials on evaluation. This material could include products such as our technical brief series (see Appendix A). The funding agency or other contractors also could create additional materials, such as a manual designed to be a "how to" for evaluation implementation. (See, e.g., Galano & Nezlet, 1991, for the development of a training manual for evaluating prevention programs that was written in clear and nonintimidating language for service providers.)

Sponsor Meetings/Workshops on
Evaluation Design and Implementation

Our initial meeting of all program grantees in Richmond drew favorable comments, in part because grantees were afforded the opportunity to network with each other. Workshops could not only teach the practical aspects of evaluation but also facilitate the sharing of information and evaluation experiences, which could be useful.

Provide Assistance with Record
Keeping and Database Management

Accurate record keeping is a necessary component for any evaluation process. Assistance could include funding for computers, software, and instruction in their use to the service provider agencies. The funding agency also could provide templates for standard forms and records that parent education programs might use. For example, when we began our work in Virginia, we were informed that the required monthly reporting form was so poorly designed that it took an inordinate amount of time to fill out and submit. As one program director said, "My administrative assistant begins to cry every month when we have to complete the form!" One of the first activities that we undertook was to redesign this form so that it provided needed information in a way that was easy to record and collect.

These suggestions assume that service agencies want more support and involvement from the central funding agency with respect to evaluation. Each requires an investment of resources (time and/or money) on the part of the funding agency as well as the grantees. Although this may appear to divert resources from service provision, the commitment to evaluation is essential to the implementation of *effective* prevention programming. No funding agency can expect grantees to demonstrate an active effort at evaluation without modeling its own commitment, as an agency, to evaluation. As discussed in previous chapters, information obtained from evaluation can and should be useful for the programs in their own operations and for the central office in its own policy decisions regarding funding priorities. It is important that the information produced from evaluation be used at both levels. The funding agency may be able to facilitate this use by providing feedback on the information included in the monthly and annual reports. Feedback can occur by communication with individual programs or perhaps through some form of shared communication, such as newsletters, that highlight evaluation efforts and results.

DEVELOP GENERAL FUNDING CONSIDERATIONS

Although it may be helpful to determine minimum costs to establish prevention programs for administrative reasons, the diversity of programs and their community contexts make it difficult. Localities may be able to generate cost estimates of service delivery in their own communities, but for state and national planners, the same program may vary widely in cost, depending on the region (rural/urban) or the state and the cost-of-living index for that region. General economic factors would influence not only estimates of the costs of parent education but also characteristics of the programs themselves. Thus, standard cost estimates of parent education programs cannot be made without accounting for particular program characteristics that can affect funding decisions. In the following section, we make recommendations regarding several of these characteristics.

Acknowledge that Programs Have Different Resource Requirements

Funding must remain sensitive to program needs. When budgeting and allocating funding dollars to prevention programming, a number of factors should be considered: 1) program type, 2) program phase, 3) location, and 4) staff and volunteers.

Program Type   The costs of making parent education services available vary according to the type and phase of the program. For example, weekly home-visiting programs may entail more transportation costs than a parent support program. Educational classes may require the purchase of a curriculum and supplemental materials. Because program type must be matched to community need, the costs of implementation may vary.

Program Phase   Costs vary according to the phase of program development. Initial start-up costs may emphasize public awareness; networking and developing community contacts; or reviewing, developing, and purchasing materials, among others. Program maintenance may entail different staff and resource expenditures as programs change priorities or expand.

Location   Physical location is a cost issue. Some programs require a meeting area; others only need office space for staff. Affiliation with a larger group, such as a private or nonprofit agency, can facilitate sharing of overhead costs but may entail greater administrative requirements. Free-standing programs can retain flexibility and autonomy but may lack the structural support and community recognition of a larger agency. Programs located in public agencies (e.g., the departments of social services or health) benefit from the resources and stability of local government but may also carry some "baggage" of being affiliated with these agencies (e.g., departments of social services and child protective services work).

Staff and Volunteers   The number of staff needed to administer a program effectively and efficiently affects costs. Paid staff may have a greater commitment to the program, as well as more time, but entail salary and benefits costs. Community volunteers can provide free assistance, foster community ownership, and provide outstanding service; but they engender administrative management, recruitment, retention, and training efforts and may feel less commitment to the program than paid staff. Even so, many programs rely heavily on volunteers (by choice or by necessity) to maintain their desired level of services under limited budgets; this is probably a positive situation in most cases.

Identify the Necessary Minimal Administrative Conditions

Providing direct services to parents and families requires a significant amount of administrative and, in most cases, fund-raising work. Programs often appear to feel a tension between direct services and administrative concerns. More successful programs seem able to meet minimal administrative conditions; they are able to complete paperwork for funding sources, maintain records documenting program activities, and prepare recruitment and class materials. They do this in a variety of ways; some are housed within larger social services organizations with administrative help, whereas others delegate administrative work to a staff member or volunteer as one of their job duties. Specifying who is responsible for administrative concerns and setting aside priority time for this work is essential, even if this requires taking some time away from direct service provision. Programs with computers may be better able to complete paperwork and store information in a timely fashion, as long as staff are trained appropriately or have access to technical assistance.

Provide the Resources and Commitment to a Minimal Level of Evaluation

As discussed in previous sections, to ensure that good ideas are translated into effective prevention projects, programs must be able to document and evaluate what they do. Evaluation can be implemented at a variety of levels, ranging from documenting services provided and clients served to evaluating program effectiveness. Whatever the degree of evaluation, all levels require a minimal commitment of resources for entering information, developing record-keeping forms, selecting measures, and using a computer database (if possible). For more advanced evaluative techniques, assistance in project design and data analysis may be necessary. This assistance could be obtained from in-house personnel, from community volunteers with relevant experience, or through partnerships with local colleges and universities. Evaluation must become a budget category for these programs.

The commitment to evaluation fosters the planning necessary for effective preventive interventions. Although evaluation does require some commitment of time and resources (e.g., to developing valid measures and to implementing some more rigorous experimental design than is usually the case) the information that it provides can document who is being served, how the program is being implemented, the strengths and weaknesses of the current approach, and what effects the program is having. This information can be used to improve programming and to suggest additional approaches. In sum, we concur strongly with the conclusion of Thompson and Wilcox (1995) that

> advances in understanding . . . of the most feasible strategies for preventing and treating . . . [child maltreatment] . . . remain contingent on the commitment of behavioral scientists to create policy-relevant knowledge and on the willingness of federal agencies to provide appropriate administrative and financial support. (p. 793)

CONCLUSION

We conclude this book by emphasizing our belief that parenthood is an extremely complex and demanding job and that parent education can help parents to perform this job more effectively. We view parent education neither "as a panacea for poverty, mental illness, crime, and divorce" (Wandersman, 1987, p. 207), as some of its more ardent proponents have, nor "as an intrusion into family life and a threat to individual freedom and cultural diversity" (p. 207) as some of its opponents have. Rather, for us, parent education is one central part of the family support movement and has great potential as a contributor to the well-being of our society. Nevertheless, we need much more systematic documentation of the various types of programs in varying ecological contexts to determine what its actual potential is, especially as a component of a public policy whose goal is to eradicate child maltreatment in all of its forms and guises. As we have emphasized throughout this book, both careful process and outcome evaluations must be implemented as integral parts of the prevention programs that are initiated. The literature and our own investigations suggest much promise, but we still have much to learn. The nation's children and families deserve no less!

Topical Briefs
for the Practitioner

appendix • A

This appendix contains summaries, or "topical briefs," of key issues that have been raised throughout this book. Although most of these topics have been covered in the preceding chapters, the information is reformatted here for use by program staff as training or reference material. The goal is to provide an immediate, usable resource for the busy practitioner. There is no need to obtain permission to copy and distribute these briefs.

CONTENTS

These briefs were prepared by the Community Research Group under the auspices of a grant from the Virginia Department of Social Services.

PARENT EDUCATION AS A PREVENTIVE INTERVENTION

The alarmingly high incidence and prevalence of child abuse and neglect in the United States suggest an urgent need for prevention at the community level. In the 1960s, a governmental shift in policy encouraged state intervention "in the best interests of the child" when the parents were unable to perform their child-rearing roles adequately. Many of the programs are designed to prevent or end child maltreatment or family violence by improving family functioning. These programs benefit families in two separate but related ways: 1) by increasing parenting knowledge of child development and effective discipline and 2) by decreasing parental distress through expanding social support networks. Given our state of knowledge about the nature of family violence, does it make sense to expect parent education programs to prevent abuse?

PARENTING KNOWLEDGE

Justifications for parent education as an intervention for improving family functioning (generally) and preventing abuse and neglect (specifically) have been based on several lines of developmental research. Although limitations exist, these lines of research converge on the conclusion that parental behavior does affect development throughout childhood. For example, some research has found that teaching mothers about the emotional development of young children will minimize the occurrence of child abuse in groups at high risk (e.g., parents from low-income or isolated settings, teen mothers), on the basis of findings that abusive parents have more inappropriate expectations and demands for their children.

Mental health professionals have found that parents who interpret children's developmental limitations as deliberate noncompliance are likely to experience frustration and anger. For example, the difficult phases of colic, awakening at night, separation anxiety, exploratory behaviors, negativism, poor appetite, and toilet-training resistance have been described as the "seven deadly sins" of childhood. These are frustrating for any parent, but in the context of families who are at high risk for maltreating their children and who are not prepared or able to cope with them, these behaviors are likely to precipitate harsh punishment or episodes of abuse. It is one goal of parent education programs to prevent abuse by teaching parents to expect and deal with such difficulties.

Education about nonviolent disciplinary alternatives is another focus of parenting classes. Parent education programs provide a means for parents to learn effective parenting practices from sources other than their own upbringing. Bavolek and Comstock (1985), for example, wrote in their Nurturing Program curriculum that "to offset the generational perpetuation of dysfunctional parenting practices, education in appropriate parenting and child rearing is viewed as the single most important treatment and intervention strategy" (p. 3). If physical abuse itself is conceptualized as an inappropriate and extreme form of discipline, then it follows that abusive parents typically lack an awareness of appropriate discipline.

Although these empirical studies of abusive parents' knowledge of typical child development are few in number (Rosenberg & Reppucci, 1983), several studies have found these parents to be surprisingly knowledgeable about discipline alternatives and describe typical responses to misbehavior that very often are appropriate techniques. Thus, abusive parents as a group should not be presumed to have poor parenting skills. Given the resilience demonstrated by children when rearing environments are improved, however, knowledge of child development and basic child-rearing practices may lessen the stress of parenting for the parent and improve the child's chance for healthy development, in spite of the presence of other "risk" factors.

STRESS AND SUPPORT

Above and beyond the delivery of information on parenting skills, the social support functions of parent education programs may be essential components of comprehensive prevention services. Support-based parent education programs provide information and assistance in a social context, through either parenting group formats or individual home visitors. For many parents who lack a support network, parent education classes or home visits provide a viable way to meet others who are under similar stresses.

The transition to parenthood has been associated with the negative stress factors of increased physical demands, strains in the marital relationship, emotional stresses, and the realization of opportunity costs and restrictions, especially for young, single parents. A "real world" paradigm of looking at abuse prevention emphasizes the situational nature of abuse and suggests that the most salient risk factors may be the situational demands that place the highest levels of stress on those who are predisposed to abuse, in the absence of sufficient support systems. Approaches that seek to reduce stressors vary from support systems with ambiguous or broad-based goals to specific behavior modification programs designed to change a particular type of behavior. Parent education programs for adolescent and adult parents are viewed as important means of removing nonfacilitating environments from family members' lives.

Other parent groups concentrate on humanistic support of parents at risk. They use informal discussion and linkage to appropriate community services. They assume that the provision of social support will have a positive effect on family functioning and that knowledge per se is not enough to change behaviors and attitudes; however, social support may need to be matched to specific stressors (e.g., child behavior problems, family economic difficulties) in order to be effective. Groups may serve different supportive functions from individuals. The value of "kitchen talk," or informal conversations, is important for group members to grow closer by sharing experiences (Powell, 1989).

Unfortunately, it is unclear whether parent support programs are effective in reducing stress and, if they are, which characteristics of the program are effective and which specific stressors are being reduced. Whether increasing parenting knowledge leads to decreased parental stress or whether parenting groups directly alleviate stress, teasing out the differential effects of parent education and support orientations requires careful research. It is also unclear whether an individualized home-visiting program or participation in a support group is more effective for any given individual. Nevertheless, parenting education using these techniques appears desirable. There is wide variability in "parent education," including support groups, community resource networking, home-based programs, and the more traditional lecture/discussion courses. The service providers include professionals such as nurses, social workers, and trained volunteers. The programs can be sponsored by public or private agencies or organizations. The programs may be available to all parents or specific target groups. Though diverse approaches may be effective (depending on one's criterion), identification of a "best" type of program has been unsuccessful. With respect to the clients who are actually served, parents' participation in various types of support and education groups or home-visiting programs may be related to their levels of environmental stress, social networks, and dispositional or demographic characteristics.

EVALUATIONS

Evaluations have yielded tentative support for the use of parent education. Simple evaluative research generally has supported the effectiveness of parenting groups. Educational approaches generally involve the teaching of democratic parenting methods in which the purposes or goals of a behavior are analyzed; the interconnected nature of thoughts, feelings, and behaviors is used to describe the mutual influences of parents and children on one another. Several studies have indicated that parents in more behavior-oriented programs display more physical contact with their children than do controls or parents in nonbehavioral educational parent classes. In one example, the use of child behavior management flash cards (featuring developmental and behavior expectations) in a parenting class with pregnant and parenting teens resulted in knowledge changes that were sustained over 3 months. Many other studies of educational parent classes have documented short-term knowledge and attitude changes among parents. Other studies, however, have found parent education classes to be poorly targeted, sparsely attended, and generally ineffective in changing the knowledge of abuse indicators or appropriate expectations, even for those parents who did regularly attend.

On the whole, parent education shows some promise as an indirect means of preventing child maltreatment, with improved knowledge potentially leading to attitude and behavior changes. Most published materials for abuse and neglect prevention programs, however, have undergone little or no experimental testing. The different curricula also vary in terms of reading level and difficulty, target groups, and approaches that may be more or less effective with various participant groups.

Programs that serve families at risk most successfully have several characteristics in common: 1) formal and informal communication occurs across community organizations, such that parent education and support services do not compete with other services; 2) services for parents are well-coordinated across agencies; 3) programs serve the needs of parents and children; and 4) staff rely on group process techniques more than on a fixed syllabus of topics. Powell (1989) noted a shift from standardized, curriculum-based classes to individualized programs that are culturally responsive and contextually relevant to the family. He also argued for the implementation of programs with sustained contacts (i.e., at least 3 months) in order to achieve the most pervasive and sustained effects on family functioning. A multifaceted approach to preventing maltreatment suggests that education about children's competencies and demands is an important part of abuse prevention but that it must be accompanied by efforts to give support and reduce the situational problems that are interfering with the parents' childrearing.

REFERENCES AND SOURCES FOR FURTHER INFORMATION

Bavolek, S.J., & Comstock, C. (1985). *Nurturing Program for parents and children birth to five years: Program implementation manual* (2nd ed.). Park City, UT: Family Development Resources, Inc.

Powell, D.R. (1989). *Families and early childhood programs.* Washington, DC: National Association for the Education of Young Children.

Rosenberg, M.S., & Reppucci, N.D. (1983). Abusive mothers: Perceptions of their own and their children's behavior. *Journal of Consulting and Clinical Psychology, 51,* 674–682.

THE FIRST STEP: A NEEDS EVALUATION

Prevention programs are founded on the notion that the community is in need of some form of prevention services. The idea for a new program can be generated from a variety of sources—perceptions of community members or service providers, changes in agency priorities, media reports of social problems, or governmental initiatives, among others. Although the pressure to start a program can be great once an idea has been generated, evaluating the community's needs thoroughly is an important first step. A more complete understanding of a community's needs and resources will provide a stable framework on which a successful prevention program can be built.

The needs evaluation process involves gathering information from a variety of sources about a variety of topics. Before a needs assessment is conducted, the people or agency involved in developing the prevention project usually has some idea of the target group, the broad categories of intervention that might be useful, and the negative aspects of the condition to be prevented. For example, an agency might want to target teen mothers with some sort of educational/support intervention to alleviate some of the stress and to compensate for lack of parenting knowledge in young mothers. With that very broad background of ideas, the next step in program planning is the needs evaluation itself. Important steps in the needs evaluation process include the following:

1. *Describe the target group* (age, sex, socioeconomic characteristics, geographic distribution).
2. *Identify major stresses* affecting the target group.
3. *What problems* (as a result of stress) within the target group should be reduced or eliminated with a prevention intervention?
4. *What skills* does the target group need to develop to cope with stress/crisis?
5. *Identify the agencies or groups* in the community that must be involved in planning for this target group. Which person(s) need to be involved?
6. *What steps will be taken to secure the interest and cooperation* of the community groups or agencies?
7. *Establish several tentative objectives* for the intervention project.
8. *Identify intervention strategies* to achieve these objectives.
9. *How will the program be evaluated* to identify needed *administrative* changes while the project is under way?
10. *How will the project be evaluated* to determine the extent to which *intervention objectives* have been met for the target group?
11. *What level of resources* (information, money, support, space, expertise) will be needed? What sources for these resources should be approached? (adapted from Wisconsin Department of Health and Social Services, cited in Price & Smith, 1985, p. 30)

Perhaps the most time-consuming part of a needs evaluation is assessing local services to determine where the gaps are. If you are already involved with the service community, then you may be somewhat familiar with available services. If not, then you may want to make initial contacts with easily identifiable groups or agencies such as the Community Services Board, Department of Social Services, or local advocacy groups. Regardless of where you start, it is important to speak with service providers and other interested parties about their own agencies as well as their familiarity with other community services and needs. This assessment can be done formally with standardized interview or survey protocols or informally through discussions with relevant people.

Koss and Harvey (1991) identified five dimensions by which local services can be assessed:

- *Availability:* What is being offered?
- *Accessibility:* Which people can actually receive the services?
- *Quantity:* How many programs are offered, and how many people can be served?
- *Quality:* How good is the available programming?
- *Legitimacy:* Does the community believe in the providers and services?

These questions are then applied to the relevant services. For example, a needs assessment of parent education services could be applied to available parent education classes, support groups, outreach activities, workshops, and home-visiting programs, as well as other educational activities in a given community. Although it may appear to delay the implementation of a good program, needs assessments are crucial to an accurate understanding of the community's needs. Without such an understanding, even the best-intentioned program may fail because it was implemented improperly or failed to meet existing needs. Information from a thorough needs evaluation can strengthen funding applications and provide a solid foundation for effective programming.

SOURCES FOR FURTHER INFORMATION

Koss, M.P., & Harvey, M.R. (1991). *The rape victim: Community and clinical interventions.* Beverly Hills: Sage Publications.

Price, R., & Smith, S. (1985). *A guide to evaluating prevention programs in mental health.* Washington, DC: U.S. Government Printing Office. (DHHS Publication No. ADM 85-1365)

EVALUATION: MAKING IT WORK FOR YOU

Although many service providers and policy makers agree that evaluation is an important component of any service program, in reality, few effective evaluations are required, funded, and executed for child abuse treatment and prevention programs (Starr, 1990). A number of practical barriers may serve to prevent systematic evaluation of prevention programs. Barriers include lack of funding, lack of time, and lack of knowledge. Often, evaluation is thought to be a large-scale project involving large amounts of staff, time, and money. In reality, evaluation does require varying degrees of time and effort. If done well, however, evaluation can be integrated into the everyday operations of prevention programs, providing critical information for service delivery and funding requests.

Given the realities of limited funding and staffing for most prevention programming, including child abuse and neglect, the desire to focus scarce resources on direct services is understandable. The lack of evaluation, however, truly does a disservice in the long run to service providers, policy makers, and especially program recipients. Policy makers want to fund programs that work, service providers want to meet their clients' needs effectively, and clients want to have their problems addressed. None of this can happen without the knowledge gained from some form of evaluation. This brief discusses the advantages of incorporating evaluation procedures into a prevention program and outlines which types of evaluations are appropriate.

THE BENEFITS OF EVALUATION

- *Evaluation enables you to fine-tune service delivery and adapt to the changing needs of your clients.* Information obtained from sound evaluative techniques can help ensure that services adapt to the changing needs of special groups. Evaluative feedback can fine-tune service delivery and provide evidence of unanticipated benefits. If parent education programs increase parental knowledge (the stated goal) but serve the indirect purpose of empowering parents to become more involved in their child's schooling, then that program benefit needs to be documented.
- *Evaluation feedback can determine whether you are effectively reaching your target group.* Systematic evaluation can also enable service providers to determine whether the stated target group is actually being reached. Demographic and assessment information may show that education program clients are not at risk, low-income parents but instead are middle-income parents who already exhibit adequate levels of parenting skills and knowledge. This type of information may indicate that client recruitment efforts should be adjusted to reach the original target group. The products

of a program evaluation can help program administrators serve clients better by delineating which aspects of the program are successful and which aspects need adjusting or reformulating.

- *Evaluation data can make your program more competitive for funding.* Evaluation data can also serve to justify program efforts to policy makers and other funding sources. Solid information about clients, program activities, and outcome measures provides a comprehensive picture of program achievements and may help providers acquire additional or continued funding. Scarce financial resources require that program efficacy justify significant expenditures. If a parenting education program can document its clientele, service delivery, and changes in outcome measures, then it might be more competitive in a grant funding decision or a round of governmental budget cuts than would other existing programs based solely on good ideas without good data.

Evaluation is an ongoing process that can be integrated into the continued existence of a prevention program. Depending on the intended use of information obtained from an evaluation, one or more types of evaluation may be appropriate. Needs, process, and outcome evaluations each serve a different purpose for a prevention program, although they may overlap in time frame. Needs assessments are covered in another brief and is not addressed here. Efficiency evaluations can provide information about the costs and benefits of a program, but, due to space limitations, this type of evaluation is not reviewed here either.

PROCESS EVALUATION

Once a needs evaluation has been completed, goals and objectives have been defined, and a program has begun, a process evaluation can provide information about the way in which the program is being implemented. Monitoring the implementation process can serve as a method of quality control for the intervention in deciding whether the service is delivered in the intended manner. If parent support groups were intended to serve as the primary service for parents, but attendance suggests that most parents are involved with the program's child care service, then any successes or failures of an outcome evaluation may not necessarily be attributed to the support groups. Modifications of original proposals are not intrinsically negative. Indeed, adapting a program to a particular community's needs can be vital to the success of a program. If changes are made in the course of service delivery, however, then process evaluation data gathered to assist in program replication must reflect those changes, and goals and objectives must be modified accordingly.

A number of questions regarding program implementation can guide a process evaluation. They should focus on comparing the intended or planned service delivery with the program as it is actually being implemented. Example questions in a process evaluation include the following:

- Are participants successfully retained across the length of the program?
- Are program goals and objectives clear, concrete, and measurable? Is programming consistent with the goals and objectives?
- Are program orientations appropriately matched to participants?
- Are programs implemented according to the original intent and design? If not, then are the modifications appropriate?
- Are appropriately trained staff and/or volunteers utilized to implement programs?
- What kinds of data are maintained by the programs regarding program implementation? Are data used to modify programming when appropriate?

Terms such as *appropriate, effective,* and *successful* indicate that some criteria must be developed, either by the evaluator or the program staff (or both) by which implementation can be evaluated.

Examining process can determine whether the appropriate target group is being served and how effectively the program is reaching them. Target groups may go unserved for a number of reasons, including potential clients' lack of awareness of services; practical barriers, such as access to transportation or program costs; or lack of appropriate referrals from other agencies. Even if target groups are reached, information from a process evaluation may suggest that particular program strategies are inappropriate or ineffective. A standard parent education program may reach the targeted group of low-education mothers, but the curriculum format may rely too heavily on verbal and reading skills and thus exceed the literacy levels of participants. This type of mismatch, if uncorrected, may lead to retention problems.

At this point unintended consequences of a program, both positive and negative, can be discovered. An educational workshop series designed for parents at risk may have unintended labeling effects, preventing some parents from identifying themselves as in need of services or leading parents who do attend to view themselves as inadequate. Alternatively, a program that relies on volunteer "program graduates" to facilitate discussion may serve the unintended purpose of empowering and educating those volunteers as well as the program participants.

OUTCOME EVALUATION

An outcome evaluation is designed to assess the effectiveness or impact of a project in terms of its goals and objectives. More common, the outcome evaluation should ultimately help answer the question, "Does this program make a difference?" Of any type of intervention, it is perhaps the most difficult to conduct effective outcome evaluation research for prevention programs for several reasons. These include the complexities of working with agency staff and clients, obtaining information from many different people, and trying to contact clients after a program is completed. Improvements in parenting skills may demonstrate effects for years, and improved child outcomes may not surface until adolescence or adulthood. In the shorter term, true knowledge and behavior change must be demonstrated to last beyond the intervention itself—tracking participants for extensive follow-up can be difficult. These difficulties do not make outcome evaluation impossible; instead, they underscore the need for systematic planning and assessment to ensure that outcome evaluations are valid and useful.

Parent education programs designed to prevent child abuse can utilize a number of outcome indices. Individual programs can measure success by adopting a "small wins strategy." This strategy involves identifying particular factors associated with child abuse that an intervention tries to affect and measuring change. Particularly for parent education programs, these factors can include (but are not limited to) the following:

- *Stress:* individual and family stress; parenting stress and general life stress, including poverty and unemployment; the control of anger and use of coping strategies
- *Developmental expectations:* lack of knowledge of child development, skill deficits, inappropriate expectations
- *Child management:* poor parent–child interactions, skill deficits, problem-solving deficits, ineffective child control
- *Social support:* family and governmental/social services support, lack of knowledge of available resources, inability to gain access to resources, insularity

It is easy (especially for funding sources and legislators) to get caught in the trap of using the ultimate outcome measure—the reduced incidence of child abuse—as the only true outcome measure. Child abuse prevention is the ultimate goal of most programs, but it is important to recognize that child abuse is a complex phenomenon occurring within the interaction of individual, family, and societal forces. True reduction of child abuse and neglect in the general population will depend on comprehensive, multifaceted, long-term strategies. Certainly, we hope that participants in parent education programs are less likely to abuse their children than are other groups at similar risk. Indeed, the number of abuse incidents among program participants may be an appropriate outcome measure (with caveats of confidentiality, permission, and so forth). Outcome evaluations of parent education programs, however, should take a broader view of appropriate outcome measures, both short term and long term.

Ultimately, an effective outcome evaluation should provide information on whether objectives have been achieved, what specific changes have occurred, and why those changes occurred. The need for specific, concrete, measurable objectives is underscored here. Useful objectives will lead to outcome measures that can document change in the level of the criterion variable before and after the intervention, preferably compared with a control group. Participants in a special home-visiting program may demonstrate higher scores on parenting behavior assessments and knowledge tests than a group of parents who were provided only the normal services—access to parenting resource materials.

Data can be used to identify the program elements that are most effective. If educational programming creates behavior change only when in the context of larger comprehensive family services, then short-term parenting programs may not be an effective sole strategy for child abuse prevention. Outcome data can show which parts of a program are working and where resources should be targeted. Moreover, the data can document program worth to external funding agencies, a crucial component of competitive grant applications.

REFERENCES AND SOURCES FOR FURTHER INFORMATION

Galano, J., & Nezlek, J.B. (1986). *Evaluating prevention programs: A training manual*. Richmond: Virginia Department of Mental Health, Mental Retardation and Substance Abuse Services, Office of Prevention, Promotion, and Library Services.

Posavac, E.J., & Carey, R.G. (1989). *Program evaluation: Methods and case studies*. Englewood Cliffs, NJ: Prentice Hall.

Price, R.H., & Smith, S.S. (1985). *A guide to evaluating prevention programs in mental health*. Washington, DC: U.S. Government Printing Office. (DHHS Publication No. ADM 85-1365)

Rossi, P.H., Freeman, H.E., & Wright, S.R. (1979). *Evaluation: A systematic approach*. Beverly Hills: Sage Publications.

USING GOALS AND OBJECTIVES
TO IMPROVE PROGRAMMING

Primary prevention projects often begin with a strong commitment to promoting health and preventing negative outcomes. These commitments provide a guiding philosophy on which prevention programming depends, but concrete goals and objectives can help ensure that the program remains true to its intended purpose and that ideas are translated into service delivery. Identifying measurable goals and objectives, however, can become one of the most difficult activities in prevention programming. As a result, vague goals often are identified quickly in an effort to move directly to service provision. Service delivery can be greatly facilitated, however, by investing time in the development of concrete measurable goals and objectives. This brief focuses on the importance of goals and objectives; how they are developed; and how they can be used successfully to guide future programming, enhance service delivery, and strengthen applications for funding.

WHY GOALS AND OBJECTIVES ARE IMPORTANT

Once the needs of a particular community have been determined and a service delivery format has been selected, concrete goals and objectives should be created for a number of reasons:

- *Goals and objectives make your purpose and intended impact explicit.* Without delineating and agreeing on what the activities of a prevention program are, staff may not all be working toward the same activities and outcomes. Clear goals and objectives can help ensure that all people involved with the project are on the same page. They also provide the measures of impact and outcome—program success can be defined and measured in terms of meeting goals and objectives.
- *Returning to the goals and objectives during the course of service delivery can remind staff of the intended activities and outcomes.* If the program is no longer focusing on the original goals and objectives, then this indicates that either 1) the program has unnecessarily strayed from its intended purpose and needs to get back on track; or 2) the program is intentionally changing in response to something (e.g., changes in population, potential duplication of services), and perhaps goals and objectives need to be reformulated.
- *Goals and objectives enable staff to communicate more effectively about accountability.* Accountability is both internal, in terms of management and staff responsibility, and external, in terms of the criteria by which project success is judged. Determinations of whether goals and objectives have been met can provide feedback to program administrators regarding strengths and weaknesses of implementation. This feedback can also be

used to provide concrete measures of success, as well as areas that deserve more attention, to potential and current funding agencies.

HOW TO CREATE GOALS AND OBJECTIVES

Project goals are general statements that specify the end condition that should occur as a function of the program. Goals should be flexible statements about intended results that connect the program to the larger purpose. For example, the goals of a parent education program may be to increase parents' capability to effectively raise their children or to increase parents' capacity to cope effectively with parent–child conflict. Goals should be usable, practical, and compatible with each other:

Agency purpose:

- General statement with room for flexibility
- Sets the general mission for the agency
- Seldom changed

Program goal:

- General statement of results intended with room for flexibility
- States intent to carry out programs as means to achieve agency purpose
- Seldom changed but more often than purpose

Program objective(s):

- Specific statement with criteria for evaluation built in
- Changed every program budget period (year)

Service goal:

- General statement of the desired end
- Stated for each service unit (e.g., case, group)

Service objectives:

- Specify conditions or behaviors that are intended as outcomes and time for appearance of outcome
- Stated for each service incident (Price & Smith, 1985, p. 49)

Objectives are more specific statements of outcomes that reflect progress toward or achievement of a goal within a specific time frame. Objectives should be measurable, specify the desired end, and specify the criteria that determine whether the desired result has been achieved. In other words, objectives delineate specific means by which particular outcomes will be obtained. It is important that the means to achieve objectives are delineated. Price and Smith (1985) suggested that two types of objectives should be formulated: program objectives and service objectives. *Program objectives* are specific statements of the outcomes that indicate progress toward the goal (or removal of barriers). These objectives also make the time frame explicit. For example, one outcome objective for parent education may be that 80% of parents completing the Nurturing Program in 1993 will have an accurate understanding of parenting practices as measured by the corresponding posttest. *Service objectives* specify how resources will be provided to specific clients (groups or individuals). Continuing the same example, the corresponding service objective may be that 80% of the parents participating in the August–November Parent Nurturing class will demonstrate an accurate understanding of parenting practices as measured by a minimum score of 80% correct on the Nurturing Quiz posttest, administered by the course instructor. These objectives are useful because they state very concrete criteria by which success can be demonstrated.

Objectives have several crucial elements. First, the desired result must be identified (e.g., reduced family stress, improved knowledge of child development). Second, the criteria by which we know we have achieved the desired result must be specified (e.g., 75% of families will report increased access to social support as measured by the X measure, 80% of parents will score at least 80% correct on the X child development test). Finally, the time frame in which the objective must be met is specified (e.g., by the end of the parenting class series, during fiscal year 1993–1994).

Goals and objectives require careful planning and consideration early in the process. If they are utilized properly, however, they can guide the design and implementation of successful prevention programming. Investing in the creation of sound goals and objectives will pay off in the future.

REFERENCES AND SOURCES FOR FURTHER INFORMATION

Galano, J., & Nezlek, J.B. (1986). *Evaluating prevention programs: A training manual*. Richmond: Virginia Department of Mental Health, Mental Retardation and Substance Abuse Services, Office of Prevention, Promotion, and Library Services.

Price, R.H., & Smith, S.S. (1985). *A guide to evaluating prevention programs in mental health*. U.S. Department of Health and Human Services. Washington, DC: U.S. Government Printing Office. (DHHS Publication No. ADM 85-1365)

TARGETING AND RECRUITING CLIENTS

Social services agencies begin with an idea to serve a specific group of clients who are perceived to be in need of services. An agency that has completed a needs assessment and has pulled together the necessary resources to serve clients may still face difficulties with bringing services and clients together, however. Targeting and recruiting clients in an effective manner often are challenging for agencies and prevention programs. This brief offers some suggestions for identifying potential client groups and recruiting them to participate in your program.

TARGETING CLIENTS

The group of clients to be targeted by a program may be determined by a needs assessment of community services and by the mission statement of the program. Family violence prevention programs sometimes focus on specific groups at risk for family violence, such as teen mothers or socially isolated parents. Others may focus on a broader group of all parents in a community, using a primary prevention model. Once the group is determined, the task of targeting program content and resources to meet the needs of the group is the next step. A thorough knowledge of the group of interest and the factors that place them at risk for family violence is necessary for targeting programs to the clients. The means of advertising the services must be appropriate to the group targeted as well.

A program can view recruiting clients as "marketing" services to consumers, its potential clients. The variety of options for marketing social services programs is similar to that of any other product or service. These range from television, radio, and newspaper advertisements to billboards, posters, brochures, and handouts to word-of-mouth and direct marketing. Attracting clients to social services can require a delicacy that is not possible in a public advertising campaign. Also, with funding for social programs being as it is, the expense of such campaigns can be beyond the budget of most programs. For both of these reasons, most agencies rely on the less efficient, less costly, and more personal means of communication. In many ways, such an immediate personal connection may be the most effective way of reaching out to clients and linking them to services.

For example, many programs attempt to reach teenage mothers or mothers in isolated rural areas directly through the maternity units of area hospitals. If the hospitals allow access to these mothers, then the advantages of this approach are many. Most new parents in a community can be reached, parents may be linked to services early, and agencies may gain added credibility through a hospital's recommendation. Teen mothers could also be contacted through high school nurses or guidance counselors who have contact with teens in the schools or in home-based education. Reaching the general population of parents in a community can be accomplished by sending fliers home from school with children. All of these direct means of contacting parents require the permission of schools or hospitals and involve issues of confidentiality or other personal rights of families. Newspaper ads, posters, and word-of-mouth are common means of marketing that often are within the budget of social services programs. Newspaper articles written about programs represent free advertisement and can be valuable for public relations. Public service announcements and donated advertising space also are common avenues. Another common means of advertising services is public speaking engagements at local fairs or holding open houses. Some programs even sponsor parenting fairs or child abuse awareness days in order to spread the word about their services. Sometimes marketing firms are willing to donate time and expertise to helping human services agencies. This option is always worth exploring, especially for programs that are experiencing difficulties in recruitment and that lack expertise in marketing.

NETWORKING WITH RELATED AGENCIES

Especially for programs that deal with clients mandated to attend parenting groups, a good relationship with other agencies is helpful in maintaining a source of clients. Interagency collaboration is often cited as important for getting referrals for services. Programs that are successful in getting referrals often report positive relationships with local courts, Department of Social Services, or child abuse prevention boards. As mentioned previously, relationships with schools and hospitals can be valuable assets.

"SELLING" YOUR PROGRAM

Reaching clients with the message is the first and crucial step in recruitment but clearly is no guarantee that clients will use the available services. Programs must be "sold" to clients. The two essential issues involved in selling programs are approachability and accessibility.

Approachability

Programs are designed for those in need of services, but individuals rarely like to think of themselves as in need. This issue is particularly true of programs for preventing family violence. Few (if any) parents want to consider themselves as at risk for becoming abusive. If parents perceive such programs as having been designed for abusive parents, then they are not likely to identify the services as useful for them. Making programs approachable requires careful attention to issues of labeling and social stigma. For example, programs that target a general population of parents in a community can market their education and support services to good, caring parents who wish to become better parents. Even if a program is targeting parents at risk, appealing to the competence of parents is a worthwhile approach. Programs should be tailored to the educational levels of participants. For example, a program geared toward highly educated parents should be intellectually challenging enough to engage clients, or one designed for parents with less education should avoid making clients feel "dumb" by scaling down complicated materials in handouts.

Having program staff members who are from the same community or who are perceived to be similar to clients in terms of race, gender, or culture can benefit the perception of approachability. Some programs that have used former clients as volunteer group facilitators have found that in doing so, they have improved the perception of approachability. Efforts to avoid the social stigma of these services include avoiding any mention of child abuse prevention and linking services to already approachable organizations, such as child care centers or YMCAs.

Accessibility

Even clients who view programs as being well suited to their needs may face practical difficulties in using the services. Especially when dealing with poor, isolated parents, services that require clients to arrange child care and transportation may not be appropriate. Programs that are successful in providing services to these types of clients have been those that account for these difficulties. For example, some provide van transportation to bring families to programs and set up child care or design groups such that children can attend. Many agencies bring the services to the clients through home-visiting programs or through running groups in housing projects, local churches, or community buildings. Programs that require parents to meet in groups increase accessibility by finding geographically central locations, by alternating locations within a community, or by housing meetings in buildings on a public transportation route.

Social services agencies generally have the best of intentions and work very hard to make services and resources available to those who are likely to benefit. Although many programs have waiting lists of clients seeking their services, recruiting clients can be a source of frustration if clients are unable, for a variety of reasons, to gain access to available services. Identifying a target group, determining the appropriate means of reaching them, and making services approachable and accessible can assist service providers in delivering effective programs to the appropriate clientele.

HOW TO IMPROVE CLIENT RETENTION

Keeping clients interested in staying with your prevention program is an important issue, and it poses a very significant problem for most prevention programs. After you have decided on your target group and the goals for your intervention or prevention program through a complete needs assessment and gone to great lengths to recruit clients, you begin your parent education program only to find that attendance begins to trail off rapidly from week to week. What can you do?

WHY WORRY ABOUT CLIENT RETENTION?

Is client attrition important, beyond the fact that you are serving fewer people than you had hoped to serve? Yes, in that those individuals who "drop out" may be different from those who stay with the program. For instance, the five young mothers who stopped coming to your parent support group may have been at greater risk for abusing their children than the nine who kept coming (e.g., they are more isolated, less knowledgeable about child development and disciplinary techniques, and more stressed by poor marital relationships and lack of stable incomes). In this case, you are not only serving fewer individuals, but you are also failing to retain those individuals who may need the most help. In addition, you may not know that these clients are, in fact, at greater risk if they drop out early in the program. Thus, it becomes important to work at retaining the clients that you diligently targeted and recruited.

WAYS TO IMPROVE RETENTION

- *Keep it simple.* Your first meeting is the key to getting parents interested. Keep it simple, perhaps short, and let the group get to know you and one another. After a rapport-building first meeting, move on to more of the "meat" of the program.
- *Keep interest.* Nobody, including the facilitator, wants a boring program, so be as dynamic and as warm and open as you can. Show the parents that you are there to share some information and to facilitate discussion but that the group will be both helpful and interesting.
- *Tangible rewards.* If possible, offer something in return. Tangible items such as a door prize, a free dinner at every class, or perhaps an incentive to finish or "pass" the program (e.g., a graduation party) may go a long way.
- *Make it fun.* Some programs try to make the class a fun social experience for participants so that they get to know one another and expand their social network. You might want to encourage some participants to exchange telephone numbers and carpool/bus/walk together to the program, if transportation is not provided.

- *Transportation.* Arranging transportation to and from the program is an essential element to successful recruitment and retention. Quite simply, people might not come if you do not go and get them. They may not have the means to get to you, or it may be "too much of a hassle" unless you make arrangements for them. People rarely will stand you up if they know that you are coming to pick them up. If you need to, offer the rides in the program's van for trips to the doctor or the grocery store for participants. The van or car ride to the program can also be a great time to get to know one another, in a less formal setting than that of the "class."

- *Location.* The location of your meeting place is important in terms of convenience for the participants. Participants are more likely to get to know one another if the program meets in their own community. Meetings in community settings may be more convenient and less stigmatizing than those held in government or social services offices. Location also may solve the transportation issue if the program is on a bus line in a city or meets in several places close to clients' neighborhoods.

- *Child care.* Child care is another consideration. Without a nursery or a few volunteers to take care of children while their parents are in the group, it may not be feasible for parents to attend. Some programs, such as Portsmouth's Good Beginnings, have parents and their infants attend in order to observe their interactions and alleviate the issue of child care.

- *Literacy concerns.* Consider the literacy or educational level of the participants, and tailor your materials to their needs. Some participants may stop coming to your program if they feel "dumb" or embarrassed about their inability to read, write, or understand the curriculum. Family Focus in Warsaw combats this problem by scaling down written handouts to a simpler level or by presenting pictures. If many in the class do not read or if they have a low reading level, then try to convey materials and administer evaluation instruments orally.

- *Service links.* Help participants link to other services, toward a goal of continuity of services. This will enable your clients to receive all of the services available to them without unnecessary duplications and confusion.

- *Ask what they want.* Most important and most basic (although most frequently overlooked), ask the participants what they want from the program. Once you know their needs and hopes for the program, you can plan more effectively how to help and retain the parents.

- *Reevaluate.* When you start a program, do a needs assessment (see "The First Step: A Needs Evaluation" in this appendix) to figure out which group you will serve and which orientation or means of parent education you will follow. Periodically, you should reevaluate your approach and adjust goals and objectives as necessary with respect to client retention.

These are just a few suggestions to get you thinking about how to improve client retention for your program. Of course, no program can be expected—or even needs—to do all of these things; rather, each program should select the suggestions that fit its particular needs. Some of the specifics about how you think about and work toward client retention may vary across program orientations (home visiting or class), urban or rural settings, or target groups (teen parents or adults). At a more general level, however, attention to the needs and wishes of your participants should help you to improve your program's retention of clients and make it easier for you to serve your clients in an effective manner.

REFERENCES AND SOURCES FOR FURTHER INFORMATION

Galano, J., & Nezlek, J.B. (1986). *Evaluating prevention programs: A training manual*. Richmond: Virginia Department of Mental Health, Mental Retardation and Substance Abuse Services, Office of Prevention, Promotion, and Library Services.

Kamerman, S., & Kahn, A. (1976). *Social services in the United States: Policies and programs*. Philadelphia: Temple University Press.

MANAGING STAFF AND VOLUNTEERS

The size and structure of an organization's staff is largely dependent on the scope of the organizational goals and objectives as well as funding. In social services agencies, it is not uncommon for the funding to be so minimal that small staffs are expected to perform excessive amounts of work in order to meet program goals. Therefore, managing human resources, training personnel, and monitoring job-related stress and job satisfaction become critical issues.

MANAGING HUMAN RESOURCES

Job Descriptions

Establishing clear, specific written job descriptions is helpful for several reasons. Doing so gives all members of the organization a knowledge of what is expected of them and what they can expect of others. Good job descriptions can eliminate confusion as to who is expected to perform which tasks and can be helpful in evaluating individual job performance. It is important, of course, to recognize that descriptions need to maintain flexibility and cannot cover everything, especially if the jobs are as complex as is typical in social services agencies. In writing job descriptions, it should be clear that all of the program's goals and objectives are broken down into tasks for which someone within the organization is responsible. If an evaluation of overall program goals suggests that a problem exists, then job descriptions can be useful in assessing the problem's cause.

Performance Evaluation

Although most members of social services organizations are devoted to their work and perform competently, monitoring job performance is an important component to ensure the quality of service delivery. Methods for individual job performance evaluation vary from organization to organization. Many find that annual or more frequent evaluations are useful and follow a fairly structured format for doing so. Others are less formal. Many administrators find that sitting in on programs, even those run by experienced staff, is helpful, both for supervision of staff members and for maintaining contact with clients. It is not uncommon for social services programs to use staff members who are officially employed by other community agencies. It is important that even when personnel are "borrowed," their roles should be well defined and evaluated.

TRAINING PERSONNEL

In social services programs, as in all organizations, training staff members is an important consideration. Initial training can be formal and highly structured, consisting of classroom presentations, reading of organization manuals, and supervision for a predetermined period. Some programs have developed their own training manuals for specific positions, such as home visitors or parent educators. However, staff members are sometimes given informal on-the-job peer supervision for a period of time before they feel comfortable working independently. The degree to which technical expertise or complex decision making are required for the position determines the appropriateness of the various training options. Unfortunately, given the limited resources and fast turnover associated with social services agencies, employees are sometimes placed into positions with inadequate training. It is up to individual programs to examine the written job descriptions and carefully consider the appropriate training required for competence in all aspects of the position. Although some programs are coordinated by individuals with advanced degrees in management, psychology, or social work, others have found that employees with strong interpersonal skills in relating to special client groups are just as appropriate or even more effective without such training and expertise.

After initial job training, opportunities for continuing education ideally should be made available for staff members as a component of training. Many programs have been successful in recruiting professionals from the community to conduct workshops for their staff, sometimes on a volunteer basis. Organizations often can take advantage of local or regional workshops and training on job-related issues. Although continuing education may take time away from the direct services that the staff provide, the value of maintaining and improving skills with training updates can keep staff informed of current developments and new ideas. Moreover, it creates an environment that values learning and boosts staff morale.

MONITORING JOB-RELATED STRESS AND JOB SATISFACTION

Although rewarding, the demanding, interpersonal nature of human services work can often lead to high levels of stress or job burnout. Organizations should monitor the job satisfaction and job-related stress of employees. Individuals typically are attracted to social services fields because of the intrinsic rewards of the work. The high rates of job turnover in these agencies, however, suggest that such rewards are not great enough to keep people motivated for long periods of time in the absence of extrinsic rewards. Assessing job satisfaction and stress is particularly important because burnout and high turnover are so common. Organizations can evaluate satisfaction and stress through questionnaires with established reliability and validity, through informal open-ended questionnaires, or through unstructured interviews with individuals or groups of staff members.

Social services agencies are likely to find that extrinsic rewards are inadequate, especially the typically low salaries; but an accurate assessment of the sources of dissatisfaction and stress is crucial in preventing burnout and high turnover among workers. For example, many workers report that educational opportunities that are made available to staff are valuable in meeting future career goals. But even if extrinsic rewards are not an issue or cannot be improved, job satisfaction is likely to be increased if employees sense that the organization is taking care of them. For example, staff-only workshops or retreats, periodic group evaluation, and goal setting can be helpful. When possible, debriefing (following stressful incidents) and other stress-reducing activities should be explored and implemented.

Individuals who are in charge of human services agencies have a wide variety of training and expertise in managing human resources. Regardless of one's knowledge or background in this area, managing and training staff can be challenging for any social services organization. The commitment of employees to service delivery generally is present in these settings, but it is not enough. Monitoring personnel issues is important in order to maintain service quality, staff satisfaction, and organizational stability.

INTERAGENCY COLLABORATION

Social services programs often must face the continual challenge of a scarcity of resources. In addition, the problems handled by social services programs may be too complex and far-reaching for any individual agency to resolve alone. Therefore, many agencies must rely on interagency collaboration to maximize resources and increase the effectiveness of their work. Organizations united for a common cause may constitute a "critical mass," allowing them to accomplish goals beyond the reach of any individual agency (Brown, 1984). Another incentive for interagency collaboration is provided by granting agencies, especially government, which with limited funds to award generally look favorably upon interagency collaboration while scowling at duplication of services.

Gray (1985) defined collaboration as "(1) the pooling of appreciations and/or tangible resources, e.g., information, money, labor, etc., (2) by two or more stakeholders, (3) to solve a set of problems which neither can solve individually" (p. 912). The efforts of one agency may reinforce and magnify that of another. More comprehensive services may be made available. A greater number and diversity of clients may be reached, and a better understanding of these clients may be achieved. In this regard, the work of the whole may be greater than the sum of the individual agencies.

ESTABLISHING INTERAGENCY COLLABORATION

According to Price and Smith (1985), the following questions can be used to guide interagency collaboration efforts when a structure for collaboration has not yet been established:

1. What are the other agencies and groups in the community that are involved with the target group and/or share similar goals?
2. How do these agencies interact with each other?
3. Are there planning councils or other coordinating agencies that can facilitate collaboration?
4. What steps need to be taken to secure the interest and cooperation of the other agencies and groups?

The first three questions can be addressed within the context of a community needs assessment. In conducting a needs assessment, projects can educate other agencies and groups about the services that the project will offer, highlight common goals, and begin to build an informal network. Interagency collaboration also can be encouraged through the formation of an advisory board for the project composed of personnel, including administrators and frontline staff, from other organizations. Participation by project staff on other agencies' advisory boards, planning councils, and coordinating agencies likewise can facilitate interagency collaboration. Many communities already have established service boards to oversee the activities of all social services agencies in the area.

Gray (1985) broke down the planning necessary for successful interagency collaboration into three stages:

1. Problem setting—identifying the collaborating agencies and acknowledging a common guiding purpose
2. Direction setting—articulating the values held by the participating agencies and agreeing on shared goals
3. Structuring—creating a structure to support long-term collaboration allowing for ongoing contact and negotiation between agencies

ADDITIONAL KEYS TO SUCCESSFUL COLLABORATION

Power and responsibility do not necessarily need to be divided equally between or among collaborating agencies, but they must be shared in order for true collaboration to occur (Gray, 1985). A formal agreement or contract specifying the goals and responsibilities of each collaborating agency can enable programs and agencies to work together more easily. Regular follow-up, through direct contact, telephone, or written report, of clients referred from one agency to another for service(s) can ensure comprehensive, integrated service delivery as well as help agencies remain informed of each others' activities.

FURTHER CONSIDERATIONS

Successful interagency collaboration does not come about without considerable effort and commitment. Agencies must accept a loss of autonomy in working with others. Often, unfavorable misperceptions and competitive feelings must be overcome. Collaborative work around sensitive issues, such as teenage pregnancy, can be particularly difficult. Agencies representing contrasting values may not be able to resolve their philosophical differences. These and other costs should be anticipated to the extent possible, and efforts should be taken to minimize them. The benefits from carefully planned and monitored interagency collaboration potentially can far exceed the costs. Although a formal structure for collaboration must be emphasized, the importance of informal contact between agencies should not be overlooked. Opportunities to meet informally and share experiences and thoughts can relieve stress, rejuvenate staff, and yield creative new ideas.

REFERENCES AND SOURCES FOR FURTHER INFORMATION

Brown, C. (1984). *The art of coalition building: A guide for community leaders.* New York: The American Jewish Committee.
Gray, B. (1985). Conditions facilitating interorganizational collaboration. *Human Relations, 38,* 911–936.
Price, R.H., & Smith, S.S. (1985). *A guide to evaluating prevention programs in mental health.* Washington, DC: U.S. Government Printing Office. (DHHS Publication No. ADM 85-1365)

WORKING WITH AN ADVISORY BOARD

The relationship between a nonprofit prevention program and its advisory board, or board of directors, can be both rewarding and important to the success of the program, but it often falls short of this goal. Ideally, a good, working board will allow staff to focus more heavily on service delivery by handling administrative and policy issues such as fund-raising and program development. In addition, board members may provide more access to resources in the community and can lend their particular expertise to challenges as they arise.

HOW TO SET UP AN ADVISORY BOARD

The following are some suggestions for programs setting up boards; programs with existing boards may find it helpful to review these steps in evaluating and/or revising current board structure and activities.

- Decide why you want to have an advisory board and how it will be useful to your program. Boards can have a variety of purposes (e.g., fund-raising, program development, public affairs, a combination of these roles), and it is important to have a firm idea of what you will expect from the board as a whole and from individual members.
- Once you have an idea of the board's primary functions, it is important to organize it so that it may effectively carry out this work. This usually happens through the development of a board structure, which outlines the rules that will govern the board, who will be in charge, when meetings will occur and where, and what committees will be formed. Boards often are subdivided into committees for fund-raising, program development, special events, public affairs, long-range planning, and nominating.
- Devise a board plan, specifying the objective of the board and which balance of members will best accommodate these goals. Usually, it is ideal to have a balanced mix of local business leaders, social services professionals, community leaders, representatives from local agencies, volunteers, and even clients.
- It is equally important to specify how the board will function in relation to the program staff. The director of the program usually serves as a liaison between the board and the rest of the staff. Determine whether decisions voted on by the board will be suggestions for program activity or policy that program staff are expected to follow.
- Provide written job descriptions for board members, and go over these before a member agrees to serve on the board to avoid confusion over expectations, especially regarding financial and time commitments. Also, decide whether there will be board term limits and what is expected in terms of attendance at board meetings, special events, and other program activities.

USING A BOARD EFFECTIVELY

Once a board is in place, educate board members about your program and what it does—they will be key representatives of your project in the community. You may want to bring members to program sites or have them accompany you to fund-raising meetings with local business people. Focus on individual members' strengths and interests in order to keep them motivated and involved, and provide the board with concrete "projects" to tackle. At the same time, do not be shy about holding board members to their job descriptions! If necessary, have the board chair or other board members discuss job expectations with a member who is not remaining active.

RESTRUCTURING AND REVITALIZING AN EXISTING BOARD

Many nonprofit organizations have dealt with advisory boards that have ceased to be effective. Some of the most common problems are inactive members, confusion over financial expectations, and membership that does not reflect a program's status or needs in the community. Confronting these issues may be difficult, but it can lead to a restructuring of the board to make it more effective in the long run.

- First, set up an ad hoc committee to review the existing board functions, membership, and activities, and then review their findings with the entire board.
- If a written board plan is not already in place, then challenge the ad hoc committee to devise one that specifies the purpose of the board and expectations of individual members, and have the board vote on a final plan. This can include important changes, such as term limits, written job descriptions and financial agreements, and attendance requirements.
- If possible, schedule a board retreat (this could become an annual event) for board members to review their activities, brainstorm about ways to revitalize the board, and become reacquainted with the program mission and activities. This also is a good time for members to create a "wish list" of potential board members to be recruited and nominated.

REFERENCES AND SOURCES FOR FURTHER INFORMATION

Conrad, W.R., & Glenn, W.E. (1983). *The effective voluntary board of directors: What it is and how it works.* Chicago: Swallow Press.

FUND-RAISING

Prevention projects often suffer from lack of adequate funding for a number of reasons, ranging from inadequate time and staff for fund-raising efforts to lack of knowledge about the funding process. Small programs, in particular, often find fund-raising an overwhelming task and tend to rely on a small number of funding sources (e.g., the United Way, an annual special event, a state agency funding stream). In order to provide ongoing, high-quality services to clients, however, stable funding is essential. Devising a strategic plan for seeking funds, and providing staff (or volunteers) with sufficient time and expertise to research and solicit money from a variety of sources is a worthy investment for several reasons:

- *Stable sources of funding allow you to plan for and provide high-quality direct services to clients.* If fund-raising is not an ongoing, planned activity, then a program may have to rely on inadequate, intermittent sources of funding. This can interrupt or even halt the provision of direct services and lead to "emergency" fund-raising, which tends to take even more time away from services and is very stressful for staff, volunteers, and potential donors. Setting annual and long-term fund-raising goals to match projected services and outlining methods for achieving those goals can help ensure that service needs will be met consistently.
- *Foundations and corporate donors, in particular, tend to support programs with explicit service and budgetary goals.* Most private foundations, government agencies, and corporate donors tend to support programs with explicit service and budget plans. Although preparing budgets, writing grant proposals, and documenting program effectiveness can be time consuming, they are critical factors in funding decisions made by large funding sources. In addition, these funding sources usually prefer not to be a program's sole source of financial support; showing that your program is well-supported by individuals and businesses in your local community tells potential grantors that you are an important presence in the community with long-term staying power.

THE FIRST STEPS TOWARD EFFECTIVE FUND-RAISING

One of the first steps that a program can take toward conducting more effective fund-raising is to set fund-raising as an explicit priority within the organization. This may require setting some time aside from direct services; undeniably, successful fund-raising requires administrative work and a commitment to researching funding sources and soliciting gifts throughout the year.

Whatever funding sources you are interested in tapping, there are some initial steps that must be taken:

- Document your program's mission, goals, and objectives so that you and potential funding sources have a clear idea of what your program does, the client group that it serves, and why your program is necessary to meet community needs.
- Create an immediate and long-range plan, including current services provided and funds necessary to continue, as well as projected or ideal services and budgetary needs for the next 5- and 10-year periods. This information will help you when grant proposals require budget sections. Do not forget to include nonfinancial needs, such as office and meeting space, or administrative needs, such as computer hardware.
- Design a strategic fund-raising plan, including a rough number of potential foundations, corporations (for financial or in-kind gifts), and individuals (for both large, personally solicited gifts and direct-mail campaigns). This should include a balance of funding sources (i.e., you may end up going after a few large foundations while sending a large number of direct-mail requests to individuals).
- Research potential funding sources—it does not do you any good to spend time, energy, and money trying to get money from foundations, corporations, or individuals that are not interested in what you do. Foundations and corporations will mail annual reports and guidelines for applying (including proposal deadlines) upon request.

HINTS FOR GOING AFTER FOUNDATIONS, CORPORATIONS, AND INDIVIDUALS

Different sources of funding often require slightly different fund-raising tactics.

Soliciting Individual Donors

- Do not overlook your advisory board members both as sources of funds (you should decide whether adopting a "give-or-get" policy is what you want, and write this expectation into board members' job descriptions) and as people who can ask other professionals for funds. Board members often have good business contacts in the community.
- Decide whether direct-mail campaigns can help your program, and coordinate a mailing to individual donors.
- Draw up a list of "heavy hitters" in your community who may be appropriate for larger individual donations.
- One-time or annual special events may be particularly efficient in raising a large amount of funds from individuals and/or corporate sponsors.

Going after corporate money

- Local businesses often are the best supporters of community programs. Research corporations in your area, and request information on their philanthropic giving guidelines.
- Set up a recognition program so that levels of corporate support are tied to some form of thanks (e.g., listing on special events programs).

Writing foundation grant proposals

- Do your research! Request funding guidelines from foundations that appear to be interested in the work that you do. Note application deadlines carefully.

Recommended Measures for Outcome Evaluation

compiled by Deborah J. Land

PARENTING STRESS INDEX (PSI)

Author: Abidin

Purpose: To measure the amount of stress experienced by the parent as a result of the parenting role.

Description: Long form is a 101-item self-report questionnaire. Short form has 36 items. A fifth-grade reading level is necessary. Administration time is 20–30 minutes for the long form and 10 minutes for the short form. Available in both English and Spanish.

Cost: Write to obtain a price sheet.

Contact: Pediatric Psychology Press
320 Terrell Road West
Charlottesville, VA 22901

Reliability: Validity of the PSI–Long Form was demonstrated by showing that test scores were positively correlated with other measures of the same construct. The derived alpha reliability coefficients are .95 for the total score, .89 for the parent domain, and .93 for the child domain; however, the short form is recommended because of stability of factor structure and shorter administration time.

SUPPORT FUNCTIONS SCALE

Authors: Dunst & Trivette

Purpose: To measure how much participants need social support and other types of assistance.

Deborah J. Land is a Ph.D. candidate in community psychology at the University of Virginia, Charlottesville.

Description: On a 5-point scale, respondents rate how often they have or feel the need for 12 types of help or assistance.

Cost: Instrument may be copied free of charge.

Source: Dunst, C.J., Trivette, C.M., & Deal, A.G. (1988). *Enabling and empowering families: Principles and guidelines for practice.* Cambridge, MA: Brookline Books.

CHILD ABUSE POTENTIAL INVENTORY (CAP INVENTORY)

Author: Milner

Purpose: To measure a parent's potential for being abusive.

Description: A 160-item questionnaire that asks parents to agree or disagree with statements reflecting child problems, discipline, and personality characteristics. Requires a third-grade reading level. Administration time is approximately 15–20 minutes.

Cost: Write for price sheet.

Contact: Psytec, Inc.
P.O. Box 564
Dekalb, IL 60115
(815) 758-1415

Reliability: The CAP has been able to correctly identify 85% of respondents (83% of abusers and 88% of nonabusers). The reliability is over 92% for all respondents.

ADULT-ADOLESCENT PARENTING INVENTORY (AAPI)

Author: Bavolek

Purpose: To assess parenting and child-rearing attitudes that indicate high risk for child abuse and neglect.

Description: Thirty-two–item self-report questionnaire. A fifth-grade reading level is necessary.

Cost: AAPI Handbook—$17   Form A Scoring Stencil—$4
Profile/Worksheets (pkg. 40)—$7   Test Form B (pkg. 20)—$9.50
Test Form A (pkg. 20)—$9.50   Form B Scoring Stencil—$4

Contact: Family Development Resources, Inc.
3160 Pinebrook Road
Park City, UT 84060
(800) 688-5822

Reliability: The author reports reliabilities equal to or greater than .70 for each of four subscales. Test–retest reliability of the entire test is .76.

KNOWLEDGE OF CHILD DEVELOPMENT INVENTORY

Authors: Larsen & Juhasz

Purpose: To measure knowledge of child development, from birth to 3 years.

Description: Fifty-six multiple-choice questions measuring four areas: emotional, cognitive, physical, and social development. Requires an eighth-grade reading level.

Cost: Instrument may be copied free of charge.
Source: Larsen, J.J., & Juhasz, A.M. (1986). The Knowledge of Child
                 Development Inventory. *Adolescence, 21,* 39–54.

HOME OBSERVATION FOR
MEASUREMENT OF THE ENVIRONMENT (HOME)

Authors: Caldwell & Bradley
Purpose: To identify home environments that pose risks for children's develop-
                 ment and to evaluate programs designed to improve parenting skills.
Description: Administration time is approximately 1 hour. Three separate forms are
                 used:

                 1. Parents with infants form—birth to age 3
                 2. Preschool form—ages 3–6
                 3. Elementary school form—ages 6–10

Cost: Detailed Manual—$9   Observation Forms (pkg. 10)—$1
Contact: Center for Research on Teaching and Learning
                 College of Education, Room 205
                 University of Arkansas at Little Rock
                 2801 S. University Avenue
                 Little Rock, AR 72204
                 (510) 569-3422
Reliability: Internal consistency for total scores and subscales ranges from .38 to
                 .93 across the three forms.

SELF-ESTEEM SCALE

Author: Rosenberg
Purpose: To measure an individual's self-attitudes and general self-esteem.
Description: Ten questions that require the respondent to rate the frequency of a
                 feeling on a 4-point scale. Available in both Spanish and English.
Cost: Instrument may be copied free of charge.
Source: Rosenberg, M. (1965). *Society and the adolescent self-image.*
                 Princeton, NJ: Princeton University Press.

Prices are subject to change.

Additional Measures for Evaluation

compiled by Deborah J. Land

appendix • C

CONTENTS

Deborah J. Land is a Ph.D. candidate in community psychology at the University of Virginia, Charlottesville.

PARENTING

ADULT-ADOLESCENT PARENTING INVENTORY (AAPI)[1]

Author:	Bavolek
Purpose:	To assess parenting and child-rearing attitudes that indicate high risk for child abuse and neglect.
Description:	Thirty-two–item self-report questionnaire. A fifth-grade reading level is necessary.
Cost:	AAPI Handbook—$17 Form A Scoring Stencil—$4
	Profile/Worksheets (pkg. 40)—$7 Test Form B (pkg. 20)—$9.50
	Test Form A (pkg. 20)—$9.50 Form B Scoring Stencil—$4
Contact:	Family Development Resources, Inc.
	3160 Pinebrook Road
	Park City, UT 84060
	(800) 688-5822
Reliability:	The author reports reliabilities equal or greater than .70 for each of four subscales. Test–retest reliability of the entire test is .76.

CHILD ABUSE POTENTIAL INVENTORY (CAP INVENTORY)[1]

Author:	Milner
Purpose:	To measure a parent's potential for being abusive.
Description:	A 160-item questionnaire that asks parents to agree or disagree with statements reflecting child problems, discipline, and personality characteristics. Requires a third-grade reading level. Administration time is approximately 15–20 minutes.
Cost:	Write for price sheet.
Contact:	Psytec, Inc.
	P.O. Box 564
	Dekalb, IL 60115
	(815) 758-1415
Reliability:	The CAP has been able to correctly identify 85% of respondents (83% of abusers and 88% of nonabusers). The reliability is over 92% for all respondents.

FAMILY ENVIRONMENT SCALE (FES)[2]

Author:	Moos
Purpose:	To assess the social-environmental characteristics of families.
Description:	Three forms are administered to all family members. Each form has 90 statements requiring a "true" or "false" answer.
Contact:	Consulting Psychologists Press, Inc.
	3803 E. Bayshore Road
	Palo Alto, CA 94303
	(800) 624-1765
Reliability:	Normative data were collected on 1,125 normal and 500 distressed families. The instrument appears valid and reliable.

HOME OBSERVATION FOR MEASUREMENT OF THE ENVIRONMENT (HOME)[1]

Authors: Caldwell & Bradley

Purpose: To identify home environments that pose risks for children's development and to evaluate programs designed to improve parenting skills.

Description: Administration time is approximately 1 hour. Three separate forms are used:

1.   Parents with infants form—birth to age 3
2.   Preschool form—ages 3–6
3.   Elementary school form—ages 6–10

Cost: Detailed Manual—$9   Observation Forms (pkg. 10)—$1

Contact: Center for Research on Teaching and Learning
College of Education, Room 205
University of Arkansas at Little Rock
2801 S. University Avenue
Little Rock, AR 72204
(510) 569-3422

Reliability: Internal consistency for total scores and subscales ranges from .38 to .93 across the three forms.

KNOWLEDGE OF CHILD DEVELOPMENT INVENTORY[1]

Authors: Larsen & Juhasz

Purpose: To measure knowledge of child development, from birth to 3 years.

Description: Fifty-six multiple-choice questions measuring four areas: emotional, cognitive, physical, and social development. Requires an eighth-grade reading level.

Cost: Instrument may be copied free of charge.

Source: Larsen, J.J., & Juhasz, A.M. (1986). The Knowledge of Child Development Inventory. *Adolescence, 21,* 39–54.

KNOWLEDGE OF DISCIPLINE ALTERNATIVES[1]

Author: Treichel

Purpose: To measure knowledge of discipline alternatives.

Description: Twenty-nine true/false questions and one short-answer question.

Cost: A one-time copyright fee of $20.

Contact: Christa Treichel, Ph.D.
Cooperative Ventures
1272 Dayton Avenue
St. Paul, MN 55104

LISTENING FOR FEELINGS OF CHILDREN[1]

Purpose: To examine parents' affective recognition of typical children's messages.

Description: Twenty short-answer questions.

| Cost: | Instrument may be copied free of charge. |
| Source: | Gordon, T. (1970). *Parent Effectiveness Training*. New York: Peter H. Wyden Corp. |

PARENT BEHAVIOR SCALE[1]

Author:	Treichel
Purpose:	An observational form that measures parent behavior in three areas: parent–child communication, discipline, and physical care.
Description:	Thirty-eight questions that require an observer to rate the frequency of an event on a 4-point scale. The administrator must have observed the mother with her child on at least five occasions before answering the questions.
Cost:	A one-time copyright fee of $20.
Contact:	Christa Treichel, Ph.D.
	Cooperative Ventures
	1272 Dayton Avenue
	St. Paul, MN 55104

CHILD DEVELOPMENT

THE DENVER DEVELOPMENTAL SCREENING TEST

Author: Frankenburg

Purpose: To evaluate a child's development in several domains and to screen for
                   developmental delay.

Description: Assesses four aspects of a child's development: gross motor, fine mo-
                   tor adaptive, language, and personal-social.

Contact: William K. Frankenburg, M.D.
                   Department of Pediatrics
                   University of Colorado
                   Health Sciences Center
                   Box C-223
                   4200 E. 9th Avenue
                   Denver, CO 80262

STRESS AND COPING

ADOLESCENT COPING ORIENTATION
FOR PROBLEM EXPERIENCES (ACOPE)[1]

Authors:	Patterson, McCubbin, & Needle
Purpose:	To identify the behaviors that adolescents find helpful in managing problems or difficult situations.
Description:	Fifty-four questions that require the respondent to rate the frequency of an event on a 5-point scale.
Cost:	A one-time copyright fee of $5.
Contact:	Family Stress Coping and Health Project
	1300 Linden Drive
	University of Wisconsin–Madison
	Madison, WI 53706
	(608) 262-5070
Reliability:	The internal consistencies (Cronbach's Alpha) for the derived scales generally are in the range of .67 to .75 except for the Seeking Professional Support Scale, which has a reliability of .50. Validity data are equivocal.

COMMUNITY LIFE SKILLS SCALE (CLSS)[3]

Purpose:	To assess parents' ability to negotiate for themselves and for their families in the community.
Description:	Designed to be administered by an interviewer who has practiced administration according to the CLSS manual. Administration time is approximately 30 minutes.
Contact:	Nursing Child Assessment Satellite Training
	University of Washington, CDMRC, WJ-10
	Seattle, WA 98195
	(206) 543-8528

COPING HEALTH INVENTORY FOR PARENTS (CHIP)[1]

Authors:	McCubbin, McCubbin, Nevin, & Cauble
Purpose:	To assess parents' perception of their response to the management of family life when they have a child who is seriously and/or chronically ill.
Description:	Forty-five questions that require the client to rate the utility of several coping behaviors.
Cost:	A one-time copyright fee of $5.
Contact:	Family Stress Coping and Health Project
	1300 Linden Drive
	University of Wisconsin–Madison
	Madison, WI 53706
	(608) 262-5070
Reliability:	Cronbach's Alphas, computed for the items on each of the three coping patterns, resulted in reliabilities of .79, .79, and .71.

DIFFICULT LIFE CIRCUMSTANCES (DLC)[3]

Purpose: To assess stressful situations in the family environment, including problems with housing, relationships, credit, and alcohol or other drugs.

Description: Twenty-eight questions requiring a "yes" or "no" answer. Administration time is approximately 15–20 minutes.

Contact: Nursing Child Assessment Satellite Training
University of Washington, CDMRC, WJ-10
Seattle, WA 98195
(206) 543-8528

Reliability: High scores on the DLC have been related to high scores on measures of depression, physical symptoms, and lower social support.

FAMILY CRISIS ORIENTED PERSONAL SCALES (F-COPES)[1]

Authors: McCubbin, Olson, & Larsen

Purpose: To identify problem-solving and behavior strategies utilized by families in difficult or problematic situations.

Description: Thirty-item self-report questionnaire.

Cost: A one-time copyright fee of $5.

Contact: Family Stress Coping and Health Project
1300 Linden Drive
University of Wisconsin–Madison
Madison, WI 53706
(608) 262-5070

Reliability: Cronbach's Alpha has been estimated from .77 to .86 for overall reliability. Individual subscales' alphas range from .63 to .83. The test–retest reliability overall is .81 and individually ranges from .61 to .95.

HASSLES AND UPLIFTS SCALES[2]

Authors: Kanner, Coyne, Schafer, & Lazarus

Purpose: To provide an indication of how many negative (Hassles Scale) and positive (Uplifts Scale) events the respondent has experienced in the past month.

Description: The Hassles Scale consists of a list of 117 irritating, frustrating demands that characterize everyday transactions in the areas of work, health, family, friends, and the environment. The Uplifts Scale consists of a list of 135 events that may be sources of peace, happiness, or satisfaction. For both scales, respondents indicate whether each event has occurred in the past month and, if so, how severe the hassle was or how often the uplift was experienced.

Source: Kanner, A.D., Coyne, J.C., Schafer, C., & Lazarus, R.S. (1981). Comparison of two modes of stress measurement: Daily hassles and uplifts versus major life events. *Journal of Behavioral Medicine, 4*, 1–39.

PARENTING STRESS INDEX (PSI)[1, 3]

Author:	Abidin
Purpose:	To measure the amount of stress experienced by the parent as a result of the parenting role.
Description:	Long form is a 101-item self-report questionnaire. Short form has 36 items. A fifth-grade reading level is necessary. Administration time is 20–30 minutes for the long form and 10 minutes for the short form. Available in both English and Spanish.
Cost:	Write to obtain a price sheet.
Contact:	Pediatric Psychology Press
	320 Terrell Road West
	Charlottesville, VA 22901
Reliability:	Validity of the PSI–Long Form was demonstrated by showing that test scores were positively correlated with other measures of the same construct. The derived alpha reliability coefficients are .95 for the total score, .89 for the parent domain, and .93 for the child domain; however, the short form is recommended because of stability of factor structure and shorter administration time.

SOCIAL SUPPORT

FAMILY SUPPORT SCALE

Authors: Dunst, Trivette, & Deal

Purpose: To measure how much assistance participants receive from family members, friends, and other sources.

Description: On a 5-point scale, respondents rate how much assistance they have received from 18 listed sources.

Cost: Instrument may be copied free of charge.

Source: Dunst, C.J., Trivette, C.M., & Deal, A.G. (1988). *Enabling and empowering families: Principles and guidelines for practice.* Cambridge, MA: Brookline Books.

INVENTORY OF SOCIALLY SUPPORTIVE BEHAVIORS (ISSB)[1]

Author: Barerra

Purpose: To assess the frequency with which individuals were the recipients of supportive actions in the past 4 weeks.

Description: Two forms are included; one contains 40 questions, and the other is slightly shorter. Frequencies of events are rated on a 5-point scale.

Cost: Forms may be copied without charge.

Contact: Manual Barerra, Jr., Ph.D.
Psychology Department
Arizona State University
Tempe, AZ 85287-3826
(602) 965-3826

Reliability: Several studies have found total reliabilities over .90. Test–retest reliabilities vary from .63 to .88, depending on the length of time between tests.

MATERNAL SOCIAL SUPPORT INDEX (MSSI)[2]

Author: Pascoe

Purpose: To evaluate the quality and quantity of social support available to mothers.

Description: Twenty-one items to provide a quick and organized approach to assessing maternal support.

Contact: John M. Pascoe, M.D., M.P.H.
Department of Pediatrics
Clinical Science Center
600 Highland Avenue
Madison, WI 53792
(608) 263-6477

Reliability: Reliable and acceptable in terms of internal consistency and predictive validity.

PERCEIVED SOCIAL SUPPORT FROM
FRIENDS (PSS–Fr) AND FROM FAMILY (PSS–Fa)[2]

Authors: Procidano & Heller

Purpose: To measure the extent to which an individual perceives that his or her needs for support, information, and feedback are fulfilled by friends and family.

Description: The two forms each consist of 20 declarative statements to which the respondent answers "Yes," "No," or "Don't Know."

Source: Procidano, M.E., & Heller, K. (1983). Measures of perceived social support from friends and from family: Three validation studies. *American Journal of Community Psychology, 11*(1), 1–24.

Reliability: Numerous studies have documented the validity of the PSS–Fr and the PSS–Fa.

SOCIAL SUPPORT QUESTIONNAIRE (SSQ)[2]

Author: Sarason

Purpose: To determine respondents' perceived number of social supports and satisfaction with their existing social support system.

Description: The SSQ consists of 27 items inquiring to whom the respondent would reach out in specific instances and how satisfied the respondent is with that source of support. Can be used to detect change in social support over time and as a result of various interventions. Shorter versions include a 3-item (SSQ3), 6-item (SSQ6), and 12-item (SSQR) instrument.

Contact: Irwin G. Sarason
Department of Psychology
University of Washington
Seattle, WA 98195

Reliability: All of the shorter versions have been proved to have acceptable reliability and validity rating, but the complete SSQ is the preferred version.

SUPPORT FUNCTIONS SCALE

Authors: Dunst & Trivette

Purpose: To measure how much participants need social support and other types of assistance.

Description: On a 5-point scale, respondents rate how often they have or feel the need for 12 types of help or assistance.

Cost: Instrument may be copied free of charge.

Source: Dunst, C.J., Trivette, C.M., & Deal, A.G. (1988). *Enabling and empowering families: Principles and guidelines for practice.* Cambridge, MA: Brookline Books.

YOUNG ADULT SOCIAL SUPPORT INVENTORY (YASSI)[1]

Authors:	Cubbin, Patterson, & Grochowski
Purpose:	To assess the social support of parents at any stage of parenting, including new parents, and individuals in other contexts and roles.
Description:	Seventy-seven–item self-report questionnaire.
Cost:	A one-time copyright fee of $5.
Contact:	Family Stress Coping and Health Project
	1300 Linden Drive
	University of Wisconsin–Madison
	Madison, WI 53706
	(608) 262-5070
Reliability:	The overall internal reliability (Cronbach's Alpha) is .89, and the test–retest reliability is .90. Factor analyses with a varimax rotation resulted in the formation of 11 subscales. Subscale variabilities ranging from .82 to .85 were derived from a sample of 106 young parents.

SELF-ESTEEM AND PERSONAL WELL-BEING

COOPERSMITH SELF-ESTEEM INVENTORIES[1]

Author: Coopersmith

Purpose: To measure attitude toward self in social, academic, and personal contexts.

Description: Administration time is approximately 15 minutes. Two separate forms are used:

1. School form—ages 8–15 years
2. Adult form—ages 16 and older

Cost: Manuals—$10   Test Booklets (pkg. 25)—$8

Contact: Consulting Psychologists Press, Inc.
3803 E. Bayshore Road
Palo Alto, CA 94303
(800) 624-1765, ext. 300

Reliability: Internal consistency using the Kuder-Richardson estimates for several groups of students in grades 5, 9, and 12 were in the range of .80 or better. The short form has yielded reliabilities of .74 for males and .71 for females.

PERSONAL MOOD—Modified version of the Beck Depression Inventory[1]

Purpose: To measure depression.

Description: Twelve questions requiring the respondent to rate the frequency of an event on a scale of 0–7.

Cost: Instrument may be copied free of charge.

Source: Beck, A.T., Ward, C.H., Mendelson, M., Mock, J., & Erbaugh, J. (1961). An inventory for measuring depression. *Archives of General Psychiatry, 4,* 561–571.

PERSONAL WELL-BEING—Modified version of the UCLA Loneliness Scale[1]

Purpose: To measure loneliness.

Description: Seven questions that require the respondent to rate the frequency of an event or affect on a 4-point scale.

Cost: Instrument may be copied free of charge.

Source: Russell, D., Peplau, L.A., & Cutrona, C.E. (1980). The revised UCLA Loneliness Scale: Concurrent and discriminant validity evidence. *Journal of Personality and Social Psychology, 39,* 472–480.

PIERS-HARRIS CHILDREN'S SELF-CONCEPT SCALE[1]: THE WAY I FEEL ABOUT MYSELF

Authors: Piers & Harris

Purpose: To measure an individual child's self-evaluative attitudes and behaviors that have a bearing on self-concept.

Description: Eighty-item self-report questionnaire. Children read statements that tell how some people feel about themselves and indicate "yes" or "no" as to whether the statement applies to them. Appropriate for children ages 8–18. Administration time is approximately 15–20 minutes and can be done individually or in groups.

Cost: The administration manual is $37. Test booklets are an additional cost.

Contact: Western Psychological Services
Publishers and Distributors
12031 Wilshire Boulevard
Los Angeles, CA 90025-1251
(800) 648-8857

SELF-ESTEEM SCALE[1]

Author: Rosenberg

Purpose: To measure an individual's self-attitudes and general self-esteem.

Description: Ten questions that require the respondent to rate the frequency of a feeling on a 4-point scale. Available in both Spanish and English.

Cost: Instrument may be copied free of charge.

Source: Rosenberg, M. (1965). *Society and the adolescent self-image.* Princeton, NJ: Princeton University Press.

STATE-TRAIT ANXIETY INVENTORY FOR CHILDREN (STAIC)[2]: HOW I FEEL QUESTIONNAIRE

Author: Spielberger

Purpose: To provide an indication of how anxious children feel at a particular moment (A–State) and in general (A–Trait).

Description: Two 20-item self-report scales, one measuring state anxiety (A–State) and the other measuring trait anxiety (A–Trait). Intended for 9- to 12-year-old children but also may be used with older or younger children. Scales have been translated into Spanish. May be administered individually or in groups.

Contact: Consulting Psychologists Press, Inc.
3803 E. Bayshore Road
Palo Alto, CA 94303
(800) 624-1765

Reliability: Internal consistency for both scales and test–retest reliability for the A–Trait Scale is moderate. Test–retest reliability for the A–State is low.

ADMINISTRATION

DEMOGRAPHIC INFORMATION FORM[1]

Purpose: To obtain basic information about all program participants.
Description: Nine questions.
Cost: Instrument may be copied free of charge.
Contact: Children's Trust Fund
444 Lafayette Road
St. Paul, MN 55155-3839
(612) 296-5437

GOAL ATTAINMENT SCALING (GAS)[1]

Purpose: To measure a participant's specific goals.
Description: The respondent charts his or her goals and ranks them according to their significance.
Cost: Instrument may be copied free of charge.
Source: Kiresuk, T.J., & Sherman, R. (1968). Goal attainment scaling: A general method of evaluating comprehensive community mental health programs. *Community Mental Health Journal, 4*(6). Adapted from Pietrzak, J., Ramier, M., Renner, R., Ford, L., & Gilbert, N. (1990). *Practical program evaluation: Examples from child abuse prevention.* Newbury Park, CA: Sage Publications.
Contact: Children's Trust Fund
444 Lafayette Road
St. Paul, MN 55155-3839
(612) 296-5437

PARTICIPANT FEEDBACK FORM[1]

Purpose: To gather information about how participants feel about a program.
Description: Twenty-five questions that require the participant to rate an objective on a 6-point scale and 6 additional short-answer questions.
Cost: Instrument may be copied free of charge.
Contact: Children's Trust Fund
444 Lafayette Road
St. Paul, MN 55155-3839
(612) 296-5437

REFERRAL FOLLOW-UP FORM[1]

Purpose: To help track participants' completion of referrals.
Cost: Instrument may be copied free of charge.
Contact: Children's Trust Fund
444 Lafayette Road
St. Paul, MN 55155-3839
(612) 296-5437

SATISFACTION WITH CHILD CARE[1]

Purpose: To measure how children or their parents feel about the adequacy of the child care component.

Description: Three separate forms are used:

1. Birth to age 3—for adults to complete
2. Ages 4–6—to be read to children by child care workers
3. Ages 7 and older—for children to read and complete independently

Cost: Instruments may be copied free of charge.
Contact: Children's Trust Fund
444 Lafayette Road
St. Paul, MN 55155-3839
(612) 296-5437

SERVICE TERMINATION FORM[1]

Purpose: To help monitor participants' reasons for discontinuing use of a program.
Cost: Instrument may be copied free of charge.
Contact: Children's Trust Fund
444 Lafayette Road
St. Paul, MN 55155-3839
(612) 296-5437

JOB SATISFACTION

JOB SATISFACTION SURVEY

Author:	Spector
Purpose:	To measure job satisfaction, particularly in human services, public, and nonprofit sector organizations.
Description:	Thirty-six questions rated on a 6-point scale. Measures satisfaction with pay, promotion opportunities, fringe benefits, contingent awards (appreciation and recognition), supervision, co-workers, nature of work itself, communication, and work conditions.
Cost:	Instrument may be copied free of charge.
Source:	Spector, P. (1985). Measurement of human service staff satisfaction: Development of the Job Satisfaction Survey. *American Journal of Community Psychology, 13*(6), 693–713.

MASLACH BURNOUT INVENTORY (MBI)

Authors:	Maslach & Jackson
Purpose:	To assess individual occupational burnout among human services workers and others whose work involves intense interaction with other people. The MBI elucidates the relationship between specific individual or organizational factors and the development of burnout, as well as the association of burnout with certain physical or psychological conditions. Caution must be used, however, in interpreting individual factors.
Description:	Measures emotional exhaustion, depersonalization, and lack of personal accomplishment. Twenty-two items rated on two Likert scales, one measuring frequency and the other measuring intensity. Administration time is 20–30 minutes.
Cost:	Instrument may be copied free of charge.
Source:	Maslach, C., & Jackson, S.E. (1986). Burnout in organizational settings. *Applied Social Psychology Annual, 5,* 133–153.

MINNESOTA SATISFACTION QUESTIONNAIRE

Authors:	Weiss, Davis, England, & Lofquist
Purpose:	To measure intrinsic and extrinsic aspects of job satisfaction. To provide an internal indicator of the correspondence between the employee's preferred reinforcers and the reinforcers present in the job.
Description:	Measures satisfaction with working conditions, pay, employee policies, and perceptions of internal rewards. Long form contains 100 items rated on a 5-point Likert scale and requires 15–20 minutes. Short form contains 20 items and requires only 5 minutes.
Cost:	Manual—$4.50 Short Form (minimum of 50)—$.35/form
	Sample—$10.50 Long Form (minimum of 50)—$.60/form

Source: Weiss, D.J., Davis, R.V., England, G.W., & Lofquist, L.H. (1967). *Manual for the Minnesota Satisfaction Questionnaire.* Minneapolis: University of Minnesota.

SELF-DIAGNOSTIC SURVEY

Purpose: To measure the degree of burnout experienced by employees, particularly human services employees.

Description: Measures emotional exhaustion, depersonalization, and personal accomplishment. Twenty-two items rated on a 7-point scale. Requires 20–30 minutes to administer.

Cost: Manual—$15   Testing Packet (pkg. 25)—$9
Demo Data Sheet (pkg. 25)—$9   Scoring Sheet—$4

Contact: Consulting Psychologists Press, Inc.
3803 E. Bayshore Road
Palo Alto, CA 94303
(800) 624-1765

RECOMMENDED MEASURES

The following measures were selected by the University of Virginia evaluation team and successfully piloted at several VFVPP-funded projects. These measures were chosen according to their potential utility, ease of administration, and simplicity (see Appendix B).

Adult-Adolescent Parenting Inventory (AAPI)
Child Abuse Potential Inventory (CAP)
Home Observation for Measurement of the Environment (HOME)
Knowledge of Child Development Inventory
Parenting Stress Index (PSI) Short Form
Support Functions Scale
Self-Esteem Scale

---

[1]Information on these evaluation instruments was obtained from Center for Evaluation Research. *Children's Trust Fund evaluation instrument battery.* State of Minnesota Department of Human Services.

[2]Information on these evaluation instruments was obtained from Daro, D., Abrahams, N., & Casey, K. (1990). *Parenting program evaluation manual* (Second Edition). The National Center on Child Abuse Prevention Research, a program of The National Committee for Prevention of Child Abuse.

[3]Information on these evaluation instruments was obtained from the Virginia Children's Trust Fund's *Proposed trust fund short-term outcome measures packet.*

The Good Beginnings Curriculum

The lesson plan for each weekly session consists of objectives for the parents, activity sheets, discussion topics and points, materials for distribution, and a planned opportunity for mother–infant interaction.

Class Topics

- Bonding and Communication—"My Baby's Diary" worksheet (what my baby did/what my baby was "saying") and "Teen Parenting: Baby's First Year Quiz, Part I"
- Growth and Development—"Showing Baby" activity and "Child Development Quiz"
- Keep Your Baby Healthy—"Teen Parenting: Baby's First Year Quiz, Part II" and "Thermometer Readings" activity
- Responsible Parents—"Parental Expectations Test" and "Family Feud" activity
- Infant CPR I—skills practice
- Infant CPR II—Red Cross CPR test
- Options—"Discipline Quiz" and "Win, Lose, or Draw" activity
- Sexually Transmitted Diseases and Family Planning—"AIDS and STDs Test"
- Self-Esteem and Support Session—"Panel Questions" and "Time of Your Life" activity
- Substance Abuse Prevention—"Street Talk" guest speaker and "My Attitude Quiz"
- Nutrition—"Meal Planning and Preparations" activity

Note: To request the full curriculum, contact the Good Beginnings program director at Child & Family Services of Southwest Hampton Roads, Inc., 1805 Airline Blvd., Portsmouth, VA 23707.

Materials in Clients' Files

At hospital:

- Bolton's parenting risk profile
- Medical records and information from nursing staff
- Face sheet, consent form, and hospital release of information consent form

At-home visit:

- AAPI (pre-program)
- Observations of mother–infant interactions and home environment
- Information about the program
- Referral/recommendation

At program:

- Record of outside resource utilization and referrals
- Attendance
- Process goals monitored
- Weekly quizzes and activity sheets
- Seven-day diary of mother–child interaction
- Facilitator's case notes on each mother–child dyad
- Periodic satisfaction surveys (for given classes)
- AAPI (post-program)
- Satisfaction survey (post-program)
- Parent follow-up (2-month follow-up call, documents: whether mother is in school, whether mother is pregnant, child health, specific referrals, and agency usage)

Risk Factors (Observed or by Interview)
Used in Screening (from Bolton, 1990):

- Single parent
- Broken family
- Income below poverty line
- Inadequate housing
- Family or marital discord
- High stress/lack of tolerance
- Feelings of loss of control
- Heavy, continuous child care responsibility
- Spousal abuse

- Lack of knowledge of child development/unrealistic expectations
- Inability to provide health care for children
- Impulsive behavior
- Personality disorders
- Alcohol or other drug abuse
- Parental history of abuse as child
- Depression
- Close spacing of children
- Views child as abnormal
- Lacks nurturing behavior
- Lacks bonding to child
- Poor self-image
- Inappropriate discipline
- Emotional instability
- Lack of support systems
- Geographically or socially isolated

REFERENCES

Abidin, R.R. (1982). *Parenting skills: Trainer's manual* (2nd ed.). New York: Human Sciences Press.

Allan, J. (1994). Parenting education in Australia. *Children and Society, 8*(4), 344–359.

Allen, M., Brown, P., & Finlay, B. (1992). *Helping children by strengthening families: A look at family support programs.* Washington, DC: Children's Defense Fund.

Allen, J.P., Kuperminc, G., Philliber, S., & Herre, K. (1994). Programmatic prevention of adolescent problem behaviors: The role of autonomy, relatedness, and volunteer service in the Teen Outreach Program. *American Journal of Community Psychology, 22*(5), 617–638.

Altepeter, T.S., & Walker, C.E. (1992). Prevention of physical abuse of children through parent training. In D.J. Willis, E.W. Holden, & M. Rosenberg (Eds.), *Prevention of child maltreatment: Developmental and ecological perspectives* (pp. 226–248). New York: John Wiley & Sons.

Anastasiow, N. (1988). Should parenting education be mandatory? *Theories in Early Childhood Special Education, 8,* 60–72.

Andrews, S.R., Blumenthal, J.B., Johnson, D.L., Kahn, A.J., Ferguson, C.J., Lasater, T.M., Malone, P.E., & Wallace, D.B. (1982). The skills of mothering: A study of parent–child development centers. *Monographs of the Society for Research in Child Development, 47*(6, Serial No. 198).

Armstrong, K.A., & Fraley, Y.L. (1985). What happens to families after they leave the program? *Children Today, 14,* 17–20.

Atkins, M. (1986). The Welcome Baby Program: A community-based volunteer prevention model of caring, sharing, and support for new parents. *Infant Mental Health Journal, 7,* 156–167.

Barnett, W.S. (1985). *The Perry Preschool program and its long-term effects: A benefit–cost analysis.* Ypsilanti, MI: High/Scope Educational Research Foundation.

Barrick, J.D. (1988). Parental involvement in child abuse prevention training: What do they learn? *Child Abuse and Neglect, 12,* 543–553.

Barth, R.P. (1991). An experimental evaluation of in-home child abuse prevention services. *Child Abuse and Neglect, 15,* 363–375.

Bartz, K.W. (1980). Parenting education for youth. In M.J. Fine (Ed.), *Handbook on parent education* (pp. 271–290). New York: Academic Press.

218 • References

Baum, C.G., & Forehand, R. (1981). Long-term follow-up assessment of parent training by use of multiple outcome measures. *Behavior Therapy, 12,* 643–652.

Bavolek, S.J. (1984). *Handbook for the Adult-Adolescent Parenting Inventory (AAPI).* Eau Claire, WI: Family Development Resources, Inc.

Bavolek, S.J., & Comstock, C. (1985). *Nurturing Program for parents and children: Program implementation manual* (2nd ed.). Park City, UT: Family Development Resources, Inc.

Bavolek, S.J., & Dellinger-Bavolek, J. (1989). *Nurturing Program for parents and children birth to five years: Program implementation manual.* Eau Claire, WI: Family Development Resources, Inc.

Becker, J.V., Alpert, J.L., Bigfoot, D.S., Bonner, B.L., Geddie, L.F., Henggeler, S.W., Kaufman, K.L., & Walker, C.E. (1995). Empirical research on child abuse treatment: Report by the Child Abuse and Neglect Treatment Working Group, American Psychological Association. *Journal of Clinical Child Psychology, 24*(Suppl.), 23–46.

Belsky, J., & Vondra, J. (1989). Lessons from child abuse: The determinants of parenting. In D. Cicchetti & V. Carlson (Eds.), *Child maltreatment: Theory and research on the causes and consequences of child abuse and neglect* (pp. 153–202). New York: Cambridge University Press.

Belsky, J., Ward, M., & Rovine, M. (1985). Parental expectations, postnatal experiences, and the transition to parenthood. In R. Ashmore & D. Brodzinsky (Eds.), *Perspectives on the family* (pp. 119–145). Hillsdale, NJ: Lawrence Erlbaum Associates.

Birkel, R., & Reppucci, N.D. (1983). Social networks, information seeking, and the utilization of services. *American Journal of Community Psychology, 11,* 185–205.

Bolton, F.G. (1990). The risk of child maltreatment in adolescent parenting. In A.R. Stiffman & R.A. Feldman (Eds.), *Contraception, pregnancy, and parenting: Advances in adolescent mental health* (Vol. 4, pp. 223–237). London: Jessica Kingsley Publishers.

Breakey, G., & Pratt, B. (1991). Healthy growth for Hawaii's "Healthy Start": Toward a systematic statewide approach to the prevention of child abuse and neglect. *ZERO TO THREE (Bulletin of the National Center for Clinical Infant Programs), 11,* 16–22.

Brehmer, D.A. (1995). *Communicating effectively with major donors.* San Francisco: Jossey-Bass.

Britner, P.A., Morog, M.C., Pianta, R.C., & Marvin, R.S. (1997). *Self-report measures of family functioning: A comparison of families of young children with severe cerebral palsy, mild cerebral palsy, or no medical diagnosis.* Unpublished manuscript, University of Connecticut, Storrs.

Britner, P.A., & Phillips, D.A. (1995). Predictors of parent and provider satisfaction with child day care dimensions: A comparison of center-based and family child day care. Special issue on child day care. *Child Welfare, 74*(6), 1135–1168.

Britner, P.A., & Reppucci, N.D. (1997). Prevention of child maltreatment: Evaluation of a parent education program for teen mothers. *Journal of Child and Family Studies, 6*(2).

Brooks, L.D., Spearn, R.C., Rice, M., Crocco, D., Hodgins, C., & Vander Schaaf, G. (1988, December). Systematic Training for Effective Parenting (STEP): An evaluative study with a Canadian population. *Canada's Mental Health,* 2–5.

Brown, C. (1984). *The art of coalition building: A guide for community leaders.* New York: The American Jewish Committee.

Bryant, D., Lyons, C., & Wasik, B.H. (1990). Ethical issues involved in home-visiting. *Topics in Early Childhood Special Education, 10,* 92–107.

Bureau of the Census (1992). *1990 census of the population. General population characteristics, Virginia.* Washington, DC: U.S. Department of Commerce, Economics and Statistics Administration.

Buroker, C.D. (1993). Parent education: Key to successful alternative education programs. *Journal of School Leadership, 3*(6), 635–645.

Cherniss, C. (1981). *Staff burnout: Job stress in the human services.* Beverly Hills: Sage Publications.

Clarke-Stewart, K. (1983). Exploring the assumptions of parent education. In R. Haskins & P. Adams (Eds.), *Parent education and public policy.* Norwood, NJ: Ablex.

Cochran, M., & Woolever, F. (1983). Beyond the deficit model: The empowerment of parents with information and informal supports. In I. Seigel & L. Laosa (Eds.), *Changing families* (pp. 225–246). New York: Plenum.

Cole, E.S. (1986). Active Parenting: Review and evaluation. *Techniques: A Journal for Remedial Education and Counseling, 2,* 109–114.

Conrad, W.R., & Glenn, W.E. (1976). *The effective voluntary board of directors: What it is and how it works.* Chicago: Swallow Press.

Cooke, B. (1990). Teaching and evaluating courses in parenthood education for adolescents. *Illinois Teacher of Home Economics, 33*(3), 86–88.

Coyne, J.C., & DeLongis, A. (1986). Going beyond social support: The role of social relationships in adaptation. *Journal of Consulting and Clinical Psychology, 54,* 454–460.

Crittenden, P.M., & Ainsworth, M.D.A. (1989). Child maltreatment and attachment theory. In D. Cicchetti & V. Carlson (Eds.), *Child maltreatment: Theory and research on the causes and consequences of child abuse and neglect* (pp. 432–463). New York: Cambridge University Press.

Darmstadt, G.L. (1990). Community-based child abuse prevention. *Social Work, 35,* 487–489.

Daro, D. (1988). *Confronting child abuse.* New York: Free Press.

Davis, A.A., & Rhodes, J.E. (1994). African-American teenage mothers and their mothers: An analysis of supportive and problematic interactions. *Journal of Community Psychology, 22,* 12–20.

Dawson, P.M., Robinson, J.L., Butterfield, P.M., van Doorninck, W.J., Gaensbauer, T.J., & Harmon, R.J. (1991). Supporting new parents through home visits: Effects on mother–infant interaction. *Topics in Early Childhood Special Education, 10,* 29–44.

Dawson, P., Van Doorninick, W.J., & Robinson, J.L. (1989). Effects of home-based, informal social support on child health. *Journal of Developmental and Behavioral Pediatrics, 10,* 63–67.

Dembo, M., Sweitzer, M., & Lauritzen, P. (1985). An evaluation of group parent education: Behavioral, PET, and Adlerian programs. *Review of Educational Research, 55,* 155–200.

Dinkmeyer, D., Sr., & McKay, G.D. (1976). *Systematic Training for Effective Parenting (STEP).* Circle Pines, MN: American Guidance Service.

Dinkmeyer, D., Sr., & McKay, G.D. (1982). *STEP (Systematic Training for Effective Parenting): The parent's handbook.* Circle Pines, MN: American Guidance Service.

Dinkmeyer, D., Sr., McKay, G.D., & Dinkmeyer, D., Jr. (1990). Inaccuracy in STEP research reporting. *Canadian Journal of Counseling, 24,* 103–105.

Doino, J., & Haskins, G. (1985). *The growing up together project: Proposal to the State Education Department of New York State for validation.* Buffalo, NY: Early Parenting Information for Children.

Dokecki, P.R., & Moroney, R.M. (1983). To strengthen all families: A human development and community value framework. In R. Haskins & D. Adams (Eds.), *Parent education and public policy* (pp. 257–276). Norwood, NJ: Ablex.

Dubowitz, H. (1989). Prevention of child maltreatment: What is known. *Pediatrics, 83,* 570–577.

Dubowitz, H. (1990). Costs and effectiveness of interventions in child maltreatment. *Child Abuse & Neglect, 14,* 177–186.

Egeland, B., Jacobvitz, D., & Sroufe, L.A. (1988). Breaking the cycle of abuse. *Child Development, 59,* 1080–1088.

Elwood, D.T. (1988). *Poor support poverty in the American family.* New York: Basic Books.

Epstein, A.S., & Weikart, D.P. (1979). *The Ypsilanti-Carnegie Infant Education Project.* Ypsilanti, MI: High/Scope Press.

Felton, B.J., & Berry, C. (1992). Groups as social network members: Overlooked sources of social support. *American Journal of Community Psychology, 20,* 253–261.

Feshbach, S., & Feshbach, N. (1978). Child advocacy and family privacy. *Journal of Social Issues, 34,* 168–176.

Field, T.M., Widmayer, S.M., Greenberg, R., & Stoller, S. (1982). Effects of parent training on teenage mothers and their infants. *Pediatrics, 69,* 703–707.

Field, T.M., Widmayer, S.M., Stringer, S., & Ignatoff, E. (1980). Teenage, lower-class, black mothers and their preterm infants: An intervention and developmental follow-up. *Child Development, 51,* 426–436.

Frank, E., & Rowe, D.A. (1981). Primary prevention: Parent education mother–infant groups in a general hospital setting. *Journal of Preventive Psychiatry, 1,* 169–178.

Frankel, M., & Reibstein, L. (1996, July 8). Who's hand's on, who's hand's off? The parental rights amendment. *Newsweek,* 58.

Fritz, M.E. (1989). Full circle or forward. Commentary. *Child Abuse and Neglect, 13*(3), 313–318.

Furstenberg, F., Brooks-Gunn, J., & Chase-Lansdale, L. (1989). Teenaged pregnancy and childbearing. *American Psychologist, 44*(2), 313–320.

Galano, J., & Nezlek, J.B. (1991) Evaluating prevention programs: Statewide training for decision makers and preventionists. In N.D. Reppucci & J. Haugaard (Eds.), *Prevention in community mental health practice* (pp. 11–24). Cambridge, MA: Brookline Books.

Garbarino, J. (1986). Can we measure success in preventing child abuse? Issues in policy, programming, and research. *Child Abuse and Neglect, 10,* 143–156.

Garbarino, J. (1987). Family support and the prevention of child maltreatment. In S.L. Kagan, D.R. Powell, B. Weissbourd, & E.F. Zigler (Eds.), *America's family support programs* (pp. 99–114). New Haven, CT: Yale University Press.

Garbarino, J., & Crouter, A. (1978). Defining the community context for parent–child relations: The correlates of child maltreatment. *Child Development, 49,* 604–616.

Garbarino, J., & Kostelny, K. (1992). *Neighborhood-based programs.* Report prepared for the U.S. Advisory Committee on Child Abuse and Neglect.

Garbarino, J., & Long, F.N. (1992). Developmental issues in the human services. In J. Garbarino (Ed.), *Children and families in the social environment* (2nd ed., pp. 232–270). New York: de Gruyter.

Geller, S. (1991). *Project LINK.* Richmond, VA: Department of Mental Health, Mental Retardation, and Substance Abuse Services.

Gentry, T., & Brisbane, L. (1982). The solution for child abuse rests with the community. *Children Today, 11,* 22–24.

Gordon, T. (1970). *Parent Effectiveness Training.* New York: Wyden Press.

Gray, B. (1985). Conditions facilitating interorganizational collaboration. *Human Relations, 38*, 911–936.

Gritzmacher, J.E., Schultz, J.B., Shannon, T., & Watts, J. (1981). *Child development/parent education programs.* University Park: The Pennsylvania State University, Division of Occupational Studies.

Gurman, A.S., Kniskern, D.P., & Pinsof, W.M. (1986). Research on marital and family therapies. In S.L. Garfield & A.E. Bergin (Eds.), *Handbook of psychotherapy and behavior change* (pp. 565–624). New York: John Wiley & Sons.

Hammett, V.L., Omizo, M.M., & Loffredo, D.A. (1981). The effects of participation in a STEP program on parents' child-rearing attitudes and the self-concepts of their learning disabled children. *Exceptional Child, 28*, 183–190.

Hardy, J.B., & Streett, R. (1989). Family support and parenting education in the home: An effective extension of clinic-based preventive health care services for poor children. *Journal of Pediatrics, 115*, 927–931.

Harrison, M. (1981). Home-start: A voluntary home-visiting scheme for young families. *Child Abuse and Neglect, 5*, 441–447.

Haskins, R., & Adams, D. (1983). Parent education and public policy: Synthesis and recommendations. In R. Haskins & D. Adams (Eds.), *Parent education and public policy* (pp. 257–276). Norwood, NJ: Ablex.

Hawkins, J.D., Catalano, R.F., & Associates. (1992). *Communities that care: Action for drug abuse prevention.* San Francisco: Jossey-Bass.

Jackson, M.D., & Brown, D. (1986, November). Use of Systematic Training for Effective Parenting (STEP) with elementary school parents. *School Counselor*, 100–104.

Kadushin, A., & Martin, J.A. (1981). *Child abuse: An interactional event.* New York: Columbia University Press.

Kagan, S.L., Powell, D.R., Weissbourd, B., & Zigler, E.F. (1987). Past accomplishments: Future challenges. In S.L. Kagan, D.R. Powell, B. Weissbourd, & E.F. Zigler (Eds.), *America's family support programs* (pp. 365–380). New Haven, CT: Yale University Press.

Kamerman, S., & Kahn, A. (1990, Winter). If CPS is driving child welfare: Where do we go from here? *Public Welfare*, 9–13.

Kaufman, J., & Zigler, E. (1992). The prevention of child maltreatment: Programming, research, and policy. In D.J. Willis, E.W. Holden, & M. Rosenberg (Eds.), *Prevention of child maltreatment: Developmental and ecological perspectives* (pp. 269–295). New York: John Wiley & Sons.

Kazdin, A.E. (1987). Treatment of antisocial behavior in children: Current status and future directions. *Psychological Bulletin, 102*, 187–203.

Keegan, P.B. (1994). *Fundraising for nonprofits.* New York: Harper Perennial.

Kempe, C.H., Silverman, F.N., Steele, B., Droegemueller, W., & Silver, H.R. (1962). The battered child syndrome. *Journal of the American Medical Association, 181*, 17–24.

Kessen, W. (1979). The American child and other cultural inventions. *American Psychologist, 34*, 815–820.

Kline, B., Grayson, J., & Mathie, V.A. (1990). Parenting support groups for parents at risk of abuse and neglect. *Journal of Primary Prevention, 10*, 313–320.

Koss, M.P., & Harvey, M. (1991). *The rape victim: Community and clinical interventions.* Beverly Hills: Sage Publications.

Kramer, J.J. (1990). Best practices in parent training. In A. Thomas & J. Grimes (Eds.), *Best practices in school psychology* (Vol. 2, pp. 519–530). Washington, DC: National Association of School Psychologists.

Larson, C.P. (1980). Efficacy of prenatal and postpartum home visits on child health and development. *Pediatrics, 66,* 191–197.

Leventhal, J.M., Garber, R.B., & Brady, C.A. (1989). Identification during the postpartum period of infants who are at high risk of child maltreatment. *Journal of Pediatrics, 114,* 481–487.

Lewko, J., Carriere, R., Whissel, C., & Radford, J. (1986). *Final report of the study investigating the long term effectiveness of the parenting for teens and children project.* Sudbury, Ontario, Canada: Laurentian University, Centre for Research in Human Development.

Luster, T., & Youatt, J. (1989, March). *The effects of pre-parenthood education on high school students.* Paper presented at the Biennial Meetings of the Society for Research in Child Development, Kansas City, MO.

Lutzker, J.R., Wesch, D., & Rice, J.M. (1984). Project 12–Ways: Measuring outcome of a large in-home service for treatment and prevention of child abuse and neglect. *Advances in Behaviour Research and Therapy, 6,* 63–73.

Melton, G.B., Goodman, G.S., Kalichman, S.C., Levine, M., Saywitz, K.J., & Koocher, G.P. (1995). Empirical research on child maltreatment and the law. *Journal of Clinical Child Psychology, 24*(Suppl.), 47–77.

Miller, J.L., & Whittaker, J.K. (1988). Social services and social support: Blended programs for families at risk of child maltreatment. *Child Welfare, 67,* 161–174.

Milner, J.S., & Robertson, K.R. (1989). Inconsistent response patterns and the prediction of child maltreatment. *Child Abuse and Neglect, 13,* 59–64.

Moore, K.A., Sugland, B.W., Blumenthal, C., Glei, D., & Snyder, N. (1995). *Adolescent pregnancy prevention programs: Interventions and evaluations.* Washington, DC: Child Trends, Inc.

Morgan, J.R., Nu'Man-Sheppard, & Allin, D.W. (1990). Prevention through parent training: Three preventive parent education programs. *Journal of Primary Prevention, 10,* 321–331.

Mulvey, E.P., & Britner, P.A. (1996). Research on law and mental health issues affecting minors. In B.D. Sales & S.A. Shah (Eds.), *Mental health and law: Research, policy, and services* (pp. 319–356). Durham, NC: Carolina Academic Press.

National Institute of Mental Health (1994). *The prevention of mental disorders: A national research agenda.* Unpublished report.

Newberger, C.M., & White, K.M. (1989). Cognitive foundations for parental care. In D. Cicchetti & V. Carlson (Eds.), *Child maltreatment: Theory and research on the causes and consequences of child abuse and neglect* (pp. 302–316). New York: Cambridge University Press.

Newberger, E. (1983). The helping hand strikes again: Unintended consequences of child abuse reporting. *Journal of Clinical Child Psychology, 12,* 307–311.

Nystul, M.S. (1982). The effects of Systematic Training for Effective Parenting on parental attitudes. *Journal of Psychology, 112,* 63–66.

O'Connor, L. (1990). Education for parenthood and the national curriculum: Progression or regression? *Early Child Development and Care, 57,* 85–88.

Olds, D.L., & Henderson, C.R. (1989). The prevention of maltreatment. In D. Cicchetti & V. Carlson (Eds.), *Child maltreatment: Theory and research on the causes and consequences of child abuse and neglect* (pp. 722–763). New York: Cambridge University Press.

Olds, D.L., Henderson, C.R., Chamberlain, R., & Tatelbaum, R. (1986). Preventing child abuse and neglect: A randomized trial of nurse home visitation. *Pediatrics, 78,* 65–78.

Olds, D.L., & Kitzman, H. (1990). Can home visitation improve the health of women and children at environmental risk? *Pediatrics, 86,* 108–116.

Osofsky, J.D., Hann, D.M., & Peebles, C. (1993). Adolescent parenthood: Risks and opportunities for mothers and infants. In C.H. Zeanah (Ed.), *Handbook of infant mental health* (pp. 106–119). New York: Guilford Press.

Parsons, B.V., & Alexander, J.F. (1973). Short-term family intervention: A therapy outcome study. *Journal of Consulting and Clinical Psychology, 41,* 195–201.

Patrick, L.F., & Minish, P.A. (1985). Child-rearing strategies for the development of altruistic behavior in young children. *Journal of Primary Prevention, 5,* 154–168.

Patterson, G.R., Chamberlain, P., & Reid, J.B. (1982). A comparitive evaluation of a parent-training program. *Behavior Therapy, 13,* 638–650.

Pianta, R., Egeland, B., & Erickson, M.F. (1989). The antecedents of maltreatment: Results of the Mother–Child Interaction Research Project. In D. Cicchetti & V. Carlson (Eds.), *Child maltreatment: Theory and research on the causes and consequences of child abuse and neglect* (pp. 203–253). New York: Cambridge University Press.

Pillai, V., Collins, A., & Morgan, R. (1982). Family Walk-In Centre-Eaton Socon: Evaluation of a project on preventive intervention based in the community. *Child Abuse and Neglect, 6,* 71–79.

Popkin, M.H. (1989). Active Parenting: A video-based program. In M.J. Fine (Ed.), *The second handbook on parent education: Contemporary perspectives* (pp. 77–98). San Diego: Academic Press.

Powell, D.R. (1984). Enhancing the effectiveness of parent education: An analysis of program assumptions. In L.G. Katz (Ed.), *Current topics in early childhood education* (Volume 5, pp. 121–139). Norwood, NJ: Ablex.

Powell, D.R. (1988). Emerging directions in parent–child early intervention. In D.R. Powell (Ed.), *Parent education as early childhood intervention: Emerging directions in theory, research and practice. Annual advances in applied developmental psychology* (Vol. 3, pp. 1–22). Norwood, NJ: Ablex.

Powell, D.R. (1989). *Families and early childhood programs.* Washington, DC: National Association for the Education of Young Children.

Price, R.H., & Smith, S.S. (1985). *A guide to evaluating prevention programs in mental health.* Washington, DC: U.S. Government Printing Office. (DHHS Publication No. ADM 85-1365)

Reppucci, N.D., & Aber, M.S. (1992). Child maltreatment prevention and the legal system. In D.J. Willis, E.W. Holden, & M.S. Rosenberg (Eds.), *Prevention of child maltreatment: Developmental and ecological perspectives* (pp. 249–266). New York: John Wiley & Sons.

Reppucci, N.D., & Haugaard, J. (1988). Prevention of child sexual abuse: Myth or reality. *American Psychologist, 44,* 1266–1275.

Richett, D., & Towns, K. (1980, April). *Education for parenthood: Eighth graders change child rearing attitudes.* Paper presented at the Annual Meeting of the American Educational Research Association, Boston.

Roberts, R.N., Wasik, B.H., Casto, G., & Ramey, C.T. (1991). Family support in the home: Programs, policy, and social change. *American Psychologist, 46,* 131–137.

Robinson, M.A. (1992). Management in the South Carolina Resource Mothers program: The importance of supervision. In E. Fenichel (Ed.), *Learning through supervision and mentorship to support the development of infants, toddlers, and their families: A source book.* Arlington, VA: National Center for Clinical Infant Programs.

Rogers Weise, M.R. (1992). A critical review of parent training research. *Psychology in the Schools, 29,* 229–236.

Rosenberg, M.S., & Hunt, R.D. (1984). Child maltreatment: Legal and mental health issues. In N.D. Reppucci, L.A. Weithorn, E.P. Mulvey, & J. Monahan (Eds.), *Children, mental health and the law* (pp. 79–101). Beverly Hills: Sage Publications.

Rosenberg, M.S., & Reppucci, N.D. (1983). Abusive mothers: Perceptions of their own and their children's behavior. *Journal of Consulting and Clinical Psychology, 51,* 674–682.

Rosenberg, M.S., & Reppucci, N.D. (1985). Primary prevention of child abuse. *Journal of Consulting and Clinical Psychology, 53,* 578–585.

Rossi, P.H., Freeman, H.E., & Wright, S.R. (1979). *Evaluation: A systematic approach.* Beverly Hills: Sage Publications.

Sarason, S.B. (1972). *The creation of settings and the future societies.* Washington, DC: Jossey-Bass.

Sarason, S.B., Zitnay, G., & Grossman, F.K. (1971). *The creation of a community setting.* Syracuse, NY: Syracuse University Press.

Schmitt, B.D. (1987). Seven deadly sins of childhood: Advising parents about difficult developmental phases. *Child Abuse and Neglect, 11,* 421–432.

Schweinhart, L.J., & Weikart, D.P. (1988). The High/Scope Perry Preschool Program. In R. Price, E. Cowen, R. Lorion, & J. Ramos-McKay (Eds.), *14 ounces of prevention: A casebook for practitioners* (pp. 53–66). Washington, DC: American Psychological Association.

Seidman, E. (1987). Toward a framework for primary prevention research. In J. Steinberg & M.M. Silverman (Eds.), *Preventing mental disorders: A research perspective* (p. 219). Washington, DC: U.S. Government Printing Office. (DHHS Publication No. ADM 87-1492)

Seppanen, P.S., & Heifetz, J. (1988). *Community education as a home for family support and education programs.* Cambridge, MA: Harvard University Press.

Showers, J. (1991). Child behavior management cards: Preventive tools for teens. *Child Abuse & Neglect, 15,* 313–316.

Siegel, E., Bauman, K.E., Schafer, E.S., Saunders, M.M., & Ingram, D.D. (1980). Hospital and home support during infancy: Impact on maternal attachment, child abuse and neglect, and health care utilization. *Pediatrics, 66,* 183–190.

Starr, R.H. (1990). The need for child maltreatment research and program evaluation. *Journal of Family Violence, 5,* 311–319.

Summerlin, M.L., & Ward, G.R. (1981, December). The effect of parent group participation on attitudes. *Elementary School Guidance Counseling,* 133–136.

Teleen, S., Herzog, B.S., & Kilbane, T.L. (1989). Impact of a family support program on mothers' social support and parenting stress. *American Journal of Orthopsychiatry, 59,* 410–419.

Tetzloff, C.E., & Barrera, M. (1987). Divorcing mothers and social support: Testing the specificity of the buffering effects. *American Journal of Community Psychology, 15,* 419–434.

Thompson, R.A. (1995). *Preventing child maltreatment through social support: A critical analysis.* Beverly Hills: Sage Publications.

Thompson, R.A., & Wilcox, B.L. (1995) Child maltreatment research: Federal support and policy issues. *American Psychologist, 50,* 789–793.

U.S. Advisory Board on Child Abuse and Neglect. (1991). *Creating caring communities: Blueprint for an effective federal policy on child abuse and neglect.* Washington, DC: U.S. Government Printing Office.

U.S. Advisory Board on Child Abuse and Neglect. (1993). *The continuing child protection emergency: A new national strategy for the protection of children.* Washington, DC: U.S. Government Printing Office.

U.S. Department of Health and Human Services, National Center on Child Abuse and Neglect. (1996). *Child maltreatment 1994: Reports from the states to the National Center on Child Abuse and Neglect.* Washington, DC: U.S. Government Printing Office.

Virginia Department of Mental Health, Mental Retardation, and Substance Abuse Services. (1988). *A plan of prevention services: Phase I: Pre-natal to age 18.* Richmond, VA: Author.

Virginia Department of Social Services. (1993). *Maltreatment reports and identified service needs.* Unpublished data, Richmond.

Virginia Vital Statistics. (1993). *Teenage pregnancies (Live births, induced terminations, and natural fetal deaths) 1991.* Richmond: Virginia Department of Health, Center for Health Statistics.

Vondra, J. (1990). The community context of child abuse and neglect. *Marriage and Family Review, 15,* 19–38.

Wald, M.S., & Cohen, S. (1988). Preventing child abuse: What will it take? In D. Besharov (Ed.), *Protecting children from abuse and neglect* (pp. 295–319). Springfield, IL: Charles C Thomas.

Wandersman, L.P. (1987). New directions for parent education. In S.L. Kagan, D.R. Powell, B. Weissbourd, & E.F. Zigler (Eds.), *America's family support programs: Perspectives and prospects* (pp. 207–227). New Haven, CT: Yale University Press.

Wasik, B.H., Bryant, D.M., & Lyons, C. (1990). *Home visiting: Procedures for helping families.* Beverly Hills: Sage Publications.

Webster-Stratton, C. (1984). Randomized trial of two parent-training programs for families with conduct-disordered children. *Journal of Consulting and Clinical Psychology, 52,* 666–678.

Weick, K.E. (1972). Small wins: Redefining the scale of social issues. *American Psychologist, 39,* 40–49.

Weinman, M.L., Schreiber, N.B., & Robinson, M. (1992). Adolescent mothers: Were there any gains in a parent education program? *Family and Community Health, 15*(3), 1–10.

Weiss, C.H. (1972). *Evaluation research: Methods for assessing program effectiveness.* Englewood Cliffs, NJ: Prentice Hall.

Weissbourd, B. (1987). A brief history of family support programs. In S.L. Kagan, D.R. Powell, B. Weissbourd, & E.F. Zigler (Eds.), *America's family support programs* (pp. 38–56). New Haven, CT: Yale University Press.

Weissbourd, B., & Grimm, C. (1981). Family Focus: Supporting families in the community. *Children Today, 10,* 6–11.

Weissbourd, B., & Kagan, S.L. (1989). Family support programs: Catalysts for change. *American Journal of Orthopsychiatry, 59,* 20–31.

Wekerle, C., & Wolfe, D.A. (1993). Prevention of child physical abuse and neglect: Promising new directions. *Clinical Psychology Review, 13,* 501–540.

Wetzel, L.L. (1990). *Parents of young children: A parent education curriculum.* St. Paul, MN: Toys 'n Things Press.

Wiehe, V.R. (1992). Abusive and nonabusive parents: How they were parented. *Journal of Social Service Research, 15,* 81–93.

Williams, R.E., Omizo, M.M., & Abrams, B.C. (1984, November). Effects of STEP on parental attitudes and locus of control of their learning disabled children. *School Counselor,* 126–133.

Willis, D.J., Holden, E.W., & Rosenberg, M.S. (Eds.). (1992). *Prevention of child maltreatment: Developmental and ecological perspectives.* New York: John Wiley & Sons.

Wilson, M.N. (1986). The black extended family: An analytical consideration. *Developmental Psychology, 22*(2), 246–258.

Winans, T.R., & Cooker, P.G. (1984). The effects of parent education on the marital dyad: An examination of systems theory. *Journal of Marital and Family Therapy, 10,* 423–425.

Wolfe, D.A. (1987). *Child abuse: Implications for child development and psychopathology.* Beverly Hills: Sage Publications.

Wolfe, D.A. (1991). *Preventing physical and emotional abuse of children.* New York: Guilford Press.

Wolfe, D.A., Edwards, B., Manion, I., & Koverola, C. (1988). Early intervention for parents at risk of child abuse and neglect: A preliminary investigation. *Journal of Consulting and Clinical Psychology, 56,* 40–47.

Wolfe, D.A., Reppucci, N.D., & Hart, S. (1995). Child abuse prevention: Knowledge and priorities. *Journal of Clinical Child Psychology, 24*(Suppl.), 5–22.

Wolfe, D.A., Sandler, J., & Kaufman, K. (1981). A competency-based parent training program for child abusers. *Journal of Consulting and Clinical Psychology, 49,* 633–640.

Wolfner, G.D., & Gelles, R.J. (1993). A profile of violence toward children: A national study. *Child Abuse and Neglect, 17,* 197–212.

Zigler, E., & Black, K.B. (1989). America's family support movement: Strengths and limitations. *American Journal of Orthopsychiatry, 59,* 6–19.

Zigler, E., Hopper, P., & Hall, N.W. (1993). Infant mental health and social policy. In C.H. Zeanah, Jr. (Ed.), *Handbook of infant mental health* (pp. 480–492). New York: Guilford Press.

Index